Inside the Dark Web

Inside the Dark Web

Erdal Ozkaya and Rafiqul Islam

CRC Press
Taylor & Francis Group
Boca Raton London New York

CRC Press is an imprint of the
Taylor & Francis Group, an **informa** business

CRC Press
Taylor & Francis Group
6000 Broken Sound Parkway NW, Suite 300
Boca Raton, FL 33487-2742

© 2019 by Taylor & Francis Group, LLC
CRC Press is an imprint of Taylor & Francis Group, an Informa business

No claim to original U.S. Government works

Printed on acid-free paper

International Standard Book Number-13: 978-0-367-23622-9 (Hardback)

Library of Congress Cataloging-in-Publication Data
A catalog record for this book has been requested

Visit the Taylor & Francis Web site at
http://www.taylorandfrancis.com

and the CRC Press Web site at
http://www.crcpress.com

Contents

Acknowledgements

My deepest gratitude goes to my wife, Arzu, and two kids, Jemre and Azra, for all your support and endless love. I know I steal a lot of time from you and spend it in my career; that's why I cannot thank you enough. Your endless love and support is just motivating me to do even more.

My parents—they never went to school; they never had a chance to read and write. But all their life, they worked really hard for me to get an education and no words can explain how thankful I am for all that you have done. The same credit goes to my brothers, Sedat & Serdal; they supported me during my early education, and this simple line of thanks cannot reflect the respect I have for both of you.

My special thanks to Dr. Rafiqul Islam for his unwavering support and collegiality throughout this journey. Your patience, motivation, and guidance has helped me throughout my research while I was completing my Doctorate and writing this book.

Authors

Dr. Erdal Ozkaya is a leading Cybersecurity Professional with business development, management and Academic skills who focuses on securing the Cyber Space & sharing his real-life skills as a Security Adviser, Speaker, Lecturer and Author.

Erdal is known to be passionate about reaching communities and creating cyber aware campaigns and leveraging new and innovative approaches and technologies to holistically address the information security and privacy needs for every person and organization in the world. He has authored many cybersecurity books as well as security certification courseware and exams for different vendors.

Erdal has the following qualifications: Doctor of Philosophy in Cybersecurity. Master of Computing Research, Master of Information Systems Security, Bachelor of Information Technology, Microsoft Certified Trainer, Microsoft Certified Learning Consultant, ISO27001 Auditor and Implementer, Certified Ethical Hacker (CEH), Certified Ethical Instructor and Licensed Penetration Tester. He is an award-winning technical Expert and Speaker: His recent awards are: Microsoft Circle of Excellence Platinum Club (2017), NATO Center of Excellence (2016) Security Professional of the year by MEA Channel Magazine (2015), Professional of the year Sydney (2014), and many speaker of the year awards in conferences.

He also holds Global Instructor of the year awards from EC Council and Microsoft. Erdal is also a part time lecture at Australian Charles Sturt University

Erdal's Twitter: https://twitter.com/Erdal_Ozkaya

Erdal's Blog: www.ErdalOzkaya.com

Dr. Rafiqul Islam has more than 15 years of teaching and research experiences at different universities in Australia and overseas. Currently, he is working as an Associate Professor in Computing at Charles Sturt University (CSU), Australia, and leading the Cyber Security Research Group (CSRG) since 2014. He has a strong research background in cybersecurity with a specific focus on malware analysis and classification, dark web, authentication, dark web threat analysis, security in the cloud, privacy in social media, and Internet of Things (IoT). Dr. Islam has been involved, as General Chair, Cahir, and member of the organizing committee in a number of international conferences and acting as a member of an editorial team of different international journals. He has a strong publication record and has published more than 160 peer-reviewed scholarly research papers, book chapters, and books. His contributions have been recognized as evidenced by numerous national and international recognition and awards.

Introduction

The dark web is an internet content that exists in the World Wide Web ecosystem but is only accessible through specific software/browser. The anonymity around dark web paves way to plenty of illegal activities leading to cyberattacks. Having a sound knowledge around dark web will act as an important skill for cybersecurity professionals.

The aims of this book are to provide a broad overview of emerging digital threats and computer crimes, with an emphasis on cyberstalking, hacktivism, fraud and identity theft, and attacks on critical infrastructure. The book also analyzes the online underground economy and digital currencies and cybercrime on the dark web. The book further explores how dark web crimes are conducted on the surface web in new mediums, such as IoT (Internet of Things) and peer-to-peer file sharing systems.

The reader will also be able to understand dark web forensics and mitigating techniques.

This book will start with the fundamentals of dark web along with explaining the threat landscape of dark net. The book will then introduce the Tor browser, which is used to access the dark web ecosystem. The book will continue to look on the deep dive into cybersecurity criminal activities in the dark net and will analyze the malpractices used to secure your system. Furthermore, the book will also dig deeper into forensics of dark web, web content analysis, and threat intelligence, IoT, crypto market, and cryptocurrencies. This book will act as a comprehensive guide for those who want to understand dark right from the scratch.

About This Book

This book will help to understand/learn

- The get up and running with the core concept of dark web.
- Different theoretical and cross-disciplinary approaches of the dark web and also the evolution of the dark web in the context of emerging crime threats.

- The forms of cybercriminal activity through dark web and the technological and "social engineering" methods used to undertake such crimes.
- The behavior and role of offenders and victims in the dark web and analyze and assess the impact of cybercrime and effectiveness of their mitigating techniques on the various domain.
- How to mitigate cyberattacks happening through dark web.
- The dark web ecosystem with cutting edge areas like IoT, forensics, and threat intelligence and so on.
- The dark web-related research and applications and up-to-date on the latest technologies and research findings in this area.

Who This Book Is For

This book is targeted towards cybersecurity professionals or aspiring cybersecurity enthusiasts who want to upgrade their skills by understanding the concept of dark web. Your one-stop guide to intrude the dark web and build a cybersecurity plan.

Chapter 1

Introduction to Cybersecurity and Dark Web

Introduction

The digital universe is huge, and the internet and World Wide Web (WWW) are much bigger than what we see through our regular browsing. The internet and its users are rapidly growing due to emerging applications of information technology (IT), and it is expected to continue to grow. However, the rapid growth of internet has left it susceptible to misuse and abuse which becomes significant threat and challenge in cyberspace around the globe. A big number of cybercriminals are trying to make illicit attempts every day to gain the access of unauthorized data through the internet. The majority of internet users are accessing the web through normal browsers such as Microsoft Internet Explorer, Mozilla Firefox, Google Chrome, and Apple Safari. The web accessed by a normal browser is called as surface web; however, a large part of the content remains hidden in the deep website. According to the literature, the modern search engines index only a very small part of the web, and a large amount of the web contents are concealed as it is in the deep website. The term dark web is part of the deep web which is targeted by the majority of cybercriminals, and they are doing criminal activities within the dark site of the web which is called dark net. This chapter will describe the following:

- Explanation of cybersecurity and cybercrime
- Web and its categories
- Dark web and its terminologies

- Origins of dark net
- Dark web software.

Cybersecurity and Cybercrime

The expansion of internet has created a great opportunity among the users in different domains, for instance, academic, government, business, and industry sectors. However, this growing development has also created the opportunity to exploit vulnerabilities to attack the infrastructure and system, conduct espionage, and wage cyberwar. Therefore, the cyberspace needs to ensure the users are secure so that they can protect their privacy and safety in the cyber world. The term cybersecurity has been adopted by government and industry, and is understood as the process by which computer networks and databases of national interest are protected, for example, large corporations and government agencies including civilian, military, and law enforcement.

Cybersecurity

The term cybersecurity, also known as computer security and IT security, refers to the technologies, processes, and practices to safeguard from unwanted access of software, hardware, data, program, and intellectual property by cybercriminals over the internet. It is also considered to control the physical access of hardware and/or cyber physical infrastructure. Cybersecurity also refers to protect data from exfiltration, various code injection attacks (CIA) such as SQL injection and XSS, or any type of service disruption.

According to the International Telecommunications Union (ITU), cybersecurity is defined as

> the collection of tools, policies, guidelines, risk management approaches, actions, training, best practices, assurance and technologies that can be used to protect the cyber environment and organization and user's assets. Organization and user's assets include connected computing devices, users, applications, services, telecommunications systems, and the totality of transmitted and/or stored information in the cyber environment. Cybersecurity ensures the attainment and maintenance of the security properties of the organization and user's assets against relevant security risks in the cyber environment. The security properties include one or more of the following: availability, integrity, and confidentiality.

CIA (confidentiality, integrity, and availability) is the basic principles of cybersecurity. Confidentiality means that the information which is classified or sensitive must remain so and be shared only with appropriate users. Availability means that the information and systems must be available to those who need it. Integrity means that the information must retain its reliability and not be altered from its original state.

Cybersecurity includes different elements such as application security, information security, network security, and disaster recovery. Cybersecurity includes different activities and operations aiming at the reduction and prevention of threat and vulnerabilities and having in place policies for protection, incident response, recovery, data assurance, law enforcement, and military and intelligence operations relating to cyberspace security. It defends the systems from hacking and virus attacks.

Consequently, cybersecurity has had growing importance in the cyber world due to the increasing reliance on computer systems, smart devices, wireless networks such as Bluetooth and Wi-Fi, and the growth of the internet. Cybersecurity involves protecting the information and systems we rely on every day—whether at home, office, or business.

Cybersecurity touches practically all activities and all citizens around the globe; it provides tremendous opportunities for enhancing human development as well as achieving better integration in the information society. It also supports wider access to knowledge and education, as well as to the development of policies and strategies.

In legal and regulatory institutions, the lack of cyberspace security undermines the realization of the full potential of the IT revolution. Consequently, special attention is needed to prevent cyberspace from turning into a source of danger for states and citizens, and to prevent the appearance of a cybercrime haven. The prevention of cybercrime is a key objective of cybersecurity.

Cybercrime

According to Interpol definition, the cybercrime refers as follows:

> Cybercrime is a fast-growing area of crime. More and more criminals are exploiting the speed, convenience, and anonymity of the Internet to commit a diverse range of criminal activities that know no borders, either physical or virtual

> **– Interpol**

Cybercrime is used most often by social scientists and is understood as the process by which criminals target computers or use computers as tools in the commission of a crime. The emphasis is on the offender and the victim. This focus on individual criminals and offenders means an expansive exploration of both crimes, including romance scams, online fraud schemes, cyberbullying, and online extremism.

Cybercrime or computer crimes are "offences against confidentiality, integrity and availability of computer data and systems" and "computer-related offences," not limited to computer-related forgery, intentional illegal computer system access, intentional illegal interception of computer data transmission, intentionally interfering with data without approval, systems interference, and misuses of electronic or computer devices.

Cybercrime costs billions of dollars to business during cyberattacks that cause direct damage and continue disrupting the business operations after the attack.

Due to the financial loss and business disruption, there are more targeted efforts to control the attacks. In addition, why the efforts are becoming more targeted is because our consumer lives are mostly online and a significant portion of attacks are difficult to detect.

In recent years, the cybercrime efforts are increasingly becoming more targeted by means of the time and cost of performing an attack versus the payback.

According to Australian cybercrime online report, the term cybercrime refers to "crimes which are directed at computers or other devices, and where computers or other devices... are integral to the offence." This definition broadly defines the types of activities performed by cybercriminals. Their operations either target specific computer networks by developing and deploying various forms of malicious software (such as viruses) or exploit these networks to further their own criminal agendas (phishing, identity theft, fraud, recruitment, etc.). The security experts are working hard to protect cyberspace from the growing cyberattacks including deliberate attempts. Therefore, cybersecurity is an important area that is needed to safeguard the details of internet users.

There has been a dramatic growth of malicious activities within the cyberspace. It is a major concern that thousands of new sophisticated malware and spam are released in an attempt to damage computer systems, or steal or destroy their data (Table 1.1).

Table 1.1   Differences between the Concepts of Cybersecurity and Cybercrime

	Cybersecurity	Cybercrime
1	Applied science-oriented coding and engineering strategies for making networks more secure	Pure science-oriented theoretical understandings of how and why crimes are committed
2	Science, technology, engineering, and mathematics (STEM) disciplines in particular computer science, computer engineering, IT	Social science disciplines: criminology, psychology, sociology
3	The primary law enforcement bodies are federal	The primary law enforcement bodies are state and local
4	The victims of interest are government and corporate networks	The victims of interest are individuals
5	The crimes are more focused on computer network; software and/or hardware is the target (malicious software, code injection, XSS, DoS attacks)	The crimes are more focused on computer as tool (identity theft, romance scams, cyberbullying, fraud)
6	Corporations and governments	Families and individuals

Web and Its Levels

The term dark web is part of the WWW and known as invisible/hidden web. The content on the dark web remains hidden and cannot be searched through conventional search engines. The content only exists on personal encrypted networks or peer-to-peer configurations, and it is not indexed by typical search engines. Therefore, the large part of the internet that is inaccessible to conventional search engines is known as deep web (invisible web). Everyone who uses the web virtually visits what could be reflected as deep websites on a daily basis without being aware.

The deep web is the anonymous internet where it is much difficult for hackers, spies, or government agencies to track internet users and have a look on which websites they are using and what they are doing there.

Web Levels

There are various levels of deep web; for instance, the lower level (level 1) is generally comprised of the "open to public" part of the web, and the upper level (called level 5) is known as dark web which is not accessible by normal web browser and needs to get The Onion Router (Tor) network or some other private network. The following table gives a brief understanding of the level of dark web:

Table 1.2 Dark Web Levels

Level 1	Common web
Level 2	Surface Web Reddit Digg Temp email services
Level 3	Bergie Web Google locked results Honey ports Freehive, Bunny Tube, etc.
Level 4	Charter Web Hacking Groups Shelling Networking AI theorist Banned videos, books, etc.
Level 5	Onion sites Human trafficking, bounty hunters, rare animal trade Questionable materials Exploits, black markets, drugs
You can learn more about dark web at: Parker A. et al., Introduction to Deep Web, IRJET, V 4, I 6, 2017.	

Web Categories

This section describes the three different levels of web such as the public web, the deep web, and the dark web.

Public web: It typically refers to the unencrypted or non-dark net. This traditional WWW has relatively low-base anonymity, with most websites routinely identifying users by their IP address.

Deep web: It refers to internet content that is not part of the surface web. This means that instead of being able to search for places, you have to visit those directly. They're waiting if you have an address, but there aren't directions to get there. The internet is too large for search engines to cover completely; thus, deep web is largely present. The deep web generally mentions the web pages which are invisible by traditional search engine.

Dark web: It is part of the WWW and part of the deep web which can only be accessible by specific software, configurations, or authorization, often using nonstandard communication protocols and ports. The Onion Router is used to access the dark website which is called Tor network.

The following figure shows the differences between deep web, dark web, and internet.

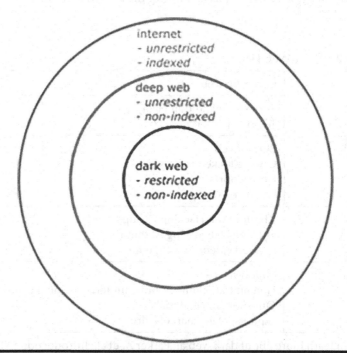

Figure 1.1 Differences Between Deep Web, Dark Web, and Internet.

Dark Net

The term dark net is part of dark deep web, and it is a collection of networks and technologies used to share digital content. The dark net is hidden from the users who use to surf with normal or standard browser, and it is also hiding the web address and server locations. The following table shows the difference between surface web, deep web, dark web, and dark net.

Table 1.3 Differences Between the Surface Web, Deep Web, Dark Web, and Darknet

	Surface Web	*Deep Web*	*Dark Web*	*Dark Net*
Description	Content that search engine can find	Content that search engine cannot find	Content that is hidden intentionally	–
Known as	Visible web, indexed web, indexable web, lightnet	Invisible web, hidden web, deep net	–	Underbelly of internet
Constitutes	Web	Web	Web	Network
Contents	Legal	Legal+illegal	Illegal	Illegal
Information Found	4%	96%	–	–
Browser	Google Chrome, Mozilla Firefox, Opera, etc.	–	Tor Browser	Freenet, Tor, GNUnet, I2P, OneSwarm, RetroShare

The Implication of the Dark Web Crime

Security in the dark web is crucial for building confidence and security in the use of information technologies so as to ensure trust by the information society. Lack of security in cyberspace undermines confidence in the information society. This is especially the case with many intrusions around the globe resulting in the stealing of money; assets; and sensitive military, commercial, and economic information. With information flowing through boundaries of different legal systems connected to different networks around the globe, there is a growing need to protect personal information, funds, and assets, as well as national security. As a result, cybersecurity is gaining interest by both the public as well as the private sectors.

With the emerging applications of computer and IT, cybercrime has become a significant challenge all over the world. Thousands of cybercriminals attempt every day to attack against computer systems to illegally access them through the internet. Hundreds of new computer viruses and spam are released every month in an attempt to damage computer systems, or steal or destroy their data. Such threats are expensive, not only in terms of quantity but also in terms of quality. In recent years, experts are becoming more concerned about protecting computer and communication systems from growing cyberattacks including deliberate attempts to access the computer systems by unauthorized persons with the goal of stealing crucial data; to make illegal financial transfers; to disrupt, damage, or manipulate data; or execute any other unlawful actions.

As computer security has advanced, maintaining network persistence has grown harder. As per Australian Cyber Security Centre (ACSC) report, the culture has adapted to this environment, focusing on low-risk, high-reward targets to achieve their goals, with a focus on the development of social engineering methodologies to implement new attacks.

Further to this, the ubiquitous nature of the internet has allowed these nefarious individuals to gain increasingly detailed profiles of individuals through exploitation and analysis of their digital footprints. This has resulted in higher rates of spear-phishing attacks, identity theft and fraud, and the development of highly specialized malware tools.

There are many risks and pitfalls in cybersecurity incident that can seriously affect computer and network systems. It can be due to improper cybersecurity controls, man-made or natural disasters, or malicious users. The following section mentions some major incidents in the cyberspace.

Ransomware

The ACSC report indicates that the ransomware is a type of post-exploitation denial-of-service (DoS) attack that uses malware to stop legitimate network user(s) from accessing the content of their device(s) or the system. It is typically accompanied by a request for payment (ransom demand) from the victim, to unlock compromised computer. Modern forms of ransomware use encryption to encrypt the data on compromised systems. This forces the victim to pay the ransom, in exchange for the decryption key.

Payment is typically demanded through Bitcoin or other cryptocurrencies due to the anonymity associated with its use. The instructions are released through a "ransom message" that explains how the payments are to take place. The adversary typically demands monetary payments according to what the targeted company or individual can afford. This information is gained through the scanning phase of the compromise. Some forms of ransomware also include payment increases to encourage the prompt delivery of the funds into their respective accounts. It is important to note that "paying the ransom doesn't always result in the data being unlocked" (Table 1.4).

Malware, Worms, and Trojan Horses

These spread by email, instant messaging, malicious websites, and infected non-malicious websites. Some websites will automatically download the malware without the user's knowledge or intervention. Other methods will require the users to click on a link or button.

Table 1.4   Recent Ransomware Variants

Ransomware Type	Summary
WannaCry	It can self-propagate through a network through the exploitation of vulnerabilities within Windows operating systems (released by the Shadow Brokers). This type of ransomware encrypts "176 different file types and appends. WCRY to the end of the file name". Once complete, it issues a ransom letter to the victim asking for payment via Bitcoin
Crysis	Self-propagation properties allow for reinfection of victim's machines if any compromised devices remain within the network. Interestingly, AV firm ESET has developed a decryption algorithm which will restore the data affected by the Crysis strain of ransomware
PETYA	Utilizes the same vulnerability as WannaCry; however, the compromise occurs through an M.E Doc software update. This software is integrated into Ukrainian Government systems. PETYA overrode the master boot record on the system, allowing the adversary to gain command and control of the device
SAMSAM	Ransomware targeted at hospitals and other healthcare systems. It exploits unpatched servers and uses these to travel through the network, compromising each machine. SAMSAM encrypts the data on the compromised system
Locky	"Widely distributed by spam as a macro attachment". The latest file extensions are renamed ".diablo6" or ".lukitis". This type of ransomware is primarily distributed through spam emails. The emails contain "a malicious Microsoft Office file or a ZIP attachment"

Botnets and Zombies

A botnet, short for robot network, is an aggregation of compromised computers that are connected to a central "controller." The compromised computers are often referred to as "zombies." These threats will continue to proliferate as the attack techniques evolve and become available to a broader audience, with less technical knowledge required to launch successful attacks. Botnets designed to steal data are improving their encryption capabilities and thus becoming more difficult to detect.

Distributed Denial-of-Service Attack

The distributed denial-of-service (DDoS) refers to an attack that successfully prevents or impairs the authorized functionality of networks, systems, or applications by exhausting resources.

Scareware

It's a fake security software warning. This type of scam can be particularly profitable for cybercriminals, as many users believe the pop-up warnings telling them their system is infected and are lured into downloading and paying for the special software to "protect" their system.

Social Network Attacks

Social network (SN) attacks are major sources of attacks because of the volume of users and the amount of personal information that is posted. Users' inherent trust in their online friends is what makes these networks a prime target. For example, users may be prompted to follow a link on someone's page, which could bring users to a malicious website.

Key Hitches

The Key Hitches are considered one of the most challenging threats in cyberspace which can be a rapidly and constantly evolving nature of security risks; therefore, the security experts can keep up with it. Furthermore, it imposes new types of commercial, professional, and social paradigms, giving rise to a number of legal and technical problems that must be addressed on the basis of respecting its special nature and needs. Hence, a different approach and different methodologies than what has been adopted are needed.

Cybersecurity has never been simple. And because attacks evolve every day as attackers become more inventive, it is critical to properly define cybersecurity and identify what constitutes a good cybersecurity.

Categories of Crime

This section gives some overview of various cybercrimes and their attack pattern. At the outset, the cybercrimes are broadly categorized into three broad categories, specifically crime against a(n):

- **Individual level**: This type of cybercrime can be in the form of cyberstalking, distributing pornography, trafficking, "grooming," etc.
- **Property level**: This type of cybercrime steals a person's bank details and siphons off money, misuses credit card details to make numerous purchases online, runs a scam to get naive people to part with their money, uses malicious software to gain access to an organization's website, or disrupts the systems of the organization.
- **Government level**: Although not as common as the other two categories, crimes against a government are referred to as cyber terrorism. If successful, this category can wreak havoc and cause panic among the civilian population. In this category, criminals hack government and military websites, or circulate propaganda. The perpetrators can be terrorist outfits or unfriendly governments of other nations.
- **Cybercriminals through SN**: Social media has become an integral part of daily life. Intruders can find this technology an attractive vehicle to commit cybercrimes. Cybercriminals use this platform and exploit it to steal user credentials, identity, and other classified information. There are various steps and methods used to carry out cyberattacks on SNs:
  - **Target**: Cybercriminal communicates with an individual via a social media outlet. The message passing through SN contains a link to a fraudulent website or an attachment which initiates an installation file. The most frequently targeted social media networks are Facebook, Twitter, and LinkedIn.
  - **Infect**: Cyberattackers use malware payloads to infect a user's computer or network. Types of malware include Trojan horse, BotNet, or FakeAV. In the past, pop-up ads and attachments containing viruses were the primary methods of delivering malware. Sophisticated techniques are now used to compromise legitimate websites in order to spread malware through holes in a user's OS.
  - **Attack**: Armed with a network of "zombie" machines, perpetrators can attack an enormous scale or target specific individuals. The attacks can hypothetically be carried out on any individual, corporate office, government, or online retailer connected to the internet. The attacks can also persist for long periods of time, as proxy connections and IPs can be constantly changed by the attacker.
  - **Control**: The infected machine, commonly defined as a "zombie," contacts a public server that the attacker has set up as a control plane to issue commands. The infected machine will first be controlled to recruit other machines using the same process of scanning for vulnerabilities.

Malicious Activities in the Dark Web

The malicious activities in the dark web are considered one of the serious threats. Through this malicious activities, the intruder is either trying to disrupt the normal computer operation or gather sensitive information from private computer systems. Antivirus (AV) vendors are receiving a huge number of distinct malware samples per day.

This problem is very important as the proliferation and exponential increase of malware has continued to present a serious threat to the security of information systems. Furthermore, with the development of ever more sophisticated methods of evading detection, malware has posed serious challenges to combat it. Moreover, due to the continuous changes in malware design, anti-malware (AM) strategy that has been successful in a given time period will not work at a much later date.

Taxonomy of Malware

With the rapid development and popularity of the internet, malware has become more and more complicated and evolved into more and more types, from the very first appeared virus, worms, Trojan followed by the currently notorious rootkits. Here I attempt to clarify the meaning of each of these terms to help understand what they are and their potential dangers. The following figures show the taxonomy of malware.

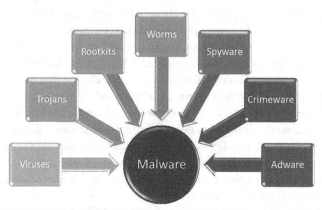

Figure 1.2   Taxonomy of Malware.

Challenges of Malware in Cyberspace

The malware is now the biggest challenge among the cyber community due to their unpredictable and sophisticated attack patterns. For instance:

Enterprise networks: The enterprise networks are challenged by the growing sophistication and obfuscation technique of malware with unknown threats.

Financially motivated attacks: Cybercriminals commonly take advantage of exploits in web browsers, plug-ins, and document readers to compromise end users with Remote Access Trojans (RATs). RATs allow hackers to maintain access while evading detection and compromise sensitive user information such as bank account credentials. Ransomware attacks encrypt all user files. To obtain the key needed to decrypt the files, the victim must pay a ransom to recover their data. The success of ransomware attacks seems to indicate that they will increase over time.

Email: Email-based malware is used to deliver an executable code to the host and then replicate it out. Today, social engineering is going into email deliveries, such as embedding compromised documents in encrypted zip files while providing the password in the email, or disguising the file type, such as making an executable file look like a PDF file.

Mobile malware: Mobile malware attacks are general information-stealing malware, which tracks what you are doing, gets your credentials, or hijacks transactions, including financial ones. Mobile devices introduce security risks when they are used to access company resources; they easily connect with the internet and third-party cloud services, and with computers with security postures that are potentially unknown and outside of the enterprise's control.

Cloud network: The term cloud network is actually considered as cloud-based network, is a combination of WAN (wide area networking) or internet-oriented access techniques through which one can access the resources of network tools and technologies from a centralized third-party provider. It is related to the idea of cloud computing, where computers and resources are interconnected and shared with all their stakeholders. Due to its hyper connectivity nature in the cloud system, there is a serious concern and growing probability of malicious activities.

1. Compact network topology—In cloud-computing environment, the packed network topology of clouds coupled with the likelihood of homogeneous software exploitation could allow rapidly propagating malware to propagate even faster than the classical network. This makes detection of malware more challenging compared to the non-cloud atmosphere.

2. Insecure interfaces and APIs—Cloud-computing providers expose to a set of software interfaces or APIs that customers use to manage and interact with could services. The securities, as well as accessibility of cloud services, depending on the security of APIs, which initiates the complexity of new layered API's. This complexity of new layer APIs makes malware detection more challenging as it allows malware running on one virtual machine (VM) to execute code or access data on another VM.

3. Virtualization—One of the problems in the cloud is virtualization which introduces an increase in software complexity and hence increases the

opportunity for vulnerabilities and hardware sharing. There is always a risk of an improper implementation or configuration of complex software that makes more defenseless of detecting malicious software.

Malware Analysis

The taxonomy of malware detection methods largely employs two features for extraction processes: (i) static features—extracted from executables and (ii) dynamic features—extracted from runtime behavior of executables. The following figure gives an overview of classical malware analysis, in particular malware feature analysis.

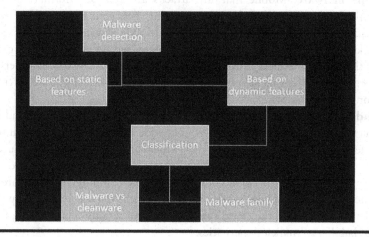

Figure 1.3   Classical Malware Analysis.

Static Analysis

Conventional malware detection and classification systems are based on static features extracted from executables by reverse engineering. The static feature extraction process is based on four different types of features:

- Portable executable (PE)
- Byte-sequence n-grams
- Function length
- String features.

The following figure illustrates a high-level overview of static malware analysis method. In this figure, the WEKA (https://cs.waikato.ac.nz/ml/weka/) interface is given as classification and evaluation as it is well-known classification algorithm developed by machine learning group at the University of Waikato.

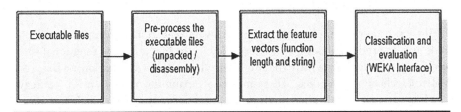

Figure 1.4 Overview of Static Malware Analysis.

Dynamic Analysis

Dynamic analysis is the behavioral analysis of malware which is time-consuming as each malware sample must be executed for a certain time period and its actions logged all within a controlled environment to ensure that it cannot infect an active platform. This controlled, virtual environment is quite different from a real run-time environment, and the malware may act in different ways in the two environments resulting in an inaccurate picture of the malware in the logs. The following figure gives an overview of the dynamic analysis process.

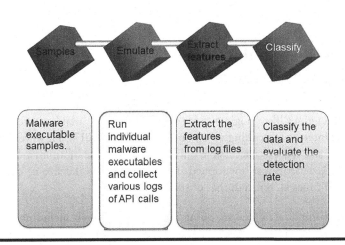

Figure 1.5 Overview of Dynamic Analysis.

Additionally, some malware behavior is triggered only under certain conditions (via a specific command or interaction with a human, for example), and this cannot be picked up in the virtual environment. On the other hand, it has been suggested that dynamic extraction is a necessary complement to static techniques as it is significantly less vulnerable to code obfuscating transformations.

Defense against Malware

While a substantial number of various malware detection techniques based on static and dynamic analyses have been studied in the literature, the recent malware proliferation technique with dynamic nature has attracted attention among the AM researchers and vendors. These malware capabilities render an AV strategy which has been successful in a given time period not to work at a much later date. Moreover, because malware evolves with time and eventually becomes unrecognizable from the original form or because completely new malware is designed which is unlike any known malware and so would not be detected by AV software constructed to detect known types of malware.

It is obvious from the current literature that present malware detection methods will not easily detect future malware. To solve this problem, researchers also proposed cumulative timeline analysis (CTA) that retains high accuracy over an extended time period. This technique provides strong support for the argument that both static and dynamic features are needed in malware detection and also that these features can be chosen in such a way that they leverage better results when they act independently and so complement each other. By extracting both static and dynamic features from executables and by accumulating these features over intervals in the 10-year period, the technique provides a high-accuracy malware detection method that retains very close to the same accuracy along the entire timeline.

The Dark Web in the Context of Emerging Crime Threats

The emerging crime and threat are now ongoing development in the dark site of the web. Search engines like google provide access to freely available content which is 0.3% of the internet, according to the study of Kristin (2017). However, deep web is of massive size which is accessible only through the use of anonymous browser such as TOR. Kristin also mentioned in the report that the size of deep web is 4,000–5,000 times larger than that of surface web.

Numerous criminal activities are going on in the deep web including drug dealings (selling or buying), contract for assassinations, pornography industry including child pornography, sales of human body organs, human trafficking and sex trafficking, transactions for illegal shipment of arms, sales of stolen goods, sales of hacked cyber identity information, terrorism activities, and many more. The easiest way to browse is hidden wiki and deep search engine. These sites provide link access to many other links in deep web. The following figure shows a snapshot of deep search interface (Tor access only).

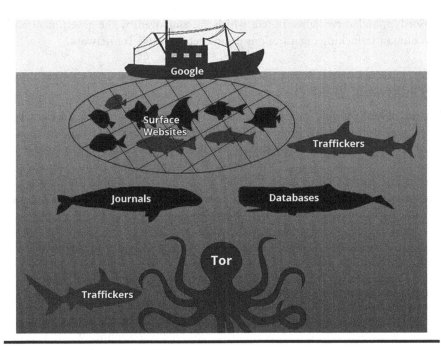

Figure 1.6 Dark Web activities.

(Source: Human trafficking)

Figure 1.7 Snapshot of Deep Search Interface.

Human Trafficking and Sex Trafficking

Human trafficking and sex trafficking are a large part of crimes (homeland) and have extremely increased due to online forums, chat services, and anonymousness of the deep web. Human traffickers do negotiate and make contracts to recruit victims for human trafficking and sex trafficking. They can easily avoid detection, censorship, and surveillance system which are employed by the government and anti-human trafficking organizations using deep web and Tor network.

Pornography Industry

Victims of human trafficking and sex trafficking, particularly women, are exploited by pornography industry. Peak mentioned in a report that once a male or female signs the agreement for accomplishing the acts, traffickers force them by fear of assassination for pornography production. The sex traffickers record video without the consent of victims. Then, pornography industry distributes those to interested parties. Traffickers also publish those recordings and photos in their website, as reported in Covenant Eyes (2011). Many websites are hosted in the deep web. Similar to human and sex traffickers, pornography industry uses deep web, social media, and online forums to recruit or kidnap victims but hide their identification.

Assassinations and Its Marketing

According to the Daily mail report (2013), criminals are using deep web to sell their assassin skills. A number of websites including MailOnline, White Wolves, and C'thuthlu provide advertisement for criminals mentioning that they can be hired for $10,000 in the United States and $12,000 in Europe. This ranges from 40,000 to 15 million of hire price for a police officer to a high-ranking politician.

Figure 1.8   Silk Road.

(Source: Silk Road: http://silkroadvb5piz3r.onion/index.php)

Drug Transactions

Anonymity of deep web access has led significant increase in drug transaction from the deep web which has created digital black market for drug. Criminals are using deep web for drug dealings, because there is no need for face-to-face communication for buying/selling drugs. One of the examples is Silk Road website that sold the drug for over a billion dollar.

Where drug is posted by the courier company DHL ((Dalsey, Hillblom and Lynn) International GmbH) or drop shipping. A statistics has been provided in following figure.

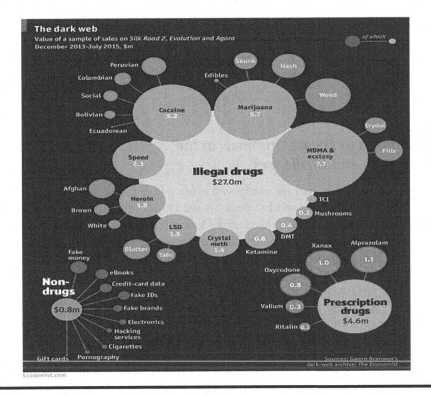

Figure 1.9   Statistics of Drug Transactions.

(Source: Economist)

Child Pornography

Children are using social media and many applications for communicating with their peers, friends, and family members. Often children come in contact with many strangers without their parent's knowledge. Many of these applications such as Omegle and Ask.fm hide the identity of their users (CyberSafetyCop).

This facilitates pedophiles to interact with the children. Pedophiles and related criminals are using deep web massively for child pornography, sharing photos and porns. One of the known companies is freedom hosting which uses 550 servers all over the Europe offering space to anyone for hosting porn from children (the US mulls). The statistics show that the FBI (FBI report in 2017) arrested several hundreds of pedophiles from the United States and international territories, which involve 2,000,000 users, 23,000 explicit images, and 9,000 video files with explicit sexuality in operation pacifier.

Terrorist and ISIS Use the Dark Web

ISIS uses dark web as a weapon for terrorism, where they provide live streaming and recording of mass execution of prisoners. They use the dark web as broadcasting media where they upload small video clips. The report published in June 20, 2017 by Singer and Brooking indicated that they used the dark web to recruit the soldiers around the world.

Techniques to Locate Criminals in the Deep Web and Challenges

Social media and deep web are jointly used to identify criminal activities. Different media including YouTube and Facebook are used to identify suspects. The US law enforcement agencies are using Metasploit Decloaking Engine and Memex systems by indexing the deep websites in an intelligent way to identify the criminals in the deep web [darpa], particularly the human traffickers. Bitcoin is the virtual money in the deep web [news.vice]. Law and policing agencies are also using Bitcoin flow in the deep web to locate criminals. The criminal's websites are monitored; purchases of contraband merchandise are also used by the agencies for this purpose. One of the successful examples of identifying criminals from the deep web is the Silk Road server. The FBI identified the location of the server in Iceland data center. Although TOR is anonymized, this was identified due to a misconfiguration in Silk Road's login page which described the IP addresses and physical location of the server. The FBI has also been successfully able to hack into the underground discussion board dark mode where criminals join every day, share information, and discuss about their criminal activities.

Although there are some successes in identifying the criminals, still there are more challenges to overcome. One of the biggest challenges is international borders which hinder further investigation and make it time-consuming. Privacy law stops the surveillance and information-gathering operations. The anonymity of deep web is also a big challenge to follow the money trail and criminals. The IP addresses and names are frequently changed in the deep web by criminals, so it is difficult to track.

To identify criminals in the deep web in a better and efficient way, more researchers are required such as cyber black market economics and logistics, technologies for counter anonymity, and building the cyber threat vectors that can characterize and asses the crime. Finally, the techniques of collecting digital evidence should be such that they are collected, retrieved, and analyzed by following the law of the country to avoid further problems in the court.

Summary

This chapter provides the fundamentals of cybersecurity and the dark web. The chapter started with a high-level overview of cybersecurity and cybercrime, how cybercrime becomes more targeted, and what criminal activities are going to happen in the deep dark web. The chapter further explores the WWW and its categories and various web levels. Some basic terminologies of the dark web and dark net alongside their consequences are discussed. The chapter further explores the threat landscape in the dark web and how to access the deep dark web. The basic idea of malicious software (malware), the taxonomy of malware, and the analysis of malware by both static and dynamic methods are discussed in this chapter.

A detailed analysis of the dark web in the context of emerging threats and their impact on various domains are also presented.

Questions

1. Describe with an example the main differences between cyberwar and cybercrime.
2. Define cybercrime. Explain, why cybercrime efforts are becoming more targeted.
3. What are the characteristics of malicious software?
4. Why are malicious insiders a focus of security experts?
5. List the terms that relate to the cybercriminal behavior involving computers.
6. What is extortion? How do criminals engage in online extortion?
7. Briefly explain the general categories of cybercriminals in modern society.
8. Distinguish between surface web and deep web in terms of threat intelligence.
9. Define with an example the traditional and contemporary techniques used by organized crime groups.
10. Explain with an example the technique used in social engineering.

Further Reading

The reader can explore the following materials and websites for further understanding:

Amores R., Paganini P., *The Deep Dark Web: The Hidden World*, Vol. 1. Seattle, WA: CreateSpace Independent Publishing Platform, 2014.

Bartlett J., *The Dark Net: Inside the Digital Underworld*. Brooklyn, NY: Melville House, 2016.

Bishop M., *Introduction to Computer Security*. Boston, MA: Addison Wesley Professional, 2004.

Chen H., *Dark Web: Exploring the Data Mining the Dark Side of the Web*. New York: Springer, 2012.

Eric A.F., Cybersecurity issues and challenges. *In Brief*, Congressional Research Service (CRS) Report- R43831, August 12, 2016. Available: http://crs.gov.

Henderson L., *Darknet: A Beginner's Guide to Staying Anonymous Online*. Seattle, WA: CreateSpace Independent Publishing Platform, 2013.

https://turbofuture.com/internet/A-Beginners-Guide-to-Exploring-the- Darknet.

https://theguardian.com/technology/ 2009/nov/26/dark-side-internet- freenet.

https://deepweb-sites.com/.

ITU Publication, Understanding cybercrime: phenomena, challenges and legal response, September 2012. Available: www.itu.int/ITU- D/cyb/cybersecurity/legislation.html.

Kim P., *The Hacker Playbook: Practical Guide to Penetration Testing*. Seattle, WA: CreateSpace Independent Publishing Platform, 2014.

Lee N., *Counterterrorism and Cybersecurity: Total Information Awareness*, 2nd edn. New York: Springer, 2015.

Nikola Z., Computer security and mobile security challenges, ResearchGate, 2015. Available: https://researchgate.net/publication/298807979.

Rogers D., *Mobile Security: A Guide for Users*. Copper Horse Solutions Limited, 2013.

Singer P.W., Friedman A., *Cybersecurity and Cyberwar: What Everyone Needs to Know*. New York: Oxford University Press, 2014.

State of Alabama Information Services Division, Why cyber security is important. Available: www.cybersecurity.alabama.gov, Retrieved on 20 November 2016.

Wu C.H., Irwin J.D, *Introduction to Computer Networks and Cybersecurity*. Boca Raton, MA: CRC Press, 2013.

Chapter 2

Threat Landscape in Dark Net

The dark net, due to its anonymity, has seen the breeding and commercialization of threats. Criminals, terrorists, hackers, assassins, drug peddlers, and customers have been flocking on this corner of the internet. There have been a number of shops that have been established in order to serve the needs of most of the visitors of the dark web. There have been some quite successful black markets created on the black net, often specializing in the sale of drugs. There has been a significant growth of terrorism in the dark net over the previous 5 years. Terrorists can now communicate, raise funds, plan attacks, recruit, and spread propaganda without the fear of being tracked and caught. Hacking tools and services are being sold in stores on the dark net. Malware targeted at specific hardware has also been listed for sale. Fraudulent activities are being carried out on the dark net. The dark net is no longer famous for its anonymity; people are mostly hearing about it for their first time when law enforcement agencies catch up with the culprits that it is hiding. The threat landscape is still growing with new black markets rising from the ashes of the ones taken down by legal enforcement agencies. This chapter will go through the threat landscape on the dark net and discuss it in the following topics.

Emerging Crime Threats in Dark Net

The dark net is facilitating new and dangerous types of criminal activities that are perpetrated by nameless and faceless people. The attackers are tech savvy, they know how to hide their tracks, and they operate on the dark net that protects their anonymity. They are therefore hard to track let alone catch. They have often outmatched the capabilities of police agencies worldwide and led to a spurge of notorious illegal activities on the dark net.

Dark Net Black Markets

It is estimated that annual revenues earned on the deep web due to illegal activities are on the upward of $100 million.[1] This amount is mostly held in Bitcoin. With the recent fluctuations in the prices of Bitcoin, this revenue is likely to be more than that. Several crackdowns on the deep web have also indicated that the illegal activities on the deep web generate a lot more than could be imagined. A bust on a notorious deep web marketplace for drugs by the FBI led to the seizure of $34.5 million in 2015.[1] In May of the same year, $80,000 in Bitcoin were nabbed during the crackdown of firearms and drugs marketplaces.[1] These statistics are likely to be higher today, only if there will be more successful crackdowns to give out this data. The following are details about the dark net black markets that were or are still being used by vendors to list different types of illegal goods and services.

Silk Road

Focusing on Silk Road, a reliable network of selling and distributing drugs had been created, and law enforcement agencies could do very little to stop it for a long period of time.[2] Transactions used to take place in the highly secure and anonymous dark net with the payments being done in Bitcoin to avoid traces to the transacting parties. Authorities apprehended Ross Ulbricht who was sentenced to life imprisonment.[2] It was thought that this would be a deterrent to similar markets or to anyone that would assume the name Dread Pirate Roberts.[2] It was a norm for a new head to take over the role of heading Silk Road with the name Dread Pirate Roberts. The tough sentence handed down was thought to bring an end to the online sale of drugs. However, it seems that the opposite happened. The use of the dark net just gained more publicity, a publicity that would lead to more dire consequences. Ross Ulbricht's case brought a lot of attention which served as free advertising to this online evil of buying drugs. There were arguments that he was innocent, there were other arguments that the FBI used illegal ways to get the evidence that was used in his case, and there were other arguments that he was not even the head of the Silk Road. All this had unadvertised consequences of getting to people that there was a way to buy drugs online anonymously. Media coverage on this issue was careless enough to explain how the Silk Road operated, the browsers that would be used to access it, and the form of payment that would be done. This led to the growth of this evil as authorities would discover in 2017.

AlphaBay

Following the free advertising that online drug sale had received in between 2013 and 2015 due to the case of Silk Road, a new online black market emerged to fill the gap that had been left.[3] This new market would take up the former customers of the Silk Road as well as the new customers that had just heard about dark net drug markets. In mid-2017, the FBI was able to take down the largest drugs black market on the dark net that was called AlphaBay. This market, just like Silk Road, connected drug sellers with the online customers. However, AlphaBay was said to be ten times bigger than Silk Road. There was a record of 250,000 drugs listed on the site at the time that the FBI cracked down the site.[3] Alongside these were weapons and hacking tools. With the threat of terrorism and public shootings, the sale of guns was a huge concern. The vast distribution networks of the black market were an assurance that users would get the items they would order. Therefore, anyone with sufficient purchasing power could get hands on a deadly arsenal of weapons. The fact that there were so many items on the site meant that there was a big and ready market. The FBI said that the users on the site were well above 200,000.[3] Even more shocking, the black market was able to reach sales of up to $800,000 each day.[3]

This online drug syndicate used to operate like eBay. It made money by taking a cut of the sales made. For each item displayed on the site, a given percentage would go to it as commission. At the time of the 2017 crackdown, the FBI said that the black market had made tens of millions of dollars. In the years prior to the crackdown, authorities were able to purchase and receive drugs and fake IDs from the site. The arrest of the founder of this dark net eBay-styled drug store, Alex Cazes, was less controversial as that of Ross Ulbricht. Authorities were able to find him through an email that he had configured to send recovery emails to users. He had used an email that was tied to a PayPal account and one that he had also used to post on a troubleshooting website. These small slipups turned out to be the only chance that authorities had to arrest the brains behind the market.

What was visible in the arrest of Cazes was that law enforcement agencies still have a long way to go when it comes to apprehending criminals on the dark net. It took over 2 years for the authorities to pick up on an open hint, that the founder used his email address to send recovery emails to users. This was a huge flaw that should have been picked up very early in an investigation on a black market that had made $1 billion worth of transactions. The methods being used to nab dark net criminals are therefore wanting. Authorities are still playing catch up, and they are out-phased by the criminals on the dark side of the internet.

As has been the trend, the fall of one big drug market results in the rise of another. Silk Road fell and AlphaBay, which was ten times larger than Silk Road, raised. The demand for these drugs is only going up. The media has only been giving free advertisement to these dark net drug stores by explaining how they are accessed and the tools one needs to use to access them. There is a high probability that another black market on the dark net is being established and it will be even bigger than AlphaBay. In response to this type of speculations, the FBI director said that this was the nature of crime, it never really goes away and thus has to be constantly fought. http://pulselive.co.ke/bi/tech/tech-the-fbi-just-took-down-alphabay-an-online-black-market-for-drugs-that-was-10-times-bigger-than-silk-road-id7023493.html

Hansa

This was the much-expected successor of AlphaBay after law enforcement agencies put an end to it in June 2017. However, this was not to be as the legal agencies had already proliferated Hansa and within a month, they also brought it down.[4] Impersonating as site administrators, Dutch officers were able to collect sensitive information such as usernames and passwords that allowed them to close down the black market just before it rose to its glory. Hansa was no different from AlphaBay in terms of the items that it sold. There were drugs, weapons, and fake identity cards on sale. With the efficient distribution networks that the black market used, these items could be smuggled to their customers within and also outside of the Netherlands. It also had an encouraging user base which was being served by close to 8,000 vendors by the time of closure.

Dream Market

This is a dark net site that is still active and running at a time when most other dark net black markets have been taken down by law enforcement agencies.[6] Its merchandise is no different from the likes of Silk Road and AlphaBay. It has drugs, stolen data, consumer goods, and counterfeit currency, among other things.[5] All the transactions are carried out using Bitcoin. The black market has an added advantage to buyers in that it offers escrow services. Therefore, payments are released to sellers after buyers acknowledge receipt of goods. There is also an active support team that handles disputes between sellers and buyers. There is even a chat forum where sellers, buyers, and moderators can interact with each other.

There is speculation that Dream Market will grow to be bigger than AlphaBay if the FBI or any other law agency does not take it down. Currently, customers that used to shop for drugs and other things on AlphaBay are streaming into this black market. Vendors that used to post items for sale in Silk Road and AlphaBay are also joining this market. It also has a commendable structure that is normally visible in some e-commerce stores such as eBay. The fact that there is a support team to deal with any misunderstandings between customers and sellers means that the market is well thought out. The founder(s) seemingly had a long-term vision of this type of business. With strengthened ties between customers and the vendors, the market might just grow faster. It will also be adopted by many others. News media have been giving dark net websites' free coverage each time FBI takes down a black market. The biggest free advertising that media did was in 2015 during the shutdown of Silk Road 2.0 that was headed by Ross Ulbricht. The shutdown of AlphaBay also received a lot of coverage. Among the things that news media were covering was how to access these dark net stores and how to buy products listed therein. With all the public awareness that is out there, the knowledge that the large black markets have been shut down leaves Dream Market at an advantage. New buyers will keep streaming into the market.

There are however some fears about the survival of this black market. A common tactic that law enforcement agencies have shown in previous shutdowns is that they first infiltrate the black markets. They pretend to be customers, vendors, and even site administrators as they interact with other users of the site. All this time, the law enforcement agents will be collecting incriminating evidence that can be used to put people on the black market in jail. It is said that before AlphaBay was shut down, law enforcement agencies had infiltrated the site and had been collecting information about the transacting parties. In the last month of its operations, the site was claimed to be run by law enforcement agencies who had already apprehended or put out of power the real site admins. There are fears that Dream Market is in this state. It is not explainable how this market has been able to survive after the vigorous takedown of other large black markets. It is probable that indeed law enforcement agencies are already in control of the site. In the case of AlphaBay, the law enforcement agencies that had taken over the site changed some files that users used to get after transactions so as to track them. There was a time that they made Excel invoices that when downloaded and opened by users, the files would send back the IP addresses of the machines that they had been opened in.

This black market already has 57,000 of drugs which is more than what Silk Road had.[5] The administrator of the site, who doubled as a vendor, was arrested in 2017, and this has been fueling the rumors that the site is currently under the control of the police. Bitcoin worth $500,000 at the time of arrest was also recovered from the administrator's wallet.[5] It is being said that many of the vendors in the dark net shop are now being controlled by Dutch law enforcement agents as they try to recover more information before finally shutting down the site. Furthering the doom news, some users complained that they were losing funds while transacting in the shop. A purported staff member claimed that it was because of a hard drive problem and that the lost funds would be refunded. To date, the funds have not been refunded, and it is unclear whether they will ever be. Nevertheless, Dream Market is an interesting black market on the dark net that people should look out for. Probably the law enforcement agencies will take it down, but there is also a belief that the site is stronger than AlphaBay and thus could continue supporting transactions for a long period of time. If it were weak, then probably the arrest of the administrator would have led to its end as has been the case in both Silk Road and AlphaBay.

Apple Market

In the list of the dark net sites that law enforcement agencies have already taken down is Apple Market.[7] Apple Market was an e-commerce store that featured escrow services and was seen to be quite secure and reliable by users. Even though it had fewer listings than the bigger black markets such as AlphaBay, it has an aesthetic and easy-to-use interface that was appealing to buyers. Apple Market still dealt with the normal illegal products such as drugs, accounts, cards, hacking tools, software, keygens, serial keys, and eBooks.[7] The listings depended on the vendors that put their items on the platform. The market also had a search functionality, a feature that was not available in many of the other dark net shops. It enabled users to quickly find the items that they were searching for on the site. The user interface of the site was modern with functionalities that are normally available in clear web e-commerce sites such as Amazon. The site had a feature to hold one's money through its own cryptocurrency wallet. Users would either debit or credit the wallet with Bitcoin. It was advisable, for the sake of promoting anonymity, for the user to use a Bitcoin mixer instead of sending them directly from an exchanger. The short hop from the exchanger to the Bitcoin to the Bitcoin address that the currency was being debited would be viewed as a security risk. This is because a majority of the things on this market were illegal.

Your Drug

As of November 2017, the status of this market was that it was up and running on the dark net. It is another dark net store that claims to have years of experience in the drug selling business but has expanded its businesses to the dark net markets.[6] The store claims to be a provider of the best quality drugs at the best market prices and that it sells exactly what customers want and expect. The shop is seemingly observant of security as it says that that is its number one priority. The clientele that the shop advertises to are resellers and final customers, and it assures them that it will respect their shipping times, packaging, and privacy.

Stoned 100

This is one of the trusted vendors on the dark net that has recently been featured in the Dream Market and previously on the AlphaBay market. This seller holds his external dark net presence, and it has helped him survive the recent crackdowns on AlphaBay and the current uncertainty on Dream Market.[6] The vendor is known to sell speed, ecstasy, hash, sildenafil, and weed, among other things.

QualityKing

This is another vendor from AlphaBay, Dream Market, and other markets that decided to establish his or her own dark net presence to be able to carry out business without overly relying on the big black markets.[6] This has seemingly been working well because the big markets have been focused on by law enforcement agencies and taken down one after the other. This seller has a narrow scope of goods and only advertises opioids to buyers. As of November 2017, the seller's dark net presence was still there.

MushBud

One of the longest surviving individual vendors of drugs on dark net black markets is MushBud.[6] MushBud has been present on the dark net for a long term and has passed through other black markets such as Silk Road 2, Sheep, Agora, and Abraxas. This is one of the known retailers for weed and psychedelics. The vendor has received hundreds of positive comments on dark net chat forums. This vendor was found to be up and running as of November 2017.

Fight Club

With a catchy name that has also been featured as a title of a successful Hollywood movie, Fight Club is another dark net vendor that has moved from one dark net black market to the other.[6] This vendor only specializes in the sale of illegal documents. The vendor is a seller of driving licenses of different countries and also identity cards. This vendor has been a member of sites such as Dream, Abraxas, AlphaBay, and Nucleus. As of November 2017, this vendor was confirmed to be still active on the dark net.

L33TER

This is an old vendor that is still present on the dark net. The vendor claims to be an important part of the dark net markets ever since evolution. They deal with the sale of digital and physical products with a well set up dispatch and delivery system.[6] The vendor is said to use a customer ticketing system to ensure that customers get their products at the end of the transaction. The vendor's digital products are said to have an auto dispatch whereby they get send to the customer at the completion of a payment. This vendor was confirmed to be active as of 2017 November.

Agora Market and Forum

Agora Market was one of the dark net sites taken down alongside Silk Road 2 by law enforcement agencies.[7] It was also a renowned market just like Silk Road 2 though had nagging regular downtimes. The site allowed the use of weapons alongside the usual products such as drugs and counterfeit money. The owners made revenues by charging a 4% commission on the items that were posted for sale on the market.[7] It required a referral link in order for one to visit it. However, even with all these measures, it was still taken down by legal agencies. It also had a forum for sellers and buyers to interact called the Agora Forum. This forum suffered the same fate as the market when officers came knocking.

Atlantis

This is a former marketplace that was notorious for drugs at a time when the dark net was still getting popularity. It operated till late 2013, the time at which law enforcement agencies made more frantic efforts to shut down dark net marketplaces.[7] This marketplace is said not to have been taken down by the legal enforcement units, rather, it was the owner that shut it down citing security concerns.

Blue Sky Marketplace

It was a marketplace that was taken down in 2014. It was moderately sized based on the sellers and buyers that were registered on it at the time. The marketplace charged vendor commissions ranging from 5% to 10% of the price of the products that they would post on the platform.[7] However, to attract less heat on its tail, the marketplace had banned the sale of weapons.

Caravan Marketplace

This was the first refuge site for customers that were fleeing the collapsing Silk Road 2 after the takedown by the FBI.[7] It featured listings for hard drugs, identity cards, stolen credit cards, and hacked PayPal accounts. The marketplace had an elaborate messaging system for collaboration purposes between the site's users. There were also active admins that used to resolve issues that users faced. It went down once and then another site was created to replace it in 2014. However, even the new site did not stay up that long as the law enforcement agencies took it down in early 2015.

Darknet Heroes League

This was built up to be a reliable marketplace that would feature the old-time vendors on the dark net. This would boost its reliability in the face of other new marketplaces on the dark net as users would be more certain of old-time vendors.[7] The site invited the vendors that it saw fitting its description. However, it was taken down at the time of the fall of AlphaBay and Hansa in 2017. A few months after these were taken down, it also suffered the same fate under the hands of law enforcement agencies.

Outlaw Market

This is now a defunct marketplace as of November 2017 following the takedown by law enforcement agencies.[7] It was a small market that had not yet grown but had the prospects of doing so. The marketplace offered an attractive 0% commission to vendors that wanted to list their items. However, they were still required to pay a small fee. Alongside drugs and counterfeits, the site had allowed the sale of weapons. At the time of takedown, it was first taken over by law enforcement agencies who collected some data and then proceeded to shut down the marketplace. Users had been cautioned to stop using the market when allegations came flying that the site was under the control of the legal agencies.

The RealDeal Market

It was a marketplace for the tech-savvy users that were looking for exploits to use in hacking expeditions. The marketplace offered exploits, source codes, hardware, hacking services, and the likes. Alongside the tech-related items, the marketplace also listed drugs and other normal products such as counterfeits that were being sold by other marketplaces. Its downfall came in 2017 with the site going offline on 31st of October. Legal agencies got to it and shut it down as they were taking down many other dark net sites.

Sheep Marketplace

This was a drug marketplace that died off in a dramatic way. Since there is no honor among thieves, the owner of this marketplace waited till the site accumulated quite a number of customers' Bitcoin and then ran off with them.[7] The site followed the format of many others where funds would be deposited with the site to allow a customer to make a purchase. The owner had other crafty ideas of making quick cash, and the first chance they got at disappearing with a sizeable amount of the customers' Bitcoin, he or she took it. It was a classic example of an exit scam. The site went down in December 2013.

Russian Anonymous Marketplace

It was one of the noticeable dark net market takedowns of 2017. Russian police took out the Russian Anonymous Marketplace (RAMP) which was said to be the largest remaining site after Hansa and AlphaBay went down. The marketplace had been launched in 2012 and had been quite stable except for the occasional distributed denial-of-service (DDoS) attacks that it faced.[8] It was the largest dark net site that was written in the Russian language to serve the needs of Russians on the dark net. RAMP users and admins were in disbelief when Russia took down the site as they thought that they would not suffer the same consequences that other marketplaces were going through in the hands of the FBI and Dutch police. While being interviewed by Russian media, one of the site admins said that the Russian law enforcement was not concerned with hidden services on the internet and they did not consider them as a threat. Russia was being said to have the tendency to turn a blind eye to online crime.[8] However, when the law enforcement agencies stroke, the site was taken down faster than it took the FBI to take down AlphaBay. However, tactics varied as the Russians were mostly interested in shutting down the site while on the other hand, the FBI had spent time collecting data on the AlphaBay marketplace before it was shut down.

UK Guns and Ammo

As the name suggests, this is a dark net shop that specializes in the sale of guns and ammo.[7] The shop claims to sell products only from the United Kingdom. Their preferred transaction method is through Bitcoin.

HQEB

In full, the name is High Quality Euro Bills.[7] This shop sells counterfeit currency which it claims to be of high quality. It only sells Euro Bills.

USA/EU Fake Documents Store

This store claims to sell passports to several countries on the internet and provide free delivery to customers. The store says that it has passports for the United Kingdom, the United States, Japan, and Australia.[7]

Illegal Goods and Services Offered on the Dark Net

The mentioned markets have a lot to say about the current crime threats that are emerging on the dark net. There are probably very many criminal threats, but the following are most popular.

Drugs

From the markets listed earlier, the main commodity for sale was drugs. There seems to be a never-ending demand for narcotics. Since it is at times very risky to buy drugs from street vendors, drug abusers will take the safe alternative of buying online when such an opportunity appears. Drug abusers have severally taken to internet chat forums to complain about the shutdown on some of these black markets since they used to rely on them for supplies.

Weapons

One of the most dangerous crimes being carried out on the dark net is the sale of weapons. These range from pistols to rifles and in some black markets, there are explosives. This is a big security threat since the sale of these weapons is uncontrolled and they can get to anyone. Black markets are known for effective peer reviews, and therefore, users are able to weed out the illegitimate sellers from the platforms. The vendors left are the trusted ones that are known to deliver. Therefore, there is an assurance that the weapons for sale on these platforms will eventually get to the buyers. The buyers could be terrorists, mentally troubled people, or people with vengeance goals.

Communication Channels for Terrorists

Due to the international hunting down of terrorist organizations, many communication platforms are monitored. Some are forcefully monitored as was said by Edward Snowden in 2015. He, an National Security Agency (NSA) whistleblower, quit his job at the agency and put on the public domain a lot of information about the monitoring of calls and messages on several carriers. He also said that the NSA was reading messages on other communication platforms. Terrorists are aware of this and that is why they use the dark net for their communication needs. The dark net offers them a secure space in which they can plan and coordinate terrorist activities without the fear of being tracked down. The dark net is a perfect environment for terror-related communication since it offers ready chat rooms and does not put the terrorists at the risk of easily being exposed or found out by legal agencies.

Hacking

There are specialist black hat hackers on the dark net that offer their services for hire. While browsing on the dark net, the following is a description provided by one of the hackers. The hacker first says that the least charge for a small job is €250. On the hacking skills, the hacker says that he or she is specialized in zero-day exploits, personalized Trojans, bots, and DDoS attacks. To top this up, the hacker claims to be knowledgeable of social engineering. They also say that they can cause technical troubles on websites, disrupt networks, cause economic sabotage, gather private sensitive information, and ruin persons or businesses. Among the techniques for this is framing them as child porn users.

There are other corners of the dark net where one can find malware for sale, other than just renting a hacker. The malware is normally sold based on its capabilities and detection by antivirus programs. Zero-day exploits are also sold on the dark net. Zero-day exploits target vulnerabilities that have not yet been fixed and therefore have a high chance of success.

Assassinations

Among the charges that Ross Ulbricht of Silk Road faced was hiring an assassin to take out some people that he had gotten into loggerheads with. He is said to have hired them on the dark net. Though hidden, there are some markets where one can hire assassins to take down specific people. The assassins claim to have high rates of success, and they charge differently based on the complexity of the task. Though there may be a number of bluffs on the dark net, some of the assassins for hire might be legit and will kill people for money. Due to the anonymity of the dark net, they feel protected that they cannot be tracked down. The details of how assassination deals go down on the dark net are horrifying. Since the places where these services are offered want to keep away attention from the police, they normally reject requests for proof of past work or feedback from previous customers that might be indicative of their success. Customers are asked to give proof that they have the required amounts for the assassination job and the amount is placed in an escrow service. After the assassination, the assassin provides proof that the job was completed and then the funds are released.

One of the dark net sites that offer these services is called C'thulhu which claims to be a group of former soldiers and mercenaries with lots of experience. They say that they offer solutions to common problems and that they can perform hits anywhere in the world. On their dark net site, they explain why they are the best people to work with. They say that other hitmen hired physically are risky since they can collaborate with the police once caught and threatened with a prison sentence. They may take a plea and help the police find the person that paid for their services in exchange for lighter sentences. The dark net assassins say that it is out of mutual interest that they carry offer their services on the dark net. Due to the anonymity, they cannot take the person paying for these services to prison and neither can the person take them. Their services are quite expensive as advertised on their site. The cheapest one is the beating up of a target which is charged at $3,000. The most expensive service is killing a target through an accident whereby the target is a high-ranking politician. Other services that they offer are the crippling of a target, rape, and bombing.

There are, however, reports that most of these adverts for assassinations and hit men services are a hoax. For example, Ross Ulbricht of Silk Road was initially accused by the FBI of hiring a hit man to assassinate six people. However, the FBI, later on, dropped these charges. It is said that they found out that the hit men services they were referring to were a hoax and there was no way they would stick on Ulbricht. Also, several analysts of the deep web have collected intelligence that these hit men services advertised on the dark net are hoaxes. There is also something fishy about the guarantee that the hit men give on being able to take down any target anywhere in the world.

Fraud

There are all sorts of making quick money advertised on the dark net. Most of them are through fraud. There are some shops that sell counterfeit currency. They assure that the counterfeit currency will pass the normal UV light scans. For about $600, one can get around $6,000 in some shops. There are other vendors that sell ATM cards. They place the prices on these cards based on the account balances of the ATM cards. They claim that they will ship the physical cards and provide a working PIN code for the purchaser to draw out the amounts.

Another common fraud on the dark net is the sale of hacked PayPal accounts. These accounts are also priced based on the amounts that they hold in their balances. The vendors claim that they will give the buyer the hacked logins to these accounts from where the buyer will transfer the funds to their accounts. There are two categories of accounts that are sold. The first category is composed of accounts that the hackers have verified the balances that the buyer will find. The second category is composed of a bulk of unverified accounts whereby the balances have not been checked but there is some guarantee that some money will be found in some of them. Verified accounts attract more charge than the unverified ones. While browsing the dark net, there was an advert in one of the shops selling 100 PayPal accounts for $100. This is an example of the bulk unverified accounts where the buyer is uncertain of the balance that will be contained in these accounts thus the cheap price of $1 per account.

It is important to note that for all these fraudulent accounts and ATM cards advertised on the dark net shops, no one is assured that the promised quick money will be made or they will get burned. The payment is done via Bitcoin, and there are no refunds even if one is burned. However, the dark net at times has a very effective peer-review network which will direct buyers in the direction of the trustable vendors in the dirty business.

Fake IDs/Driving Licenses

It is no lie that some of the immigrants in First World countries get in there through backdoors. Once inside, they run into a new problem of getting identity cards and driving licenses that they can use in the foreign countries. These are very powerful documents, and they can enable them to get jobs or stay away from trouble should they run into police officers. People within some countries may have been engaged in some criminal activities, and thus may seek to acquire new clean identities. There are others who simply want a fake identity that they can use to open bank accounts for fraudulent transactions, apply for loans, purchase property fraudulently, and do so many other things without jeopardizing their real identities. There are some shops in the dark net that specialize in the making of fake identity cards and driving licenses. They require the purchaser to provide a photograph and maybe desired name to be used on these fake documents. These identity cards and driving licenses differ in price based on the country that one wants to get documents for. In some dark net listings, a fake US passport, identity card, and driving were being sold for €900. For Switzerland documents, the price was slightly lower at €850. The cheapest listing was for a Germany ID, passport, and driving license which were coming to a total of €650.

Illegal Wildlife Trade

In June 2017, INTERPOL came to a finding that poachers had taken to the dark net to sell wildlife products such as rhino horns, ivory, and tiger skin among other products from endangered species.[9] It was also found out that the transactions were being carried out in Bitcoin thus making it harder to track the people behind them. In a period of 5 months, 21 advertisements surfaced that mostly offered rhino horns and elephant ivory.[9] This was a particularly disturbing finding factoring in the efforts being put to stop the sale of these products in a bid to stop poaching. It shows that poachers are responding to the increasing pressure from security agencies to take down the markets used for the illegal trade. Poachers are turning to the dark net which offers anonymity, security, and a more confident market since most of the worries about being caught are eliminated.

Child Porn

Although many of the known dark web sites that published or sold child porn have been taken down by the FBI, there are a few that remain. These sites are notorious for publishing this inhumane content and at times putting it for sale for dark net users. In multiple collaborated takedowns, most of the dark web sites that had been offering this type of content were seized and their owners arrested. However, with a little bit of digging around, some of the remnant sites can be found where dark net users are still paying to download such content. Fortunately, though, many of the large black markets on the dark net were unsupportive of the sale of such content and therefore prohibited sellers from posting about such. For example, Silk Road explicitly stated that it did not deal in child porn. There seems to be some level of decency in the mainstream black markets that recognize this crime to be on a higher level and therefore choose not to support it.

Malware for Sale

In late 2017, there was a growing concern from many security companies about the proliferation of ATM malware. Even though ATMs give the impression that they are highly secured, it seems hackers have gotten ways to exploit the hardware and software of the ATMs. Early in the year, there were manuals for sale on the dark net on how ATM systems could be compromised causing them to eject money. In dark net shops, these manuals were going for US $5,000.[10] When the FBI took down AlphaBay, they found transactions dealing with the sale and instructions on how to use the ATM malware. Some of the important information retrieved from the transaction to buy the ATM malware in April 2017 as posted on the site are as follows.

The ATM malware was being advertised by the seller as a malware that would allow one to cash out all the money loaded in an ATM machine. The seller was offering three software. The first one was to be used to check the balance in the ATM machine. The second software was to be used to cash out all the money that was loaded in the ATM. The last software was the one to be used to coordinate operations between the first and second software. The seller also promised to give instructional videos on how to use the software as well as answering any questions that the buyer wanted. Also, the seller said that the malware would work worldwide on any ATM. It would be undetectable by ATM antivirus programs. In the instruction files, the sellers explained where an ATM would be breached physically in order to expose a USB port that would be used to load the malware inside the machine.

It was reported that the instructional manual was written in broken English and was indicative that the author was a native Russian speaker. The process described in the manual was seemingly easy to follow. It first told the buyer the items that would be needed. These included USB adaptors, a wireless keyboard, a Windows 7 laptop, a drill, and a USB thumb drive among a few other essentials.[10] The buyer was to load the three programs in the USB flash disk. In an ATM, one was to follow a certain procedure to open an ATM's door and expose the USB port. He would then execute a particular program to see information about the ATM cassettes, execute another program to get a certain code, and then use the windows laptop to enter the given code and run another program.[10] The program would give out a password that would be given to the ATM to allow it to dispense all the money it held.

Even though this malware was not meant to attack the ATM users directly, it would affect their banks. The existence of the malware is a warning that criminals have found a way to make programs that can be used to dispense money from ATM machines. These programs are also on sale in the dark net for as much as $5,000.[10] Therefore, banks need to react fast to make it impossible for third parties to run their own programs on the ATM computers. Also, it might be necessary for banks to ensure that ATMs have sufficient physical security. This will prevent criminals from stepping into ATM booths and destroying the machines with drills in order to get access to the USB port. The USB port in ATM computers also needs to be better secured. It might be appropriate if the USB ports are disabled through the network until the banks need to run their own updates. If the ports are disabled, it will be impossible for the criminal entities to connect their own devices such as thumb drives which can be used to run malicious programs to steal from the machines. Banks can also better protect their ATMs with antivirus programs that are most reliable in catching malicious programs being run on the ATM computer. One of the companies that have a good reputation in dealing with this kind of threat is Kaspersky Labs. Kaspersky was among the first companies to highlight this kind of attack on ATM machines.

Botnets

One of the main cyber threats that organizations are getting wary of is DDoS attacks. A high-profile target that has suffered a DDoS attack is DynDNS, a leading

Domain Name System (DNS) company.[11] The culprits behind DDoS attacks are hackers that use botnets to send illegitimate traffic to the targets thus making it impossible for a target to process the legitimate traffic. Botnets are made up of infected computers that can be remotely controlled to participate in a DDoS attack by sending illegitimate requests to a target. The dark net has been a ready source for botnet networks advertised for sale to any willing buyers that wish to perform a DDoS attack on a target. There was one listing on the dark net that advertised the sale of a massive botnet of 100,000 computers.[11] The listing was found in AlphaBay, a big black market that was taken down by law enforcement agencies. The price for this botnet was $7,500.[11] It could be used for DDoS attacks and also to spread spam and ransomware, as the seller said.

The seller claimed that the botnet was able to generate a lot of traffic, 1 TB/s to be specific. To put this massive power of the botnet into context, the DDoS attack that took down DynDNS was said to have generated 1.2 TB/s.[11] The company, later on, said that they estimated the number of zombie computers that were sending the illegitimate requests to be about 100,000.[11] DynDNS was a big networking company, and therefore, it is safe to assume that they had all manners of protective mechanisms to handle DDoS attack up to a certain point. It can, therefore, be deduced that the botnet listed on AlphaBay would be able to take out many organizations if it generated the 1 TB traffic and directed it to their networks. Many organizations will simply not have enough protection to handle this amount of traffic and will thus be overwhelmed by it. It can be assumed that there are many other botnets on the dark net that can be purchased by any malicious-minded person.

There are other cheaper listings for a smaller number of botnets in some other shops. There are smaller offerings of a thousand botnets based in the United States for $200, while the same number of European Union (EU)-based bots is around $120. Buying in small bits helps buyers avoid getting blacklisted machines though it is more expensive. For example, it would cost $12,000 to buy 100,000 of the EU-based bots in bits while buying all at a go would cost around $7,500.

Botnets are finding a market on the dark net due to their effectiveness. They are most likely to succeed in taking down websites for the purposes of vengeance, harassment, and also for unethical business competition. If an e-commerce store takes down the website of a competitor site for a day or two, the shoppers will most likely trickle down to his or her e-commerce shop. With the advent of the Internet of Things (IoT), it is likely that botnets will get stronger and DDoS attacks will be more brutal. This is because IoT devices are small, many in number, and can generate a lot of traffic. It is only a matter of time before there are listings on the dark net of botnets made up of IoT devices. IoT malware is already being reported, and it is some of this malware that will be used to take control of IoT devices and recruit them in zombie armies of botnets.

Bitcoin Laundry

Bitcoin is not entirely an anonymous method of payment. This is because the transaction details are kept public though they are scattered. Bitcoin uses a system called Blockchain to facilitate the processing of transactions. The Blockchain technology uses an open ledger to keep track of the transactions that take place. This system is powered by peer computers scattered all over the world. To allow for the level of collaboration required by the peers to process transactions, everything is laid out in the public domain. This means that transactions conducted via Bitcoin can be tracked although with a lot of difficulties. When one wants to engage in dirty business, they want to ensure that there is no way that their crimes can be tracked to them. For example, someone hiring an assassin on the dark net will not wish to have trails in the public domain leading back to him or her.

Bitcoin laundry is a method of ensuring that it is even more difficult for one's transactions to be tracked back to them. There are dark net shops that offer this service where they mix one's Bitcoin with others. They do so by transferring the Bitcoin through many micro transactions, and they return an equivalent amount of Bitcoin to one's wallet after deducting some fees of course. The end result is that one's transactions become too many and too hard to track. At the end of the day, there are some Bitcoin holders that will want their Bitcoin to be changed back to fiat currency. To prevent the formation of a pursuable trail of some amount of Bitcoin being changed to currency and deposited in a particular bank account, there are some dark net shops that offer anonymity at this point as well. They anonymously change the Bitcoin into money and deposit it into one's bank account of choice.

Leaking of Government Officials' and Celebrities' Secrets

In the world of exposes, WikiLeaks is one of the renowned sites that publish evidence of evils carried out by a number of people. WikiLeaks has a dark net site which offers people a portal through which they can submit information about other people or organizations anonymously. On the dark net, there are many other sites that contain personal information about high-ranking politicians, law enforcement agencies, FBI agents, and celebrities. When Obama was still the president of the United States, there was a listing made in one of these sites that contained some of his personal information as well as his Yahoo and AOL email accounts. There were also IP addresses that the listing claimed were used by Obama when logging into his email accounts.

On a dark net site called Cloud Nine are more listings of notable people whereby some sensitive information about them is given out. There are listings of FBI agents, snitches to the FBI, and CIA agents. Some of the celebrities that feature in the site include Kim Kardashian and Kimberly Brown.

Bitcoin and Cryptocurrency Fraud

There are a number of dark net shops that are aimed at Bitcoin fraud, that is, their purpose is to defraud customers of their Bitcoin. The first category of shops are the ones that claim to double one's Bitcoin. It is simply impossible for a software or a system to double one's Bitcoin. The only way of getting more Bitcoin is by acquiring them from other people through purchase or receiving them as payment. The scam shops on the dark net request one to send their Bitcoin to a certain wallet from where they will be doubled and send back to them. The only problem is that once one sends the Bitcoin to the given address, the scammers disappear. It is the dark net so one cannot legally pursue the scammers or tell exactly where to look for trails that might lead to them. These fraudulent scammers have established their own shops where they specialize in stealing from customers that are looking to make quick cash from the Bitcoin-doubling systems.

The other type of Bitcoin and cryptocurrency fraud in the dark net involves a process called exit scam. This is where a shop or a vendor disappears with a customer's Bitcoin or other types of cryptocurrency that was offered as payment. The vendor fails to offer whatever the customer was buying and runs off with the payment. This type of fraud has been witnessed in new dark net shops and also in shops that are facing takedown. New shops have nothing to lose if they disappear with the buyers' cryptocurrency since the dark net is so anonymous that one can set up another shop in minutes. This type of fraud caused some reputable shops in the criminal world to assure buyers that there were mechanisms in place to prevent exit scams. One of these shops is Dream Market, it claims to be so secure such that no vendor or even the site can run off with the client's deposited Bitcoin. One of the shops that did this type of fraud was called Sheep Marketplace, and the owner decided to defraud all the customers that had made deposits to the shop's cryptocurrency wallet.

Terrorism

One of the overly negative uses of the dark net has been its use for terrorism purposes. Terrorists used to be active on many platforms, but it seems they found that the clear net was too risky because they could be monitored and traced easily. They therefore gradually reduced the posting of messages or holding discussions on clear net websites and social media platforms and started adopting the dark net. Terrorism is now breeding under the cover of anonymity that is provided by the dark net. Even though there are some Islamist chat rooms on the clear net, the radicals have found refuge in the dark web. They use these hidden chat rooms to safely communicate without the fear of being hunted down by law enforcement agencies and being found. Many governments closely monitor the surface web for inflammatory remarks aimed at encouraging terrorism and they take them down. However, they cannot replicate the same on the dark net. The dark net is more difficult to keep an eye on, and that is why terrorists are exploiting it fully. After the deadly Paris shooting in 2015, The Islamic State of Iraq (ISIS) used the dark web to spread its propaganda at the heat of the moment.[12] There were messages secured on a tightly encrypted application called Telegram that gave people links to the group's dark net site.[12] The dark net site contained a lot of information about the group and promoted its ideology to visitors. There were archives of propaganda materials, documentaries, and links to private messaging portals on the Telegram platform.[12] This was an indication that terrorists had gone under and were inviting people to the dark net site which would be harder for law enforcement agencies to track and shut down.

The activities that terrorists are carrying out on the dark web are similar to what they have been carrying out on the surface web in previous years. The dark net is being used to provide information to terrorists, recruit new members, radicalize people, contribute funds, and even to plan on how terrorist attacks can be executed. Attacks are also being coordinated on the dark net as has been revealed in some terrorist attacks. In 2013, the US NSA was able to intercept communication between two Al-Qaeda heads.[12] They got to find out that the two had used the dark net for quite some time to make plans for attacks. Terrorists have been using the Telegram software to communicate on the go. It is fully encrypted and the makers have twice offered lump-sum rewards to any hacker that could break into its encryption. A study done in 2015 on Telegram found that there was a significant increase in its usage by terrorists.[12] Terrorists are using it to broadcast their messages to very many people at a go. Several Al-Qaeda branches, as well as ISIS, have been opening up many Telegram channels to communicate to a wider audience discreetly.[12]

Fund raisings have been carried out on the dark net by terrorist organizations. There was a page created on the dark net encouraging people to support the Islamic struggle but without a trace. The page displayed an address that people would send their contributions in Bitcoin. The dark net has also been used to hide the support of terrorist groups by prominent people and countries. There are rumors that some big countries have been funding and equipping ISIS for political motives. The dark net is also being used by terrorists to acquire weapons inside of countries that they wish to carry out attacks in. Investigators believed that the Paris attack was carried out using guns that had been bought from a German vendor that had a shop called DW Guns on the dark net.[12] It is also feared that terrorists are using the dark net to sell human body organs. These organs are said to be harvested from captives. Human organs fetch quite some money on the black market as there are people desperately in need of them. The dark net is also being used by terrorist groups to sell antiquities that they have looted. Syria is one of the countries where ancient cities and towns have been attacked and ancient antiquities stolen.[12]

Conclusion of the Chapter

This chapter has defined the threat landscape in the dark net. It has highlighted it as one of the most dangerous parts of the internet. The illegal activities being carried out and procured have been discussed. The chapter has explained how big markets have been set up majorly dealing in the sale of drugs. The vastness of these markets has been outlined, one of them having had record sales of a billion dollars. The challenge of taking down these markets has been explained. The shutdown of one black net often leads to the evolution of a bigger one. When a large black market is shut down, the free publicity and advertising from news media, growth in demand from previous customers, and the search for a market by existing vendors always lead to the growth of a new market. The chapter has detailed the previous takedowns of major black markets, these are Silk Road and its successor called AlphaBay. It has also discussed a market that has seemingly survived the takedown attempts though with rumors that it is already under the control of law enforcement agencies. A detailed explanation has been given about the types of commodities and services that are sold on the dark market. Some of these are believed to be hoaxes, such as the adverts about assassins for hire. The chapter has explained how these goods and services are bought and the agreements that buyers and sellers at times have to enter into when purchasing some of the items and services. Lastly, the chapter has looked at the growth of terrorism and how the dark net has facilitated it.

Summary

This chapter focused on explaining more about the threat landscape in the dark net. There has been a rise in crime and terrorism-related activity that is either being carried out or being facilitated by the dark net. There are drugs being sold, weapons and ammunitions, fake IDs of different countries, fake driving licenses, fake currencies, hacking tools, malware, and fraudulent services being offered on different black markets. Hacking and hit men services have also been listed in some markets of the dark net. In essence, all these are leading to the breeding of crime and terror, and law enforcement agencies are having a hard time putting an end to all this. The cover of anonymity provided by the dark net as well as the ability to use cryptocurrencies to pay for these dirty deals has made the dark net ungovernable. Even when police are able to take down a big market on this part of the internet, another one springs up with more vendors, items, and customers. The chapter has combed through the markets and the illegal services and goods that they offer in a bid to better elaborate the threat landscape. The next chapter will look deeper into The Onion Router (Tor) network. It will explain what makes it so powerful and anonymous.

References

1. Fighting crime in the deep web|graduate degrees Norwich, Graduate.norwich.edu, 2018. Available: https://graduate.norwich.edu/resources-msisa/infographics-msisa/deep-web-crime-requires-new-forensic-approaches/, Accessed 28 February 2018.

2. Bilton N., The untold story of silk road, part 1, WIRED, 2018. Available: https://wired.com/2015/04/silk-road-1/, Accessed 28 February 2018.
3. Sulleyman A., The criminal marketplace police just shut down was far, far bigger than we thought, The Independent, 2018. Available: http://independent.co.uk/life-style/gadgets-and-tech/news/alphabay-down-reddit-what-is-it-dark-web-website-illegal-drugs-marketplace-us-justice-department-a7851681.html, Accessed 28 February 2018.
4. Popper N., Hansa market, a dark web marketplace, bans the sale of fentanyl, Nytimes.com, 2018. Available: https://nytimes.com/2017/07/18/business/dealbook/hansa-market-a-dark-web-marketplace-bans-the-sale-of-fentanyl.html, Accessed 28 February 2018.
5. Cuthbertson A., Drug sites on the dark web just mysteriously went offline, Newsweek, 2018. Available: http://newsweek.com/biggest-drug-markets-dark-web-offline-dream-market-684064, Accessed 28 February 2018.
6. Darknet Markets, The uncensored hidden Wiki, 2018. Available: http://uhwikiwww4e4a2fc.onion/wiki/index.php/Darknet_Markets, Accessed 28 February 2018.
7. Defunct Hidden Services, The uncensored hidden Wiki, 2018. Available: http://uhwikiwww4e4a2fc.onion/wiki/index.php/List_of_Defunct_Hidden_Services#Drugs. Accessed 28 February 2018.
8. Aliens C., Russian authorities busted RAMP, the oldest darknet market, Deep Dot Web, 2018. Available: https://deepdotweb.com/2017/09/21/russian-authorities-busted-ramp-oldest-darknet-market/, Accessed 28 February 2018.
9. N2017-080/2017/News/News and media/Internet/Home - INTERPOL, Interpol. int, 2018. Available: https://interpol.int/News-and-media/News/2017/N2017-080, Accessed 28 February 2018.
10. Zykov K., ATM malware is being sold on Darknet market, Securelist - Kaspersky Lab's cyberthreat research and reports, 2018. Available: https://securelist.com/atm-malware-is-being-sold-on-darknet-market/81871/, Accessed 28 February 2018.
11. Cybercrime in the Deep Web, Blackhat, 2018. Available: https://blackhat.com/docs/eu-15/materials/eu-15-Balduzzi-Cybercrmine-In-The-Deep-Web-wp.pdf, Accessed 28 February 2018.
12. Weimann G., Terrorist migration to the dark web, Terrorismanalysts.com, 2018. Available: http://terrorismanalysts.com/pt/index.php/pot/article/view/513/html, Accessed 28 February 2018.

Chapter 3

Malicious Dark Net—Tor Network

The name Tor is an abbreviation for The Onion Router. Tor is a software that is a key enabler of anonymity in communication. The software was initially launched in 2002 and has undergone rigorous development over the years. The software is based on Mozilla Firefox and has been imitating Mozilla's user interface. It has gained popularity with the rise of dark net stores that have gained fame due to the nature of illegal activities that they have been carrying out such as the sale of drugs. Tor is capable of directing traffic through a special network that is established and run by volunteer.

Traffic flowing through Tor passes through 7,000 relays which effectively conceal the destination location. Therefore, it is hard for the users on this network to be individually identified through traffic analysis since the chain is very long. Tor users' activities such as websites they are visiting, posts they make, messages they send and receive cannot be traced back to them. This makes Tor a safe haven for people that have something to hide, and unfortunately, there are many of these. There are also very many users of Tor that use it for the legitimate purposes that it was created for. This chapter will do an in-depth discussion of Tor and will cover it in the following topics:

- Introduction of Tor network/software
- Challenges of Tor network
- Working pattern of Tor
- Deep web and Tor
- The hidden services
- Tor users

Introduction to Tor

The primary intention of the Tor network was to protect user privacy. Tor came in as a welcome solution for those that had privacy concerns that their internet activities would be monitored. Tor was thought to establish freedom on the internet. Though it has successfully established that freedom, this achievement has not come without some major downsides. It created a room for another set of evils to be committed under the veil of anonymity. Tor also has some limitations. The network can conceal the footprints of a user's internet activity; however, its unique traffic relaying system makes it easy for online services to determine that a user is accessing them from Tor. There are some websites that have restrictions on access via Tor. Tor developers have not concentrated on implementing features in the software to prevent websites from determining when they have been accessed via Tor.

Tor's routing mechanism is complex. It implements encryption on the application layer of the OSI (Open Systems Interconnection) model. The data encrypted includes that of the IP address of the device that packets are destined for. This data, which is essential for the flow of traffic, is encrypted a number of times and then sent through a virtual circuit. The circuit is made up of multiple Tor relays that are laid in succession. When a relay receives traffic, it will decrypt one layer just to find out the next relay so that it can pass the encrypted data to it. When data gets to the last relay, which could be the 7,000th relay that the data will pass through, the data is decrypted and then sent to the destination IP address without showing the source IP address. In short, for every data packet, Tor will strip out part of the packet's header that contains information about the source. This packet is then encrypted and entered into the overlay network. The packet is then moved around the Tor servers commonly known as relays till it reaches its destination. The destination does not know the source of the packet; therefore, if intercepted, no meaningful information about the path used will be discovered.

The routing of the data is such that there is no point in the relay network where the communicating peers can be discovered through the known network surveillance tools. This is because these tools have to know the source and destination of traffic and Tor does an impressive job of hiding this information. Even at the destination, the receiver of the data cannot determine the source of it. On its website, Tor says that it protects users by bouncing communications through a network of relays. It says that these relays are all over the world and are actualized by volunteers. They say that their network prevents people's internet connections from being spied on and the websites that they are on from finding out one's physical location.

On the surface web, sensitive information is encrypted through protocols such as SSL or TLS (Transport Layer Security Protocol). These are commonly used in websites that require users to enter sensitive data such as online banking website and e-commerce stores. For example, when buying items from Amazon.com, the payment processing part is such that one's bank account data is transmitted while encrypted. This encryption is meant to prevent other parties from intercepting the data packets and reading the sensitive information. However, the packets' metadata is not encrypted. Therefore, if a third party intercepts the communication using traffic analyzer tools, they can still find out the source of the encrypted information and its destination. This is because this type of data is not encrypted by SSL or TLS. However, Tor is quite different and leaves no such traces. It encrypts the data in the packets and also the metadata after stripping out some information. Only Tor servers or relays can decrypt part of the data packets, and this is done so that they may know the next node to pass the packets to.

Usage

Tor was released to the public with the view of promoting anonymity on the internet. Since then, it has been used for both legal and illegal activities. Unfortunately, most of its users have been using it for illegal activities. It has been used by criminal enterprises, hackers, terrorists, and legal enforcement agencies. Legal enforcement agencies in the United States had been financing the Tor network, though they ceased in 2012. Tor is meant not to bring anonymity to the internet since the routes from the sources to destinations can still but not easily be traced back to users. Tor just makes it very difficult for users on its network to be traced. This feature has made Tor a very useful software for people with privacy fears and those that wish to engage in illegal activities. Tor has been freely promoted by famous dark net drug stores that have been looking for customers. News media, when covering dark net crimes, give a detailed explanation of how to access the dark net, and they mostly refer to Tor as the software for such purposes.

Tor has also been used for anonymous exposes and news leaks. WikiLeaks is a worldwide known organization that releases leaked information exposing evils perpetrated by individuals, organizations, and government. It has a dark net store where users are encouraged to use Tor to visit it and give out leaked information while remaining anonymous. There have been many submissions, some of which WikiLeaks has put on the public domain. In 2017, a UK-based newspaper called *The Telegraph* released the greatest exposes done by WikiLeaks. These were stories given to WikiLeaks mostly through its secret dark net website. If it were not for Tor, probably these stories would never have come to be known. One of the exposes was a US Apache Helicopter video footage showing US soldiers shooting and killing 15 people.[1] The US military came out to say that two of these, who were journalists, were mistaken to be carrying rocket launchers; thus, they were thought to be terrorists.[1] This admission and defense of the actions taken by the soldiers proved that the leaked footage was credible and it came to the public domain due to the dark net and software such as Tor. Hacking groups have been supporting WikiLeaks and at times emptying sensitive information that they hack to the exposed network. In 2008, for example, the famous hacking group called Anonymous gave emails they recovered from John McCain's running mate to show that she had been using her private email for official purposes to avoid laws regarding public records.[1]

British military secret documents have also been leaked to WikiLeaks through the anonymous reporting network. Some of the documents gave warnings that Chinese had an appetite for spying other countries for political, military, and other kinds of information.[1] There were other leaks from the Pentagon which termed WikiLeaks as a national security threat. The most important thing to note is that software such as Tor has made all these leaks possible. Without the cloud of anonymity, people would be scared of releasing such sensitive information for fears of being traced and identified.[1] For example, there is a likelihood that the person that released the Apache Helicopter footage showing the killing of 15 unarmed people was in the US military. Without the assurance of anonymity of Tor, this person would probably never have shared this video and the public would not come to know of this.

More uses of Tor, mostly for illegal activities, will be discussed later in the chapter. It is good to note that the main purpose of Tor, as the founders emphasize, is to be used by ordinary people that wish to maintain the privacy of their internet activities. Mostly, the intended people are those that want to avoid data-hungry websites, cookies that harvest data from browsers, cyber-spying attempts by organizations and legal enforcement agencies, and those that want to avoid censorship on the internet put on their geographical locations. The users of Tor will also be discussed further later in the chapter. Tor founders are aware that criminals have proliferated the network, but they are not ready to close it down because of the other types of users that genuinely need the network. Law enforcement agencies have also not asked for the closure of this network, in fact, they at times have been supporting it. There was a report in 2014 that NSA provided Tor with bug reports to help them improve their services. This means that the network is not viewed as a threat, it is the criminal entities that take advantage of it that are the threats hunted down by law enforcement agencies. In the FAQ section of the Tor official website, there is an acknowledgment that there are some criminals taking advantage of the network. The website says that these criminals can do bad things and are ready to break the law. Other than Tor, they have many other alternatives, some of which have even more privacy. It is only coincidence that they choose Tor. The site further says that criminals can easily switch from Tor to other better options; therefore, if the network was to be taken down, it would not stop criminals from continuing on with their criminal activities. This would only take away a very useful service from people that need it.

Lastly, the site says that Tor is useful in fighting identity theft and other crimes such as stalking. Just to prove these claims, at the heights of the allegations of the NSA spying on US citizens and other internet users, there was a dramatic increase in the number of users of Tor. To date, the biggest demography of users on Tor is from the United States. However, the recent increase in the number of users is most likely due to the illegal activities taking place through such platforms.

Working Pattern of Tor

As mentioned before, Tor uses a complex overlay network that is aimed at hiding the identities of its users and their internet activity from surveillance or traffic capture and analysis. This is all made possible by a unique working pattern of Tor that uses a different routing method. Normal routing of traffic is that the information needed to send the traffic to the next node is available in a data packet's header. A router therefore only has to read the information in the header to determine the source of the data, where it is coming from, and where it is heading. Normal routing will also try to use the shortest path to the destination. The end result is that data can be traced using surveillance and traffic analysis tools to determine where it originated from and where it is headed. If a user has visited a drugs website, it can easily be determined that the user on a particular IP address received packets from the IP address of the drugs' website. Tracing back IP addresses to users is quite simple. There are many free tools that can map the physical location of an IP address on a map. Buyers of drugs, those seeking to buy illegal firearms, those wishing to watch child porn, those trying to access some websites in countries that have censorship laws, and many others do not want to be easily identified and their locations picked up. That is why they put their trust on services that can conceal their identities. A simple way to do this is to use a proxy server. A proxy server is much different from Tor's servers, but they all use the same idea. They add a hop to a user's traffic. Proxy servers are, however, not meant to be anonymous and therefore log the traffic that passes through them. They, therefore, contain evidence pointing back to people that used them, and if law enforcement agencies want this evidence, they can easily use courts to force it to be handed to them. This is why Tor is special, it avoids all the pitfalls of normal proxy servers.

Tor uses onion routing to help conceal the identities of its users as well as information regarding the websites that they are visiting. Onion routing can be thought to be as an advanced level of routing traffic through proxy servers. There are more servers in the path to a user, and they are all created in such a way that they work towards hiding information that can be used to trace back the users. Tor's proxy servers are known as relays. They are not owned by Tor; rather, they are volunteered by people all around the globe. They continually grow in number based on the people that support the Tor project and have volunteered their devices to this cause. Each of these nodes continually encrypts data packets when they pass through them. At the end of the chain, when the data packet is almost at its destination, the last relay decrypts the packet and forwards it to the destination. Only the last relay has the capabilities to decrypt the data, this means that all other relays cannot even see the contents of the packets that they forward. Additionally, the last relay strips out information from the packet header about the source of the packet. This makes it hard for traffic analyzing tools to trace the chain used to deliver the packet. The multiple layers of encryption are what make this type of routing to be referred to as onion routing. This is because each relay adds encryption to the already encrypted data packets, thus creating multiple layers of encryption. The multiple encryption layers have a semblance with the many layers of an onion. Onion routing makes it difficult for the information to be traced back to the sources and even more difficult for it to be intercepted while in transit. Tor in full means The Onion Router.

To get a better understanding of Tor's encryption, let us consider the diagram below:

In this diagram, the source node sends data to node A. Before sending, it encrypts the data packet. Node A receives the packet, decrypts a part of it to get the information about the next node to forward to, and then encrypts the packet again. At this point, the packet has two layers of encryption. The packet is then forwarded to node B which reads data about the next node in line and encrypts the packet once more before sending to the next node. The next node will relay the packet through a forest of other nodes all of which will be adding encryption till the data packet gets to the exit node, node Z. At node Z, the packet has to be made readable to the destination computer. Therefore, node Z takes the burden of decrypting all the layers of encryption that have been applied to the data packet by the other nodes in the chain. When the packet is fully decrypted, node Z still has to make sure that the packets do not point to a source. It, therefore, goes to the packet's header and deletes the information pertaining to the source. It, therefore, appears as if node Z is the originator of the packet, even though the packet could have gone through many other of relays away from the real source. The destination gets a readable packet but cannot tell exactly where it came from. It is good to note that the other nodes cannot perform the operation done by the last node of decrypting the packet fully. Also, the nodes are chosen randomly. Encryption on Tor is done through Public Key Cryptography.[2] The intended nodes in the path are therefore only able to decrypt a certain part of the packet using their private keys in order to reveal the address of the next node.[2] The exit node has keys to decrypt all the layers of encryption that have been applied by the other nodes.[2] When a user wishes to send a response back to the source, a similar path will be used where the user's Tor client will encrypt the data packet and send it to the Tor network. Node after node, the packet will be encrypted, decrypted, and encrypted again till it gets to the final node that will deliver the response to the initial source.

The Tor network is supported mostly by volunteers. The volunteers mostly help with the addition of Tor servers, commonly known as relays. When a volunteer hosts a Tor relay, some of their bandwidth is used for the transmission of data on the Tor network. Tor does not burden the relays and only requires them to donate a bandwidth of 50 KB of data per second.[2] Though it might be minuscule, Tor has very many nodes used to transmit traffic. Each node is just one of the thousands through which encrypted data packets can be passed through. The relays help increase the anonymity of the network since they add to the number of hops that data packets have to go through before getting to their destinations. The more the hops, combined with the multiple layers of encryption, the more secure the network. If the network only had a hundred relays, it would be significantly easier for authorities to crack down on the users and find out their internet activity as well as their physical locations.

When data passes through a host that has volunteered to be a Tor node, the data is not locally stored. The relays do not know the data that passes through them. If investigations are carried out at the destination computer, chances are that volunteer nodes cannot be identified. It is believed that one cannot be charged for hosting a Tor relay, though there has never been a prosecution in court to form a precedence on whether hosts of the Tor relay network can be charged for it. There are fears that those that host the Tor relays can be charged for abating crimes done on the dark net through the dark net. The counterargument is that they cannot be charged with such crimes since they do not know the type of traffic that passes through their machines. They could as well be congratulated for helping undercover journalists to pass some information anonymously.

Challenges of the Tor Network

Tor, though very strong and anonymous, still faces some challenges. Tor does not have functionalities that can prevent traffic monitoring at its boundaries. Therefore, traffic entering or exiting from its overlay network can easily be detected. Therefore, it does not cloak the traffic that passes through it to prevent sites and traffic analyzers from knowing that it has been through the anonymity network. Due to these, there are fears that the NSA and other agencies keen on surveillance can track people that are using Tor, even though they cannot identify the type of internet activity that these people are doing. It is, however, completely legal to use Tor as per most government agencies. It, however, raises eyebrows as to why someone would start using Tor, and this could cause them to be spied on. Months to the arrest of the alleged founder of Silk Road 2, Ross Ulbricht, it was said that authorities were spying his internet traffic. As they argued in court, the times when Dread Pirate Roberts who was the site admin would log in to the site matched the time when Tor traffic would be detected from Ross's computer. This exposes the disadvantage of the lack of a cloaking mechanism from Tor to prevent the identification of traffic flowing into and out of its network. If Tor had been doing this, probably agencies would not be able to correlate the logins to the Silk Road site with any other data, and thus, the evidence they had would have been less. The following are some of the weaknesses Tor has or faces.

Website Fingerprinting

It has been found out that Tor has put more focus on resilience to website finger-printing instead of tunneling protocols. Website fingerprinting is perhaps a bigger threat facing Tor's anonymity. This is because data packets are always vulnerable before they get into the Tor network through the first relay.[3] Information about where they are headed is still visible since they will not have been encrypted and it can easily be retrieved at this stage. Third parties such as internet service providers can do this. Website fingerprinting has been carried out by websites that have wished to prevent Tor-like traffic.

Website fingerprinting is done on the website's end, that is, the point at which traffic is supposed to enter into the Tor network.[3] It can identify users hiding behind VPNs (virtual private network) and proxies too. Even though website fingerprinting may not retrieve the data passed to the user, it can lead to the tracing back of the user.

Eavesdropping

It has been mentioned that the Tor network is made up of volunteer nodes. These nodes are used to encrypt and pass the data packets to other nodes till they get to the exit node. The exit node is quite special. It is the node that has the capability to decrypt the packets fully and forward them to the client as in a readable format. This, therefore, presents a security risk. Since this node can decrypt data packets to clear text formats, they can be used for eavesdropping. They are the endpoints in the overlay network, and they are the ones that talk to the end hosts and therefore can see what the client will see at the destination. The risk is magnified by the fact that it is a node that volunteers to be an exit node, it is not chosen randomly just like other relay nodes. If someone has nefarious intentions, he or she could just volunteer an exit node and use it to purposefully read the data streaming outside the Tor network to different destinations. A researcher once tried this by volunteering five exit nodes to the Tor network.[4] He monitored different protocols in the traffic exiting the network through his exit nods. He says that he was able to recover passwords and read email streams that had been transmitted through the Tor network before this data got to the end users.[4] He observed that governments and criminal entities have interests in monitoring Tor traffic, and this was an easy way that they could use. He faulted Tor's lack of end-to-end tunneling for this weakness. If the Tor network had been fully encrypted such that decryption of the data packets would only occur at the destination, then it would be impossible for people sitting at the exit node from reading the streams of data coming off the Tor network.

Tor can also be eavesdropped on using timing analysis. This is whereby an entity monitors the time at which packets leave a server and the time at which they get to a client and then make a correlation. This would require the monitoring party to be on the watch at both ends of the communication. The time at which packets leave the source and enter the Tor network and the time at which the packets exit the Tor network and get to the client's machine can be recorded. As was mentioned, timing analysis is one of the pieces of evidence that the FBI used against Ross Ulbricht in the case where he was alleged to be the founder and head of Silk Road 2.0 which was a drug marketplace on the dark net. Therefore, timing analysis could be used in court against a user by law enforcement agencies. It is troubling to know that they can collect this evidence easily on the Tor network.

A researcher called Chloe tried to determine whether there were active rogue exit nodes on the Tor network.[5] She created a dark net website that was themed with a Bitcoin layout. It was fake and was to serve as a honeypot for people that would intercept traffic to the site. She created an unsecured login page to the site and then tried to log in and out of the site over a number of times using Tor.[5] The usernames and passwords she would enter would be transmitted in clear text instead of being encrypted. Each time she connected to the site and logged in, credential information would stream in and out of the Tor network. Her expectations were that, if Tor was completely secure and free of eavesdropping, the number of site visits and login attempts would be equal to those that she did herself. However, her eavesdropping concerns were confirmed. From her multiple site visits and login attempts, there were extra visits and login attempts that she did not perform. There were 600 new page visits and 28 login attempts.[5] Some of these attempts went through. This clearly showed that other parties had retrieved her traffic stream and read information that they used to visit the website and also retrieve the login credentials. Since she had not stored the login credentials anywhere, it meant that they were snooped by someone. Her bait worked and snoopers read her data from the exit nodes each time she visited the site. This reveals the risk that is there with the current working model of Tor. The complete decryption at the exit nodes makes it quite easy for snoopers to read the data at this point. Since it is the volunteers that choose to make their computers exit nodes, people that have interests in reading traffic from Tor users could sign up their machines as exit nodes. Both criminals and law enforcement agencies are accused of doing this. They have enlisted their computers onto the Tor network, not to support the growth of Tor but to try and monitor or eavesdrop what others do on the network.

Traffic Analysis

There have been claims that the NSA has infiltrated Tor and has enlisted many nodes of its own into the network. They are said to be aimed at enlisting many of their nodes to be entry and exit nodes into to the Tor network. These are critical points where traffic can be directly monitored before it is encrypted or after it is decrypted. Another purpose for doing this is that they be able to correlate Tor-related traffic with a particular person. The ability to pinpoint the user connecting to a certain website on Tor is quite plausible, and it is believed that the FBI and NSA use this trick once they have access to entry and exit nodes to the Tor network.[6] Since the relay network welcomes volunteers to donate their machine to be used as relay, entry and exit nodes, it can be assumed that the rumors are true that law enforcement agencies have their machines already serving these crucial roles. Traffic analysis is therefore possible and can enable the law enforcement agencies to monitor who is speaking to who.

A good example is to picture a room where many people are speaking at a go and therefore it is difficult to identify any two speakers. There are a number of ways, however, that can be used to isolate any speaking pair. The first method which is quite easy is by using their names. If the speaking parties mention the names of the persons they are talking to at the beginning of their messages, it could be possible to identify the pairs that are talking to each other. If person Bob is talking to person Alice, Bob will mention Alice's name while talking to her and Alice will mention Bob's name when responding. However, suppose that the people in the room do not mention names or give any identifiable information about their talking partners. It becomes significantly harder to identify the two people talking to each other. One way of identifying them is by observing the communication patterns that is when they are starting and stopping their communication. If Bob is talking to Alice, it is expected that when he stops talking, Alice will start responding. When Bob is talking, Alice will be quiet, and when Alice is talking, Bob will be quiet. Even if they speak an incorrigible language, there will be a way of telling that indeed Bob is speaking to Alice.

This example subtly explains traffic analysis. When a snooper suspects that two persons are communicating, in Tor's case it's a user and a website server, traffic analysis can be used to determine this. In the Tor network, the most crucial nodes to monitor will be the entry and exit nodes. The analysis to confirm whether two parties are talking to each other can be done statistically using methods such as Bayesian probability. It is a common method that is used for gathering evidence. Investigators, in most cases, have to narrow down from the evidence they have in order to find the perpetrators of a crime.

The same is applied to the Tor network. There are very many users and if just one is guilty of a crime, the others have to be slowly eliminated from the circle of focus during the investigations. After several iterations of eliminating least probable suspects, a few will remain with a very high probability of being the perpetrators of a crime. Tor does a good job at making its users anonymous. Therefore, investigations on the dark web are not as simple as those on the surface web.

On the surface web, it is easy for investigators to find the culprit's machine and location using the IP address information. If they intercept traffic between the perpetrator and a server, they can simply read headers of packets to get information about the source and destination. It is the equivalent of finding out two people talking in a crowd by listening to their names if they keep mentioning them when talking. On Tor, however, this information will not be available, and therefore, alternatives have to be used. With information about the talking parties already scrapped out, there are no links between the source and destination of a communication other than their pattern of communication. In the above example, this is represented by a snooper monitoring the communication pattern between Alice and Bob. When Alice will be talking, Bob will be quiet and when Bob talks, Alice will be quiet. Bayesian probability can be used to tie Bob and Alice together in a room filled with a crowd of people talking. The crowd, in this case, is the Tor network filled with very many users who cannot be identified by names.

If law enforcement agencies already control the entry and exit nodes in the Tor network, they can intercept packets being sent into and out of the network. They can tell that Bob is sending packets and Alice is receiving packets but they do not have evidence to tie these two together. This is because Alice is receiving from a different node than the one Bob is sending to. The anonymity function of the Tor network ensures that these two never directly speak to each other, packets are bounced between different relays before they get to their destinations. However, assuming that the time taken to bounce these packets is known and is same in all communications, the time at which Bob sends a message and the time at which Alice receives the message can be correlated. If after intercepting many packets it so happens that the times at which Bob sends messages correlate with the times at which Alice receives messages, it can be concluded that Bob is talking to Alice. On the Tor network, this will mean that a particular user is sending and receiving packets from a particular website. If the website is known to be used for illegal activities, this is evidence that can be used in court to add weight to a case.

All in all, traffic analysis is a major weakness in Tor and is reportedly being used by either criminals or law enforcement agencies on Tor's network. There are chances of success, and the only impeding factor is cost. It is expensive to own and host servers that meet the requirements of being entry and exit nodes. States could afford to purchase costly servers meant for that purpose, and criminal entities that have huge amounts gained through illegal means can also spend on similarly priced computers.[6] This is, however, too expensive of a crime for an ordinary criminal knowing that one needs to have control over a number of entry and exit nodes to be able to gather enough data for correlation purposes.

Exit Node Block

There are disadvantages of the lack of cloaking of Tor traffic to make it appear as normal traffic. There are some websites that do not appreciate users that visit them using this software that offers them the much-needed user privacy that has been lost nowadays. This unfair treatment of users using Tor has seen up to 2 million users daily being blocked from accessing some sites that they wish to access with the privacy-first focused browser.[7] Some users are not entirely being denied from visiting some surface web sites but are being offered intentionally degraded services just for using Tor. One of the companies that have been working against Tor is Cloudflare. It is a company that normally offers services that sit between a user and a web host and at times acts as a proxy for websites. It is intended to mitigate threats such as distributed denial-of-service (DDoS) that websites may face. When users on Tor try to visit sites that use the services of Cloudflare, the users are first met with Captchas that are almost impossible for Tor users to solve in order to pass a test that they are not robots. It is understandable that the service will have its alarms triggered when it detects users coming off of the same IP address which could happen to be an active Tor exit node. Repeated failures by users to solve Captcha tests given by Cloudflare leads to the assignment of a bad reputation on the IP address of the exit node making it even harder for future visitors to access the same sites.

There could be some legitimate reasons, however, for blocking access from Tor users. It is one way of combating trolls on a website. Trolling is a nuisance on some websites where users create fake profiles and use them to insult or cause aggression to other site users. Trolls are active in heated hate discussions and use anonymity as a protection mechanism so that they can get away with their crimes. Cyberbullying is another reason why websites might want to block Tor users from accessing their pages. Cyber bullies are not that different from trolls just that they bully individual users. Even though Tor might make it hard for such malicious users to be traced, it does not make it impossible. The issue is that Tor users are being blanket-banned from sites that are not even under threat from Tor traffic. It is easy for Tor users to get blocked since the exit nodes from the network are known. By feeding the exit node IP addresses to a blocking algorithm, Tor users are effectively denied access regardless of whether they have good or bad intentions. Tor is transparent and provides these IP addresses on its official surface web site. It is only unfortunate that this data is harvested by sites that want to block the exit nodes from accessing their sites. Effectively, the entire Tor user community can be locked out of sites at the will of site owners. If Tor would be obfuscating its traffic, this would not be possible, but it seems Tor has not headed that path. It has chosen to remain transparent and hence the existence of this weakness.

Bad Apple Attack

The bad apple attack can be used to reveal the IP addresses of users on Tor's network.[7] This type of an attack is orchestrated in two parts. The first part involves the exploitation of an insecure application to reveal IP addresses of Tor users.[7] The second part is where Tor itself is exploited to associate the revealed IP address with a secure application.[7] Tor is not supposed to and does not protect users against attacks at the application level.

Therefore, there is nothing much it can do to protect its users from the first part of the attack. The second part of the attack is, however, as a result of Tor's weakness. Tor's design is such that traffic streams from secure applications can be associated with traced users. Then end result is that the IP addresses of Tor users on secure applications can be known.

A research done in 2011 revealed this. After 23 days of testing the attack on six Tor network exit nods, tens of thousands of IP addresses were revealed.[8] BitTorrent was the insecure application that was used to reveal the IP addresses of the users.[8] These users were then profiled and their countries of origin determined as well as their web activities. The type of content that they downloaded on BitTorrent was also analyzed. Based on this research, it came to be known that this attack was a serious one and could be used to compromise the anonymity of users on Tor's network. It is, therefore, a significant weakness that Tor faces.

Browser Vulnerabilities

The official Tor browser is normally a modified version of the Mozilla Firefox browser. It is normally fit with a few more capabilities and some user interface (UI) elements redacted to make it more difficult to track by normal means such as JavaScript codes and cookies.

However, the reliance on this browser puts Tor at a disadvantage since the known vulnerabilities on the browser can be used against Tor. The extensive crackdown on dark net illegal marketplaces was said to be successful majorly because NSA was using a vulnerability that was present on a certain version of Firefox that Tor was using.[7] There are many other incidences where Firefox browser vulnerabilities have been used against the Tor network and Tor users. They are briefly discussed below.

Freedom Hosting Bug

During a suspected FBI crackdown on child porn sites, all the dark net sites that had been hosted by Freedom Hosting started throwing a common error message due to a hidden code in the hosting company.[7] The code was further analyzed and found that it was specifically aimed at targeting a vulnerability in Firefox that was aimed at identifying Tor users. The vulnerability was targeted at a certain Tor bundle. The code gave users the message that the sites they were visiting were down for maintenance. However, it was observed that there was an iframe on the error page that was loading some JavaScript code from Verizon.[7] Later on, Mozilla came out and confirmed that the code was targeted at exploiting a bug in Firefox's memory management feature.[7] Though it had been fixed in later releases of Firefox, the bug was still present on the Tor bundle since Tor used an older version of Firefox.

FoxAcid

The NSA is said to use its connections and persuasive powers to partner with communication companies when it aims at achieving a certain goal. The FoxAcid exploit was exposed by Edward Snowden, a former NSA staff that exposed its secrets before fleeing into an asylum in Russia. According to the documents that he provided, the FoxAcid exploit is an exploitation system that runs on Windows 2003 that is configured with multiple scripts aimed at attacking computers in different ways.[7]

With connections to internet service providers, the NSA is able to place servers with FoxAcid at optimized locations for faster than normal loading. The NSA maintains control over these servers and uses them for intelligence gathering. Since these servers are on the surface net and have normal non-onion domain names, they are unsuspicious to internet users. Surface web users can visit the domain names on FoxAcid servers without any implications.

However, when users visit these servers following a special URL, these servers become malicious and infect the browser and host computer and then gain control over it.[7] These special URLs still look normal, but they lead browsers to hostile locations in the servers where malware are downloaded and infect the user's browser. Browsers can be made to visit the servers using these URLs in several ways, the common one being a race attack.[7] This is where the servers are meant to impersonate some sites, and when a user clicks links to visit the real sites, the impersonated sites are offered to them instead. The user will hardly tell the difference since the impersonation is near perfect. Snowden reported that the special URLs are used in NSA operations where users visiting a particular site are redirected to the malicious URLs through a man-in-the-middle attack involving internet service providers.[7] Tor users are normally redirected to URLs with NSA exploits for the Firefox browser. The exploits download payloads on a user's browser that are aimed at collecting the user's location and system configuration.

Deep Web and Tor

The deep web is the part of the internet that is essentially hidden from search engines such as Google.[9] It is the biggest part of the internet as it is estimated that the surface web is minuscule compared to the size of the deep web. A particularly interesting subset of the deep web is the dark net. It is hidden but discoverable. The dark net is a network that exists on top of the internet and can be accessed using special software or tools.[9] It mainly offers anonymity to its users. There are several dark nets but perhaps the most famous one is Tor, or also known as the onion router. To access Tor, one needs special software that can get into this network. The official browser provided by Tor for this purpose is a specially modified Firefox browser called the Tor browser.[9] However, other browsers such as Chrome have put out add-ons that users can fix on them to enable them to access the Tor network. The Tor browser can be used to access websites both in the dark net and also on the surface web. Its most important use is to visit the hidden websites on the dark net that are inaccessible on the surface web. These websites built within Tor are powered by a hidden service known as Tor hidden service protocol.[9] Websites that are on the Tor network have a unique .onion URL. It is good to note that outside of Tor there exists other dark nets such as Freenet.[9] These dark nets offer similar and some have even better features than Tor. When Tor and all these other dark nets are combined, they form the dark web.[9] The dark web is the equivalent of the World

Wide Web of the surface web. The surface web is the part of the internet that many people are accustomed to and is accessible via normal browsers.

Tor's Hidden Services

The popularity of Tor has grown mostly due to the hidden services that it offers. These services are indexed by some websites where they are classified as follows.

E-Commerce Services

An important note to make about Tor's network is that any money-making venture, regardless of whether legal or illegal, is an e-commerce service. There have been a number of e-commerce stores on the dark net, most of which were discussed in Chapter 2. These stores have been selling drugs, weapons, stolen credit cards, hacked PayPal accounts, fake currency, fake driving licenses, fake identity cards, and even malware.

Most of the black markets established on Tor that have been engaging in these illegal trading activities have been tracked and brought down by law enforcement agencies. The weaknesses discussed in previous sections of this chapter are the same ones that have been used by NSA, FBI, and other legal agencies to bring to justice some of the founders of these black markets.

Communication Services

Tor offers anonymous communication services where users can exchange messages without the fears of being tracked down. This comes as an advantage at a time when the NSA has been exposed for cooperating or forcing email, social media, internet service provider, and telecommunication companies to allow them to monitor messages being sent by their users.

Instant Messaging

The instant messaging platforms on Tor include Cryptocat, TorChat, and Ricochet. The messaging platforms ensure that there is a very low chance of the participants in a communication being identified or their physical locations being determined. However, some of these chatting platforms have been reported to have flaws that can lead to impersonations and also denial-of-service attacks.

Email

Tor gives users the ability to send and receive emails on the network while remaining anonymous. This is a feature that has made it possible for users that have sensitive information and want to prevent it from being intercepted or being able to be traced back to them to share it with others. This scenario is faced by whistle-blowers, government spies, and citizens inside countries that have strict censorship rules. This adds weight as to the need for the long-term existence of Tor as these are some of the most important uses of Tor. Without the network, it would be nearly impossible for these types of users to communicate with people. However, the anonymity feature in emailing can also be abused by criminals and terrorists to communicate in ways which they cannot be easily traced and can talk with each other to share intelligence and plan on attacks. Some of the email service providers on Tor include Bitmessage.ch and Riseup.

File Storage

Tor offers file hosting services to users, a place where they can keep their digital files securely without worrying about their privacy. There are concerns that cloud storage services on the surface web come with security and privacy risks since the cloud vendors, hackers, and law enforcement agencies might try to open files on such storage platforms. On the Tor network, the chances of hacking are significantly fewer. It is also difficult for law enforcement agencies to collude with the storage service providers to get access to the files stored. Unfortunately, Tor's file storage services are also used for illegitimate purposes. The Pirate Bay, a known site that uses a peer-to-peer network to help users download pirated content and programs, uses Tor for its file storage needs. Alongside The Pirate Bay is BitTorrent that offers the same services which has also resulted in using Tor's file storage services. The most commonly used file storage system on Tor is called Free Haven. It is built to ensure that data can reliably and constantly be availed to users. It is said to be a product of MIT students.

Financial Services

Just like the surface web, Tor's network has corners where one can find financial services. On the surface web, there are sites that one can use to buy, store, and sell cryptocurrency. There are others that users can use to convert from one cryptocurrency to the other. Lastly, there are forex sites that are used to exchange currencies of different countries or regions. In Tor, operations are only carried out in cryptocurrency with Bitcoin being the digital currency of choice. Therefore, there are many sites that deal with exchange of fiat currency into Bitcoin and back. Others offer cryptocurrency wallets. A reliable company that operates both on the surface and deep web that offers these financial services is Blockchain.info.

News Archives

There are parts of the Tor's network that contain archives of news and other documents. They can be accessed to read current and old news without leaving the Tor network.

Some companies such as *The New York Times* regularly have their content posted on Tor. Other news archiving sites include BuggedPlanet and DeepDotWeb.

Whistle-blowing Sites

Due to its anonymity, Tor is obviously a ready platform for whistle-blowers to give out evidence of malpractices by individuals, governments, and companies. There are quite a number of successful whistle blows that have been done through Tor. High-ranking individuals that have committed felonies have been exposed on this network. Companies and senior staff that have failed to comply with legal obligations have been reported here. Crimes such as corruption and collusion have also been reported here. Safe havens and international banks used by the corrupt to stash away proceeds of illegal activities have been reported on Tor. The world has come to know of many crimes, injustices, malpractices, and dirty secrets through the Tor network. The assurance of anonymity has convinced many users that have evidence against big people and powerful companies and government institutions that there is a way to hand over the evidence without putting their identities at risk. Without Tor, it would be almost suicide to attempt to give evidence about these presumably big companies, people, or governments. As an adoption of the type of platform that Tor gives users to submit evidence of anonymity, some governments have encouraged their citizens to report corruption cases and other illegalities committed by known offenders through whistle-blowing sites. Italy, one of the countries advocating for the use of Tor for whistle-blowing, has recently launched its own Tor-backed whistle-blowing site meant for reporting corruption.[10] These are the legitimate uses of Tor that keep it going despite being associated with negative things such as drug trade and cybercrime.

Tor has a number of sites that are used for whistle-blowing. The most famous one is WikiLeaks that has gained popularity over the years due to the high number of high-profile crimes reported through it. There have been whistle blows touching on governments such as the US government, high-ranking politicians, businesspeople and companies that have been done through WikiLeaks. There are other less-prolific whistle-blowing sites but nevertheless, are used for the same purposes as WikiLeaks. They include GlobaLeaks, Filtrala, NawaatLeaks, and WildLeaks.

Search Engines

Just like the surface web has Google, Bing, Yahoo Search, and others, Tor's network has its own set of search engines. They are preferred for use on the dark net since they do not have intentions of capturing details about the users. Normal surface web search engines such as Google have been accused of being hungry for user data and capturing every conceivable piece of information that can be used for advertising. Dark net users, being paranoid of information such as their locations, search histories, and web activities being recorded have opted to use search engines on the dark net that are purposefully made to make them feel safe from user data collection. A particularly famous search engine that is commonly used on the dark net is DuckDuckGo. There are others such as Ahmia, BTDigg, and Searx that are options for DuckDuckGo. By default, Tor's software uses DuckDuckGo when are user does searches on the internet.

Social Media Platforms

The surface web has the likes of Facebook, Twitter, Instagram, and LinkedIn as social media platforms that internet users use to get in touch with friends, relatives, and the world. However, these platforms are plagued with user privacy issues. Some such as Facebook are accused of collecting user information from their accounts and selling it to third parties. The reliance on advertising as a revenue source of most social media platforms has led them to engage in questionable practices just to collect more user data. Some are said to even read user inbox messages to try and get any data that can be used for marketing. On the surface web, the craze to make ad revenues has made social media platforms quite unfriendly for people that have concerns about their own privacy. Tor has its own social media platforms or their equivalent where users can anonymously interact with each other. Anonymity gives the users a mask and since they are sure that they cannot be traced, they are more open and frank with each other. Some of the social media platforms on Tor are 8chan, Facebook, and The Hub.

The Users of Tor

Tor attracts a set of different users that wish to capitalize on its anonymity. There are those that have good and bad intentions when using the network. Unfortunately, the users that have been engaging in illegal activities through the network is far greater than the number of those using it for beneficial purposes. Therefore, Tor always advises its critics that it is not by design a network for illegal activities, it is just coincidental that criminals have sought refuge in it. It says that there are other dark net sites that offer far much better anonymity features that criminals can migrate to. Therefore, if it were to be closed, this would not quite solve the problem. On the other hand, its closure would be detrimental to other users that use it for the right purposes that it was meant for. One set of users are those that use it just for their privacy concerns since they do not trust the surface web. It is very hard for one to find a site nowadays that does not keep cookies in one's browser after just a single visit. These cookies record everything ranging from site usage behavior to one's web browsing habits. There are internet users that have grown tired of being monitored by websites and have therefore switched over to Tor. Another set of users are those that are avoiding cyber spying. Government agencies such as NSA have been exposed to be actively spying on people for what they call security reasons.

The spying has stretched from getting data from ISPs to gaining access to emails from email companies. The NSA has also been said to have quite a number of exploits that it can use on browsers if they are used to visit some sites. The privacy concerns are understandable and internet users have been turning to the world of Tor to escape from all this. It is just unfortunate that some government agencies have identified Tor as a threat and are actively working on ways to infiltrate it and extend their espionage activities.

Another sensitive group of users is activists. Activists, especially those against powerful opponents such as governments and big corporations, are at risk of being silenced if their true identities are discovered. On the surface web, it is very easy for an activist to be tracked down based on their internet activities. However, Tor makes it a challenge for tracking to be done. It is, therefore, a safe haven for those that have legitimate causes and wish not to be silenced by their oppressors. Another minority group of users is journalists. Journalists covering some sensitive stories that touch on powerful people or governments are also at risk of being considered threats and tracked downs. There are some harmful truths that powerful organizations and institutions will stop at nothing to have buried. However, Tor gives the needed anonymity to allow them to keep going with their stories. Lastly, there is a big percentage of Tor users that are in internet-censoring countries. In these countries, it is illegal to visit some sites or some sites have been blocked, and the only way of accessing them is by using software such as Tor. It is estimated that this is the second largest group of users on Tor. They rely entirely on this software and network to be able to get in touch with the censored world. As has been seen from the list of users, there are very many legitimate users. It is only unfortunate that media has cast more light on the criminal-minded users of Tor, and thus, this has overshadowed the appreciation of the network as an important platform for many other types of users.

Conclusion of the Chapter

The chapter has gone through Tor as a dark net that has so much to offer. The technology behind this overlay network has been discussed citing that it is volunteer-based and is composed of very many servers located all over the world. The chapter has also explained that Tor was created for a different set of reasons than the ones that it has come to be commonly associated with. It was intended to bring freedom to the internet through anonymity, but this freedom has been brought at the compromise of some evils being committed on the network. It is these evils that have encouraged law enforcement agencies to proliferate the once secure platform. The challenges that it faces, as discussed, are mostly from efforts by law enforcement agencies to try and uncover the identities of its users. The chapter has cast light on the services that are offered by the network and the types of people that use Tor. As it has been seen, the intended users of Tor direly need the network, and it has only been unfortunate that criminals have made the network their home too.

Summary

This chapter has discussed one of the most famous dark nets, perhaps one that many novices think is the whole deep web. The type of services it offers, the users, and its challenges especially with people trying to undermine its anonymity have been covered. The establishment of criminal enterprises on Tor has been highlighted in this chapter. In extension of this discussion, the next chapter discusses one of the products being made and sold by these criminal enterprises, malware. It will cover in entirety a discussion of malware and the criminal business model.

References

1. Chivers T., Wikileaks' 11 greatest stories, The Telegraph, 2018. Available: https://telegraph.co.uk/news/0/wikileaks-greatest-ever-stories-scandals/, Accessed 16 March 2018.
2. What is onion routing, make use of explains, 2018. Available: https://makeuseof.com/tag/what-is-onion-routing-exactly-makeuseof-explains/, Accessed 16 March 2018.
3. Website fingerprinting attacks and defense, B3rn3d.com, 2018. Available: http://b3rn3d.com/blog/2016/01/20/behavior-fingerprinting/, Accessed 16 March 2018.
4. Edge J., Eavesdropping on Tor traffic, Lwn.net, 2018. Available: https://lwn.net/Articles/249388/, Accessed 16 March 2018.
5. Stockley M., Can you trust Tor's exit nodes? Naked Security, 2018. Available: https://nakedsecurity.sophos.com/2015/06/25/can-you-trust-tors-exit-nodes/, Accessed 16 March 2018.
6. How to use traffic analysis to defeat Tor, Wonder How To, 2018. Available: https://null-byte.wonderhowto.com/how-to/use-traffic-analysis-defeat-tor-0149100/, Accessed 16 March 2018.
7. Attacks Against Tor, Mijpsrtgf54l7um6.onion.link, 2018. Available: https://mijpsrtgf54l7um6.onion.link/index.php/Attacks_Against_Tor#cite_note-19, Accessed 16 March 2018.
8. Blond S.L., Manils P., Abdelberi C., Kaafar M.A.D., Castelluccia C., Legout A., and Dabbous W., One bad apple spoils the bunch: exploiting P2P applications to trace and profile Tor users. arXiv preprint arXiv:1103.1518, 2011.
9. Tiwari A., What is the difference between deep web, darknet, and dark web? Fossbytes, 20018. Available: https://fossbytes.com/difference-deep-web-darknet-dark-web/, Accessed 16 March 2018.
10. Italy's anti-corruption agency embraces Tor onion services for whistleblowing, Dark Web News, 2018. Available: https://darkwebnews.com/anonymity-tools/tor/italy-agency-embraces-onion-services/, Accessed 16 March 2018.

Chapter 4

Malware

Introduction

The internet is now an efficient network for distribution of malware by attackers. It is always available, fast, and is connected to by very many people all over the globe. Malware have the ability to infect, manipulate, and destroy computing devices and networks. Some types of malware are stealthy such that victims will not know when their devices are infected or when malware are actively causing damage to them. With the increased adoption of the internet, the increase of active computing devices and significant improvements in technology, the frequency, and sophistication of malware attacks have increased. Malware attacks currently pose a threat not only to internet security but also the internet economy. Unfortunately, the efforts to fight malware proliferation have not been so successful. The biggest challenge is with users. Internet users, knowing that some are quite new or elderly, are oblivious to the means through which malware are being transmitted. They are therefore easily becoming victims. There is also technology that makes it easier for malware to be attached in files or to be automatically downloaded onto devices when certain sites are visited. Very effective malware have become listed on dark net sites. In 2017, there was an interesting listing of malware that could be used to make ATM machines to spit out all the cash in them. Similarly, powerful malware are being sold in black markets on the anonymous deep web. With challenges in knowledge and understanding of malware, it is hard for malware to be fought.

Even though different vendors of antivirus systems are putting efforts in improving the effectiveness of their programs in preventing malware, malware infections have remained the most serious threats to computers globally. Even though millions of signatures get added to antivirus knowledge bases, the attackers are even craftier. It is estimated that there are over 60 million new pieces of malware released each year. Malware creators are accessing more techniques that can produce different variants of malware that can circumvent security systems. There are those that can circumvent detections, others that can obfuscate their activities, and others that are being engineered to break through encryption. This chapter does an in-depth discussion of malware and their effects. This chapter will discuss more about malware and will do so in the following topics:

1. Malware and its classification
2. Purpose of malware
3. Criminal business model of malware
4. Malware analysis
5. Detection techniques, etc.

Learning Outcomes

In this chapter, you will explore

- What is malware
- The classification and subclassification of malware
- What malware is used for
- The criminal business model of malware
- How are malware analyzed
- The detection methods for malware.

Classification of Malware

Programs that are classified as malware are essentially malicious programs that can cause damage or disruption to computers and their networks. Generally, there are three categories which include viruses, worms, and Trojans. There are, however, other types of programs that fall into this category, and they include some hacking tools and virus code constructors. The following is a comprehensive listing of the classes of malware.

Viruses

These are malicious programs with the capability of replicating themselves using the resources of the devices that they invest. Viruses can take control of a victim's computer. As such, it can manipulate, steal, or delete data contained therein. It can also monitor browsers to capture and steal the passwords used by a user to log into online accounts such as banks and emails. Viruses can harvest a lot of sensitive information from a victim's computer. Computer viruses are also used to recruit devices into botnets by making them zombies that can send spam emails and illegitimate traffic for the purpose of performing denial-of-service (DoS) attacks. There is a particularly different type of virus that is renowned for its stubbornness called Rootkit virus. A rootkit virus is a malware that is capable of installing itself stealthily and is quite challenging to find or remove. It runs on a computer with elevated privileges and can, therefore, circumvent normal detection mechanisms such as antivirus program scans. Some antivirus programs have been added a functionality to do boot-time scans to help find and eliminate such stubborn malware. Operating systems are also receiving updates to make it more challenging for malware to get root privileges or for them to start up with the OS before security programs are even started.

Viruses are somewhat easy to contain their spread when compared to worms. This is because they do not normally use networks to propagate themselves to other computers in a network. Instead, they use a rather linear method of movement to reach remote computers. This is done in three ways. The first one is where the virus infects files located on network drives. Therefore, when other computers access and download that file, it comes with the virus. The second way is whereby a virus infects a removable storage media. When such media are inserted into another computer, the virus will be able to move to the device. Lastly, viruses can be propagated if they infect a file that is sent as an attachment to another device. When the attachment is downloaded and opened, the virus will infect the computer.

Worms

Worms are malicious programs that can easily and quickly propagate themselves to infect very many computers in a short period of time. They are also notorious for employing nefarious techniques to ensure that they reach to as many computers as possible such as sending themselves through emails to one's entire contact list. This is done without the knowledge of the user. The following is a deeper categorization of worms to help tell the different types that exist.

Instant Messaging Worm

This is a type of worm that spreads itself over instant messaging (IM) systems. This type of worm infects other computers by sending links to one's contacts on these messaging platforms. The link sent to these users will automatically download the worm and infect the IM user's computer. When it infects the user's computer, it will repeat the same process where it goes through one's contact list and sends the link to other users.

Email Worms

These are specifically propagated through emails. The worms will send themselves as attachments in emails to one's contacts in an email. The worm will activate itself either when the attachment is downloaded or opened by the recipient. Email worms come coded with methods to help them propagate over emails. Some use MS Outlook services since it is a popularly used client program by enterprises for emailing needs. Other worms use either Windows MAPI (Messaging Application Programming Interface) or their own SMTP (Simple Mail Transfer Protocol) server connections to get into a messaging platform and send themselves to other users. Email worms are crafty at finding the emails of the recipients that they target. They can read address books in Microsoft Outlook, read text files stored on hard disks with email addresses, or read email addresses in inbox folders.

P2P Worm

It is a type of a worm that is spread over peer-to-peer file-sharing networks. The worm propagates itself in a simple manner, it just copies itself to the files on the networked computers. When a peer connects to an infected computer, the files downloaded will have the worm which will infect the downloading device.

Net Worm

It is a type of worm that that only propagates itself through computer networks. This is a feature that is only present in this type of worm. The malware will search for vulnerabilities in programs being run on networked computers and use the vulnerabilities to attack the hosts. For an infection to happen, the worm will send an exploit in a packet to the hosts and these packets will contain part of the worm's code that is responsible for penetrating the target computer and activating. In other scenarios, the code will have instructions to request for the download and execution of a file that contains the main attack module. Network worms can spread very fast since they maintain their presence on the network hunting for any vulnerable devices.

Trojans

Trojan horses infect a computer through the guise of a program that users willingly download. These types of malware are known for performing actions without the authorization of users. They can initiate the deleting, blocking, modifying, or copying of data and the disruption of computer performance. However, unlike worms and viruses, they do not have the capability to replicate themselves. There are subclasses of worms based on their behaviors.

Backdoors

These are Trojans that create a secret back entry into a system or software. This backdoor access gives the attacker the power to remotely control a victim's machine. Such Trojans run their operations covertly and invisibly since they do not obtain the consent of a user. Backdoors can be used by attackers to steal data, delete files, log activities, or change the privileges of system users.

Exploit

These are malicious programs that have executable codes that can take advantage of vulnerabilities in programs running on local or remote computers. These types of malware are used in much larger attacks where they compromise a system or software, thus allowing for other malicious software or codes to be executed. Exploits are mostly used for penetration purposes into systems where other attacks will be carried out. There is a particularly unique type of exploit malware that is used to send requests to computers that will cause them to crash.

Rootkit

Trojans classified as rootkits are as evasive as rootkit viruses. They are able to hide their presence on computers and from antivirus software thereby making it hard for them to be detected. These Trojans can over a long period steal saved passwords, capture credentials, or be used to manage the victim computer during the distributed denial-of-service (DDoS) attack where the victim is one of the participants in a botnet of zombie computers. The rootkit additionally gives attackers backdoor functions that allow them to further install other malware or control the machine remotely.

Trojan ArcBomb

These malware are aimed at slowing down the operations of a computer or causing a full system crash. They mostly do this by flooding the computer's hard disks with large amounts of empty data that is stored in an archived form. They are commonly targeted at mail servers where automated processing systems handle all the incoming data. When a zipped file with an archive bomb is opened, the server gets filled with empty data and crashes. The data is referred to as empty for a reason, even though it is not null. There are three ways used to create this empty data. The first one is with malcrafted archive headers, the second one is using repeating data, and the last one is the use of identical files in an archive. In the second technique, the archive repeatedly empties the same data over and over till the storage capacity of the computer is overwhelmed. During compression and archiving, this repeating data will have been removed such that the files are small. A 10 GB file could have repeating data such that when archived it is only 1 MB. When decompression of the file occurs, the 1 MB file explodes back to its 10 GB size. In real attacks, much larger file sizes will be used.

In the last technique, the archive will have identical files that have been zipped, thus making it appear as if they are just a small-sized file. When this file is unzipped, the files are decompressed to their individual sizes and they may be just too large for the computer to handle. For instance, an attacker may archive 10,000 identical files into a small 100 MB file since compression techniques do not repeat the same data over and over to save on space. When this file is decrypted, all these files will grow back to their individual sizes and most likely overwhelm the capacity of a computer's disk.

Trojan-Banker

It is a name given to the Trojans that are specifically made to steal data from online banking systems or systems that process online payments or card payments. These Trojans capture and transmit the user data to attackers through emails, FTP connections, or web requests. Attackers will either cash out money from the affected accounts or sell these accounts on black markets. The dark net has seen a proliferation of stolen PayPal accounts that have most likely been gotten using this type of malware.

Trojan-Clicker

Trojans in this category are built to make devices visit certain websites without the knowledge or consent of the user. They can do this by sending certain commands to a browser to open certain websites or by replacing system files used to access the internet. The malware does this for three purposes. The first one is to increase the visits some websites get with the goal of maximizing ad revenue due to the increased number of views. The second purpose is to perform a DoS attack whereby many computers will be making too many requests at once to a web server, thus overwhelming its capabilities. The last purpose is to lead browsers to malicious sites that can auto download other malware to infect the computer further.

Trojan DDoS

This Trojan is specifically meant to convert a victim computer into a zombie that participates in DDoS attacks. The malware is aimed at infecting many machines, sometimes as many as 100,000, which it then uses in DDoS attacks. The infected machines are given commands to send numerous requests to a predefined address at a certain time such that the device under attack is overwhelmed and cannot process more requests. The Trojan may avoid carrying out any other functions to prevent arousing suspicion from the user. Most users whose computers are infected with the malware do not even know.

Trojan Downloader

It is a type of Trojan that can download new versions of malware onto victim computers. The malware is often used to infect visitors when they initially load a malicious website. Once it gets into a machine, it opens an avenue for other malware to get it.

It will periodically download new malicious programs such as adware. In addition to this, the Trojan will set these programs to start during the boot up of the OS.

Trojan Dropper

It is a malicious program that is used to covertly install more malicious programs on a victim's computer. The malware will download files for these malicious programs and copy them into directories on the hard disk of the victim from where they can be launched. Trojan Droppers are used to install malicious programs that may be detected by antivirus programs. The Trojan Dropper will have a non-malicious piece of code, but it will be used to download far more malicious malware file by file.

Trojan FakeAV

It is a unique malware that simulates the actions of an antivirus program on an OS for the purpose of manipulating the computer users. The Trojans will claim to be a malware removal tool so that a user can download it. Once downloaded and installed, the malware will simulate a scanning process that is meant to further fool the user that the program download is beneficial. However, the malware will start creating pop-ups alerting of malware, thus making the user get concerned about security and pay for the fake antivirus program with hopes that it will do a full system scan and remove the malware. In the worst cases, these fake antivirus programs can inhibit the operations of the OS to convince the user that they need to pay for the malware removal software to take care of the problem.

Trojan IM

It is a Trojan that targets IM platforms on a victim's computer. The aim is usually to steal user account data, particularly the login credentials. When these details are stolen, the attackers may try to defraud either the owner of the account or those in his or her contact list. The account owner may be asked to pay for some ransom for the hackers not to release some sensitive information or images that they find on these accounts. They may defraud one's contact list by asking them to send some financial aid due to an unfortunate happening that has occurred.

Trojan Proxy

These malicious programs are used by attackers to enable them to access the internet through the victim's machine. Therefore, it will appear that it is the victim visiting the sites that the attackers are visiting because their traffic is routed through the infected machine. These Trojans can be used by attacks to access sites that have blocked their IP addresses due to malicious behavior. They may also be used to escape legal consequences since it will occur as if it is another person visiting some sites and sending some malicious packets instead of the real attackers.

Trojan Ransom

It is a Trojan that is used to take hostage of a victim's computer and demand that ransom is paid so that the computer is made usable. The Trojan can modify data causing a huge hindrance to the normal functioning of programs or the OS. The user will be boxed into paying the attackers some ransom money in order for the computer to be made usable. Trojan ransoms require an attacker to send the victim another program that can restore the modified data, thus making the OS and programs to run normally.

Trojan SMS

This is a type of a Trojan that can send text messages from a mobile device on a carrier's network to a premium rate number. The victim will incur heavy charges due to the SMSs being sent to such numbers often in quick succession. The malware normally infects mobile devices especially when they are used to visit malicious websites. Also, these malware are found in some apps, and they get installed when infected apps are installed by the users. Application stores such as the Android Play Store regularly have to blacklist some of the applications published on their platforms due to the issue of Trojan SMSs. Additionally, the most common OSs have been implementing controls to ensure that a user first gives consent for a text message to be sent to a premium rate number. In 2016, there were devastating effects witnessed due to this type of malware. Several reports detailed the threats that malicious apps published on official app markets were draining user's money through the premium rate SMSs (Figure 4.1).

Welcome to the scary world of Premium SMS message fraud.

Premium SMS messages are intended to be a legitimate way for a 'content provider' to make money by somehow convincing someone to sign up to receive content via SMS, such as a joke of the day, trivia question, or something else with a 'premium' charge being automatically added to the 'subscriber's' cell phone bill.

The 'subscriber' is usually charged a fee of up to $9.99 for the 'content'. This charge may continue from month to month until the 'subscriber' sends a text reply of "STOP" to the premium SMS message content provider or calls their cell provider to have the charges stopped.

Figure 4.1   A news article on premium SMS fraud. (Source: https://lifewire.com/ protect-yourself-from-premium-sms-text-message-scams-2487773.)

Trojan Spy

This is a type of Trojan that is used to spy on whatever a user does on a computer. They can, therefore, track data being typed on keyboards, take screenshots of the computer, or access the list of all running programs on the device. This information is collected and sent back to the attackers. It is used to plan for much larger attacks on the target or to get hold of sensitive data that can be used to access some systems (Figure 4.2).

Malicious Tools

Besides the three commonly known classes of malware is a fourth class that is made up of other types of malicious programs. This is the class of malicious tools. These are programs used to create other malware, manage DoS attacks, or directly hack into other computers. However, the types of malware in this class are not a direct threat to a computer as they are used by attackers only. They, therefore, do not directly infect users and carry out their malicious functions on the victim machines.

Purpose of Malware

Malware has been in existence since the 1980s and therefore was created for a particular reason. Early malware were mostly viruses, and they mostly involved programming codes being written for dark purposes. These were mostly being used by programmers to prank other people or to showcase their prowess. Over time, things changed, and malware is no longer just about showing the prowess of programmers or about playing pranks. With the advent of the internet, it was discovered that this malware could be passed to many computers connected to the internet, and then they would pay to have the malware removed. Therefore, the main incentive that has led to the proliferation of malware is money. There has been the motivation to make illegal profits either through malware removal services. Then attackers discovered that they could do much more on victim computers such as steal valuable data. This became another avenue to amass illegal profits. If one could steal data from a business and sell it to a competitor, money would be made.

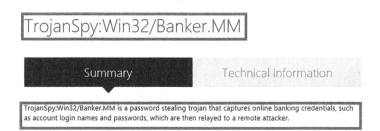

Figure 4.2   Trojan spy detected on windows.

Today, the main purpose of malware has remained to be money, although there still are other motivations. Most attackers are looking for ways to make quick money, and malware is a quick answer. If one encrypts and holds ransom several computers, the owners will probably pay up, thus giving him financial incentives to repeat the same. Businesses are hiring hackers to steal data from their competitors, thus giving hackers even more incentive to steal data upfront and sell it to the willing buyers. The use of online banking and payment systems has also made attackers figure out ways that they can use to infiltrate such transactions and take the money themselves.

Besides money, malware has been used for purely destructive purposes. A famous malware attack is one that is suspected to have been done by the United States and Israel against Iran. It involved a malware called Stuxnet that was purposefully made to destroy Iran's nuclear plant. WannaCry was rumored to have been engineered by North Korea. Malware is still being used for destructive purposes especially by attackers that have motives against the targets. These could be former business allies, enemy states, and insider threats (Figure 4.3).

Malware is being used to get access to sensitive systems by hackers. These systems may be used for specific functions, and if an unauthorized party can infiltrate them, they could use them to their advantage. Lastly, malware is used as a precursor to other attacks. Therefore, an attacker may use certain malware to soften a target. Softening a target may involve introducing a vulnerability that can be exploited in another attack or taking down some defensive functionalities of a system.

Ultimately, the purposes of malware are more and diverse. There are those that still use them for the purposes of pranking, but many people have used malware for nefarious purposes. It is the decision of the holder of a malware that determines the purpose for which the malware will be used.

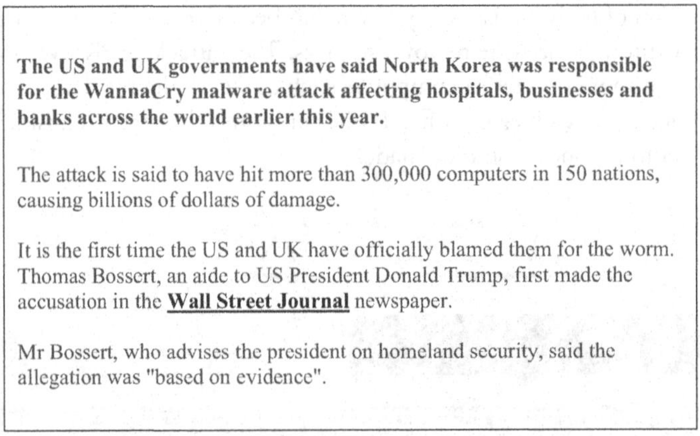

The US and UK governments have said North Korea was responsible for the WannaCry malware attack affecting hospitals, businesses and banks across the world earlier this year.

The attack is said to have hit more than 300,000 computers in 150 nations, causing billions of dollars of damage.

It is the first time the US and UK have officially blamed them for the worm. Thomas Bossert, an aide to US President Donald Trump, first made the accusation in the **Wall Street Journal** newspaper.

Mr Bossert, who advises the president on homeland security, said the allegation was "based on evidence".

Figure 4.3 A news article alleging North Korea's role in WannaCry. (Source: http://bbc.com/news/world-us-canada-42407488.)

Criminal Business Model of Malware

Researchers have come to a finding that attackers have created an underground economy where they are well organized and perform specialized tasks in the economy such as pay-per-install and malware-as-a-service. Therefore, a malware attack, particularly on corporates, should not be thought as a single event, it is backed by a chain of processes in the underground economy where several factors may have been aligned to make it successful. Financial malware schemes are made up of different elements that have been perfectly aligned such that an attack can be coordinated and financial rewards from the attack can be distributed. It is therefore of importance to understand the process of acquiring, combining, and aligning all the moving parts and their value chains.

With the quick development of the malware economy such that cybercriminals were found to be in most cases a step ahead of security teams, researchers have looked at how malware attacks happen, who or what they target, and the unique online characteristics of targets that influence the chances of success. Most importantly, the infrastructure required during the execution of financial malware has been studied leading to studies on botnets and their control servers. Another piece in the business model that has been of interest to study is the target-selection mechanism. This has been studied to help researchers find out exactly how attackers tell the targets they can hit and those they should not. The cashing-out strategy for attackers has also been studied to help explain how attackers cash out the money they get as direct proceeds of attacks. Lastly, studies have been made to find the connection between underground markets and malware, and these have led to the discovery of many underground services offered to make malware attacks successful.

From this description, it can be seen that the business model has many parts, and they all have to align from the target selection to cashing out from each successful attacks. The following is the malware scheme that has been and is still being used by cybercriminals.

Source Code Setup: Toolkits, Malicious Codes, Malware Source Codes, Exploits

This is where the first group of cybercriminals in the scheme come to play. They are the ones that source for malware and malicious codes that can be used against victims. In the underground markets, malware can be bought as exploit-as-a-service, crimeware-as-a-service, or through the purchase of exploit kits. The newer the malware and its attack techniques, the more pricey it gets.

Infection

This is where the malware gets installed on a victim's device. This can be outsourced in the malware black markets where there are people that offer the service of pay-per-install where they charge for every device installed by the malware.

Infrastructure

Some attack types require a well-reclinedinfrastructure so that the malware or attack can be effective. A good example is a DoS attack where a whole botnet is required. Alongside the botnet is a control server that will be used to command the zombie computers to send illegitimate traffic to a certain address simultaneously. In the black market, there are botnets for hire or botnets for sale if an attacker wishes to use them in the long term (Figure 4.4).

Target Selection: Attack Selection, Attack Vector

Some attacks require specific targets especially when the malware is new or expensive and there is only one chance to get it right. There are specialist cybercriminals that can study lists of potential targets and find the ones that have vulnerabilities that can be exploited. These also offer their services at a cost.

Cash Out: Cash-Out Strategies

The proceeds of the attack have to be securely routed back to the attackers. Cybercriminals will want to use a cash-out strategy that does not leave trails back to them. If trails are left, they could be tracked and put behind bars or busted in future attacks. There are specialists that offer money mule services.

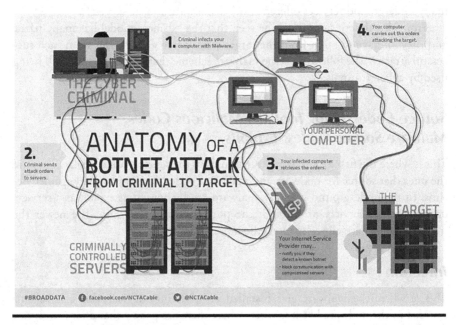

Figure 4.4 Infographic on botnets.

Part of a financial malware value chain	Underground alternative
Crimeware (source code and set-up)	Exploit-as-a-service; crimeware-as-a-service; source code for sale/free; exploit kits
Infections	Pay-per-install; drive-by downloads
Infrastructure	Botnet lease; C&C rent
Target selection	Payload, web inject/config files for sale
Cash-out	Money mule recruitment services; bitcoin exchanges; gift cards; prepaid credit cards

Figure 4.5 The financial malware scheme. (Source: https://link.springer.com/ article/10.1007/s10610-017-9336-3.)

This is where they transfer the monetary proceeds from crime to the original attackers. Mostly, money mules make money stolen difficult to trace hence to recover by moving it through multiple intermediaries. Mostly Bitcoin exchanges on the dark net are used or the money is converted to gift cards and prepaid cards (Figure 4.5).

New Value Chains

There are new value chains being used to milk money out of the malware business without necessarily having to go through the traditional scheme. We shall investigate two chains.

Value Chain 1: Man-in-the-Middle Attack on Untargeted Victims

This is where an attack can directly cash out the money from a target without having to rely on other components to make the attack successful. The process is simple. It begins with the attacker injecting malware in dynamic websites which are targeted at infecting internet users that visit them. The malware is auto-downloaded onto the victim's browser without them knowing. The target will have visited just one of the infected websites for this to happen. This type of attack will not be specifically targeted at one person; rather, it will be a wide net capturing just anyone that is infected with the malware. When the malware is on the browser and the victim visits an online banking platform, the attack will infiltrate the active session and use it to withdraw or send money to another account. Therefore, money leaves the account of the target to that of the cybercriminal without raising any suspicion on the bank's site. The cybercriminal will use one of the many money mules to withdraw the money without leaving trails (Figures 4.6 and 4.7).

As shown in the figure above, the malware scheme for this new value chain is quite different. To infect the victim's browser or device, the attacker needs a working malware. This malware can be obtained from the underground markets on the dark net through purchase or lending. This is where malware-as-a-service happens. The next step is where the attacker has to get the malware on the victim's browser for the attack to continue. To attack a banking application, the attacker needs to install the malware on the computers of users that visit certain sites and then visit their online banking platforms.

For the purpose of installing the malware on the devices of many relevant targets, the attacker might pay someone else to do that. This is where pay-per-install comes in. The person contracted to install the malware on end-user devices will be paid a certain amount or commission based on the number of computers infected. The next phase of the attack is where the malware has to infiltrate an active banking session between a target and a bank. At this point, the web session will be stolen using the malware and the attacker will be able to authorize the transfer

Novel Man-in-the-Browser attack

Figure 4.6   A depiction of the man-in-the-middle browser attack.

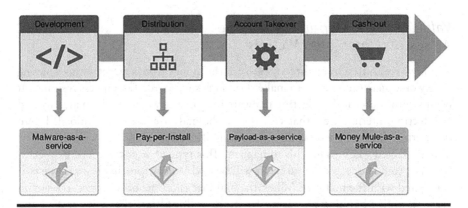

Figure 4.7   The malware scheme for the new value chain.

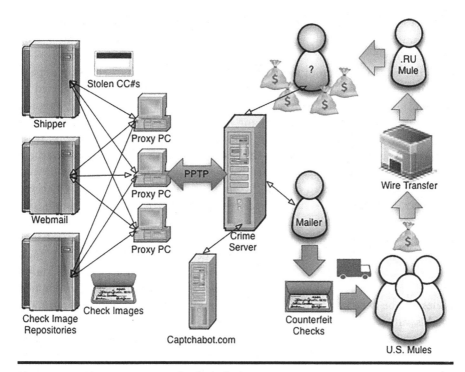

Figure 4.8 Shows money mules laundering money.

of amounts from the target's account to another account. The attacker can pay someone else to handle this through a payload-as-a-service deal. Lastly, the illegal money collected from the users has to be "sanitized" or used without exposing the end user at the risk of being arrested. This is where money mules come in and offer money-mule-as-a-service. Money mules will give the attacker money that is "safe" to use without exposing oneself to risks. This forms the value chain of the malware business (Figure 4.8).

Value Chain 2: Remote Access Tooling Targeting- Small to Medium Enterprise

Remote Acces Tooling targeting SME

Another financial malware scheme is one that uses remote access tools to target small and medium-sized enterprises. This scheme is specialized and targets non-random targets. Therefore, the potential targets are identified based on what the attacker can fetch from them and then they are first attacked using a spear phishing attempt or another similar type of attack. Employees are targeted at this stage, and those closest to an organization's funds are the primary targets. Therefore, accountants or staff working in the finance departments will be targeted. They could be spear phished and made to open file attachments with malware. The malware used here is that which that gives attackers remote access to devices. The remote access is used by the cybercriminals to observe all that takes place on the infected client. Therefore, the attackers will have full access to observe the financial systems used by the targets. Through observation, the attackers become familiar with the financial systems and practices of an enterprise. They will also find out how the system can be exploited. They then begin to attack the system. They could infiltrate the payroll and manipulate it such that when the company pays employees, money is sent to the attackers' accounts instead of the actual employees. The last step is the cashing out where money mules will be used to sanitize the money then give it back to the cybercriminals. In this value chain, the attackers are generally committed to overseeing the attack and thus might not rely on assistance from other parties as was seen in the value chain above. Therefore, other parties may only be contracted during the malware acquisition and cashing out stages. In the malware acquisition step, the attackers could buy or rent malware through malware-as-a-service undertaking. In the cashing-out step, the attackers could hire money mule-as-a-service to have the money cleansed so that it can be used. Figures 4.9 and 4.10 elaborate this.

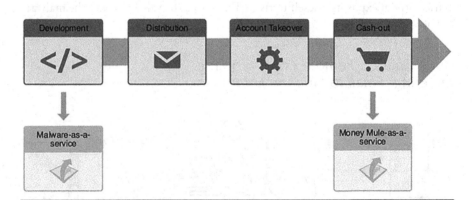

Figure 4.9 Remote access tool value chain. (Source: https://link.springer.com/article/10.1007/s10610-017-9336-3.)

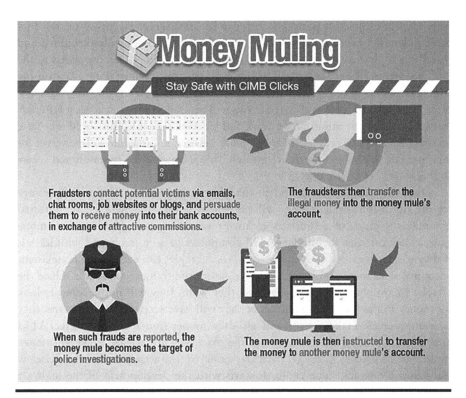

Figure 4.10   Money muling elaboration.

Value Chain 3: Remote Access Tooling against Financial Institutions

Remote Acces Tooling targeting Banks

The last value chain that we will look at is one that still uses remote access but is targeted directly at banks instead of the customers of a bank as was in the previous value chain. The attack is bold and will be targeted at getting access to the systems inside financial systems. The attack begins with an attack on one of the bank's employees where they are targeted with a spear phishing attack. Attackers will have studied a little background information about the targeted employee and find the perfect type of email to send them. The targeted employees will have to be holders of exploitable positions. This can be some senior executives or staff that directly handle transactions in the bank. When they successfully download and install the malware on their computers, the attackers will get remote access to the bank's systems. The malware will only observe the operations taking place on the compromised computers hence the need for being picky on the targets in the first place. The infected hosts within the banks will be used by the attackers for familiarization with the operations of the bank and banking systems. This could take long and attackers in this type of value chain are never in a hurry but will preserver for long periods since the rewards are greater. This is because the unmonitored access to the systems is a goldmine.

Once the attackers are confident that they have observed all that is necessary for the attack to take place, they will bounce to action. They will use the infected computers to create or authorize their own transactions or to give loans and mortgages. They can also manipulate ATM computers to do unrequested withdrawals if they will have gained such knowledge. The attackers can even create nonexistent accounts, send money to them, and then delete the transaction details. Once the attackers have obtained the money that they want, they will not necessarily look for money mules for cashing out. Since they will have access to bank systems, they can simply create a fake account and withdraw money from it or do the direct ATM attack and withdraw the money from the machines. If need be, however, money mules can be used to safely get back the money to the attackers. The figure below elaborates the attack value chain. It starts with the development of the malware to its distribution to bank employees, thus resulting in account takeover of the infected computers and cash out from the bank systems.

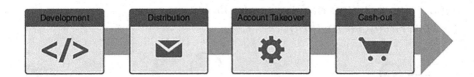

As has been seen in some of these value chains, there is the use of services from underground markets on the dark net to assist with attacks. There are those that offer malware-as-a-service on the underground markets. They either sell the malware or rent it out for attacks. There is an adequate supply of different types of malware, and they will be advertised on underground black markets. There is some level of uncertainty when paying for this service since there is no guarantee that the seller will honor the deal made. The lack of legal authorities to control activities on such markets makes it easy for the transacting parties to get away without honoring the deals they make. However, there are multiple sellers on these underground markets, and some markets have a review system where sellers build their reputation. The sellers with a good reputation get more customers and the poorly rated ones are slowly weeded out. In the malware-as-a-service business, there are three things that one can buy or rent depending on the item. These include malware source codes, infrastructure for infections, and then the malware.

Another part of the attack that is outsourced in some value chains is that of targeting or installing the malware on the target computers. For this, there are underground groups that can facilitate with getting the malware to the right targets. They can place malware on several websites and set them to only activate when an infected computer visits an online banking site. This will mean that the target is a viable one and there is money to be stolen. This is done through config files which have the domains for which the malware is to activate. Related to this is the creation of infrastructure for an attack. Some attacks such as DoS and DDoS require an infrastructure in order to be carried out. They feature an army of bots that can be used in the execution of the attack. Such bots can be procured from the dark net. An attacker can rent a botnet composed of a certain number of bots in order to use them to execute an attack.

Lastly, for the cash-out strategies, money mules are commonly used due to their expertise in the hiding evidence. They can erase the ties to an attacker from the money stolen. There are several ways through which this can be done. Mostly, cryptocurrencies are used where the money is converted into Bitcoin. It is then passed through several transactions and reassembled. It could be withdrawn as cash or used to pay for a costly item which the attacker can sell to retrieve his or her money. People or groups who offer this service are also present on the underground market.

Therefore, the underground market in the dark net offers a place for cybercriminals to create an economy based on malware. There are buyers and sellers. The sellers offer services for different parts of an attack to the buyers. These services range from target acquisition to cash out. Even though such a market may appear as not trustable due to the lack of legal regulations, there are checks in place to ensure that transactions are made and honored by all the parties involved. With such a market in place, it is difficult for cybercrime to be completely eliminated since each player in different value chains continues to innovate and come up with better services. This is why attacks have only become more sophisticated and effective. It seems that the cybercriminals are moving at a faster pace than anti-malware companies who are struggling to catch up. This is why organizations are often advised to ensure that they have cyber resilience even if they have state-of-the-art security systems. These systems could be beaten by a new malware bought through malware-as-a-service for a few dollars on underground markets.

Malware Analysis

There are some methods that can be used to analyze malware in order to find out more details about it. This is instrumental towards coming up with the mitigation measures against new malware. The following are some of these analysis types (Figure 4.11).

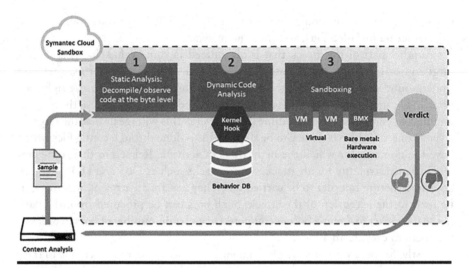

Figure 4.11 Types of malware analysis.

Static Analysis

These techniques rely on the examination of the malware's binary code so as to determine its attributes. The malware is not executed, and all the information about its execution behavior has to be obtained through the code analysis process. Static analysis is done in two ways. There is a statistical and group-matching method. In the statistical methods, the malware code will be transformed from binary to assembly code so that its fine characteristics and operations on a device such as the instructions it gives or its call patterns can be analyzed. As for the graph-matching technique, malware is analyzed against call graphs of other known malware. Therefore, their call graphs have to be built first, and then based on the call graphs of other malware in file, the new malware is classified. The weakness with these static analysis methods is that they are ineffective against malware that have been coded with polymorphism or metamorphism characteristics. Therefore, the analysis methods will yield different results when used against such malware. On the pros of this analysis method, it is quick and very effective against basic malware. It can quickly analyze a malware file and then give details about the functionalities of that malware and the malware's signature (Figure 4.12).

Dynamic/Behavioral Analysis

This is done through the observation of the malware as it executes on a host. The malware's behavior and communication to external computers will thus be monitored. Dynamic analysis is performed in sandbox environments whereby even though the malware will execute, it will not cause real harm to the computer.

Static Analysis. Static analysis techniques rely on examining the binary code to determine its properties without actually executing it. There are two types of methods of static analysis depending on the features utilized for operation: statistical and graph matching-based methods. In the statistical method, defenders transform the binary code of malware into an assembly code to extract and analyze characteristics, such as the n-grams of instruction or call patterns. The graph matching method is mainly based on similarity matching. For that, defenders build call graphs (e.g., system call graph, function-call graph, or API call graph), compare graphs with each other, and classify malware based on how well defenders match with previously known behaviors of the given malware species.

Figure 4.12   Explanation of static and dynamic analysis. (Source: https://arxiv. org/ftp/arxiv/papers/1606/1606.01971.pdf.)

Rather, the malware will only harm an operating system running inside a virtual system. The advantage of the virtual systems is that they can quickly and easily be wiped or rolled back after analysis is completed. When the malware is running, there are a number of things on the virtual machine that have to be looked at. An analyst will generally look at changes to the file system, registry, and network activity. File system changes may show when the malware is creating new files, manipulating existing files, or destroying them. Registry changes may indicate that the malware is attacking some of the aspects of the operating system. Network changes may indicate that the malware is communicating with external parties or downloading and uploading some files (Figure 4.13).

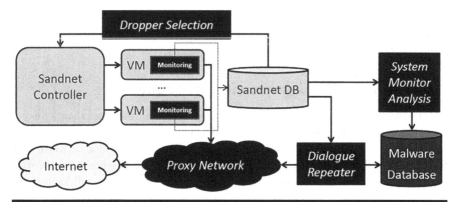

Figure 4.13   Dynamic analysis.

There are a number of sandboxes that have been built purposefully for analyzing malware behavior. One of this is Hybrid Analysis by Payload Security. Here, a user has to submit the malware files, and Hybrid Analysis conducts a static analysis of the code and then a dynamic analysis by executing the malware in a controlled environment. Another sandbox is an open source one available via GitHub called Cuckoo Sandbox. It can do automatic malware detection by running the malware files in its controlled environment. A quite different sandbox is VMRay. It is aimed at fooling malware that are not operating in a sandbox. It does this by leaving the target machine unmodified and outside of the user's control. The target machine can only be controlled from the hypervisor layer. These are just a few of the available sandboxes that can be used for dynamic analysis.

There is another technique that involves using a debugger to run the malware step by step while observing the effects that it has on a host system. It was previously very effective to analyze malware with behavioral analysis techniques till attackers learned how to defeat this type of analysis. Modern malware have built-in evasive techniques to prevent dynamic analysis. They do so by checking whether they are executing on virtual machines, debuggers, or with delayed execution being controlled by a user. The famous WannaCry ransomware that attacked computers in over 150 countries in 2017 had such a feature. When executed on a virtual machine, it would simply not run. However, when directly run on a host, the malware would immediately begin encrypting crucial files. It took static analysis to find a sloppy error in the malware source code.

Malware Detection Techniques

End-user security software are tasked with the responsibility of identifying malicious programs and files in the midst of many legitimate programs executing on a computer. The goal is to prevent the execution of the malicious programs so that they do not cause damage to the computers. There are many anti-malware programs, and these have a number of ways that they use to detect malware. The malware detection techniques vary in complexity and effectiveness. These techniques are as follows.

Signature-Based or Fingerprinting Techniques

This is whereby some aspects of the malware's file are examined and then a fingerprint is created. This fingerprint uniquely identifies the malware. The fingerprint will either represent some contents or the cryptographic hash of a malware file. Signature-based malware detection is an old method and has been an essential part of many antivirus programs. Up-to-date antivirus programs will keep virus signatures to be used to detect viruses that may try to infect a computer. However, the sole use of signature for malware detection is quickly losing importance.

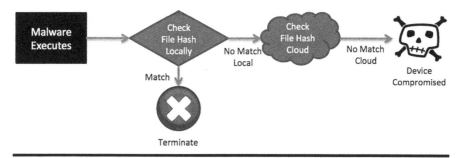

Figure 4.14   A depiction of the signature-based check.

This is because signature-based security programs cannot detect malware whose signatures it lacks. The malware will simply be let to execute since it will not be identifiable as a threat. Attackers have defeated the signature-based malware detection system by creating malware that can quickly mutate thus change their signatures but keep their malicious functionalities (Figure 4.14).

Heuristics-Based Detection

This is a method of detecting malware that involves the static examination of malware so as to determine the malicious or suspicious characteristics that it has. This method does not rely on a signature to do matching. For example, there are antivirus programs that look for rare code in suspicious files to determine whether the file is a malware. Heuristics-based detection may also involve an antivirus tool emulating the execution of a malicious file so as to determine what the file would do when executing. To avoid false positives, heuristics-based detection normally involves several checks. A file will be regarded as malicious only when it exceeds a certain threshold of risk. The con of this tool is that it can easily flag non-malicious files as malicious (Figure 4.15).

Behavioral Detection

This is where malware is identified by being let to run on a host and then its behaviors observed. Suspicious behavior such as unpacking of malware code, modifications to the host, or observation of keystrokes will identify the executable as malware. The difference between behavioral detections and heuristics-based detection is that behavioral detection does not use emulation, and once it detects a file as malicious, it labels it as a malware. Heuristics-based detection may not declare a file that it observes to execute with suspicious behaviors as malicious because that file has to meet a certain threshold of risk detection. Behavioral-detection tools borrow a lot from intrusion prevention systems which prevent the execution of a program that they observe to be acting in a suspicious way (Figure 4.16).

Top searched threats

| | THREATS 1 - 10 | 11 - 20 | 21 - 30 | 31 - 40 | 41 - 50 | MORE > |

May 09 2016 - May 16 2016	Detection of top 10000 threats	Troj/W32.Gen.txtO	HTML/Framer	XPJ-Gen.BP.2704_3	Adnd	OSX/Sploit.D	Packed/FSG	BAT/Small	Win.Troj-Agent.mnV	Program.Unwanted.1183	OSX/VSearch.B
Metadefender Core 4	89.41%	✳	✳	✳	✳	✳	⊖	✳	✳	⊖	✳
Metadefender Core 8	93.49%	✳	✳	✳	✳	✳	⊖	✳	✳	⊖	✳
Metadefender Core 12	97.47%	✳	✳	✳	✳	✳	✳	✳	✳	⊖	✳
Metadefender Core 16	98.39%	✳	✳	✳	✳	✳	✳	✳	✳	✳	✳
Metadefender Core 20	99.83%	✳	✳	✳	✳	✳	✳	✳	✳	✳	✳
Metadefender Core 20+ Custom Engines	99.88%	✳	✳	✳	✳	✳	✳	✳	✳	✳	✳

Figure 4.15   An example of heuristic-based detection.

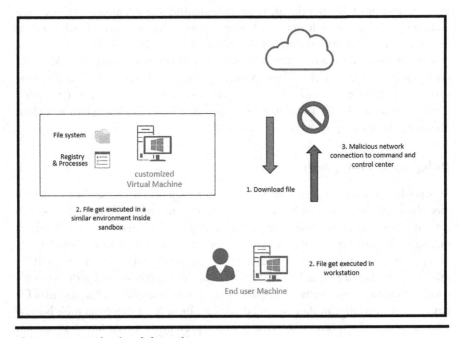

Figure 4.16   Behavioral detection.

Cloud-Based Detection

This is a new detection method that uses the power of the cloud provided by an antivirus program vendor. It creates a form of a trust-based processing system that derives intelligence from thousands of computers or even more. Data about malicious files is uploaded to the cloud by computers protected by a certain antivirus system. This data will go to the vendor's cloud from where the vendor will analyze and determine whether the file is malicious or not. Therefore, an end host will only do a bit of processing on a malicious file before sending it to a cloud engine. The cloud engine will have similar reports from other computers, and it will also determine whether the file has been reported as malware by any other computer or has previously been found to be malicious when analyzed on the cloud. The end hosts send malware characteristics and behavior to the cloud to help with the determination of whether a file is a malware or not. Cloud-based detection is far more accurate than any other method of detection since it uses the collective intelligence of many antivirus programs uploading information to the cloud combined with the processing capabilities of the cloud. Therefore, instead of an antivirus declaring a file to be a malware based on its local detection techniques, it uploads information about the suspicious file to the cloud and the cloud tells whether such a file has been reported by another computer in the community as a malware or has previously been found to be a malware (Figure 4.17).

These are the main malware detection techniques. However, their distinctions are quickly getting blurred. This is because they are normally integrated in modern antivirus systems. Therefore, an antivirus system can determine a file to be a malware using a virus signature, and when no signature exists, the program might

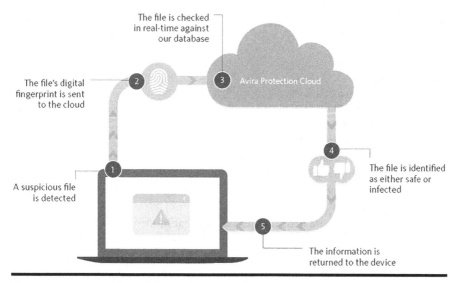

Figure 4.17 Cloud-based detection example.

turn to heuristics or the cloud to determine whether the file is malicious. Therefore, it is a common practice to find antivirus tools having a combination of malware detection techniques since it is no longer viable to use one approach to detect the malware.

Summary of the Chapter

This chapter has gone through malware. It has looked at the classification of malware into three: viruses, worms, and Trojans. Each of these has been discussed, and the subclasses of these have also been highlighted. The chapter has also examined the purpose of malware. Even though there might be many purposes for malware, this chapter has highlighted the use of malware for financial gain. Among other purposes that have been highlighted are for unfair business competition, destructive purposes, and pranking. The chapter has discussed the criminal business model of malware. Three modern value chains have been discussed. The chapter has gone through services offered by underground markets to facilitate the entire process of an attack. These include malware-as-a-service, pay-per-install, infrastructure, and money mule-as-a-service. The underground economy created by cybercriminals has been discussed under this topic. The chapter has then gone through the techniques of doing malware analysis. The paper has discussed both static and dynamic malware analysis techniques. The cons of both techniques have been discussed, and it seems that cybercriminals have devised ways to evade both these ways of analysis. Finally, the chapter has discussed malware detection techniques. It has highlighted signature-based, heuristics-based, cloud-based, and behavioral detection. The next chapter will discuss the cybercriminal activities in the dark net. It will look at the illegal activities that have been taking place on the dark net.

Questions

1. What are the main classifications of malware?
2. What are viruses and worm?
3. What is the difference between a virus and a worm?
4. Discuss four purposes of malware.
5. Explain malware-as-a-service.
6. What is a money mule (as used to cash out illegal proceeds of cybercrime)?
7. Explain the two malware analysis techniques.
8. Discuss the malware detection techniques that modern antivirus systems use.
9. What makes cloud-based detection particularly more advantageous?
10. What is the main con of heuristics-based detection?

Further Reading

The following are resources that can be used to gain more knowledge on malware:

https://link.springer.com/article/10.1007/s10610-017-9336-3.
https://arxiv.org/ftp/arxiv/papers/1606/1606.01971.pdf.

Chapter 5

Cybercriminal Activities in Dark Net

Introduction

There are lots of cybercrime activities that take place on the dark net. It has offered a breeding ground for many cybercriminals, and the results of these are slowly being witnessed. Cyberattacks are increasingly becoming more effective and also more challenging for authorities to trace where data and money stolen by cybercriminals disappear to. This is because of the structuring of the underground economy on dark nets. There are different types of actors in an attack, and each of these has been specializing and advancing their techniques. The actors responsible for creating exploits and malware have become better at it. Those that deal with money muling have also become quicker and better at ensuring that the proceeds from attacks are less traceable. When the efforts from the different actors that form a cyberattack today are combined, the end result is an advanced attack that is difficult to stop and equally challenging to investigate. This chapter will mainly focus on familiarizing you with the categories of cybercrimes, the cybercrime activities that take place on the dark net, and the new value chains that have made cyber attackers to be more effective. It will cover this in the following topics:

- Cybercrime and its categories
- Cybercriminal activities through the dark net
- Data exfiltration
- Monetization of cybercrime
- Malware-as-a-service and money laundering.

Cybercrime and Its Categories

The commonly used definition of cybercrime is a crime that involves the use of a computer and/or a network for illegal reasons. These could include fraud, identity theft, or copyright violation among other reasons. Cybercrime has been happening on the surface net for a long time. However, the increasing popularity of the dark net has given cybercriminals a more secure space that they can operate from. The main challenge that cybercriminals seek to avoid is trails of their criminal activities leading back to them. This is because if they are traced, they can be arrested and face criminal charges and probably serve long sentences. The dark net provides an almost ideal platform for cybercriminals to carry out their activities. There are several categories of cybercrimes, and these are as listed below.

Computer Fraud

This involves the misrepresentation of facts to cause someone to do or to refrain from doing something, thus leading to a loss. It is a popular type of cybercrime and has seen many people and organizations fall victim. Computer fraud involves the falsification of data through either entry of falsified data or the entry of unauthorized instructions. It may also involve the alteration, destruction, suppression, or theft of online transactions. Lastly, it may also involve the manipulation or deletion of stored data. There has been an increase in these types of illegal activities which have translated to millions of dollars lost annually. The following are the most reported computer fraud incidents by both individuals and organizations.

Business Email Compromise

This is a high-profile scam that is generally targeted at businesses. The scam is ideal when the business has partners in foreign countries to whom funds are regularly electronically sent. The scam begins with the compromise of a business email account of a high-ranking organizational employee. When the email has been compromised and is in the hands of the attackers, they will study the type of communication that the executive employee handles. In most cases, they will send an email to the accounts or finance department requesting the next payments for certain companies to be paid through new overseas bank accounts. With this instruction, hackers can create a cash cow where employees will periodically send huge amounts of money as payments to their foreign suppliers or business partners while the amounts go to hackers (Figure 5.1).

An example of such an attack was on a company called Ubiquiti Networks. Hackers created a spoofed email account of a high-ranking staff member and instructed the accountants to be sending payments to suppliers through new overseas bank accounts. By the time that the scam was realized, the company had lost

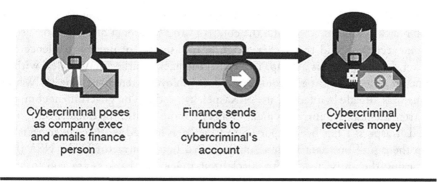

Figure 5.1   A depiction of the BEC (Business Email Compromise) attack.

http://fortune.com/2015/08/10/ubiquiti-networks-email-scam-40-million/

"On June 5, 2015, the Company determined that it had been the victim of a criminal fraud," the company writes in its 8-k form. "The incident involved employee impersonation and fraudulent requests from an outside entity targeting the Company's finance department. This fraud resulted in transfers of funds aggregating $46.7 million held by a Company subsidiary incorporated in Hong Kong to other overseas accounts held by third parties."

Figure 5.2   Ubiquiti networks attack brief. (http://fortune.com/2015/08/10/ubiquiti-networks-email-scam-40-million/.)

close to $44 million. It is, therefore, an elaborate scam that is currently in use by hackers and has been proven to be effective (Figure 5.2).

Data Breach

This is another common type of computer fraud. It is where data is leaked or spilled from a purportedly secure storage. Sensitive information ends up in the hands of hackers who either release it publically or use it as ransom to get paid a certain amount. One of the biggest data breaches for a renowned company is that of the email provider company called Yahoo. Yahoo has repeatedly been a victim of data breach where it is reported that hackers have had access to sensitive information about millions of Yahoo's users. Surprisingly, the attack has not occurred once to the company hinting that the hackers may be working closely with an insider or have been on Yahoo's systems for a significant period of time. Another significantly big hack was that of Republican National Committee's (RNC) voter data in the United States. RNC was compromised and the data of over 200 million Americans breached by the attackers. This was as a result of data being stored insecurely on Amazon S3 bucket. Uber has also been a victim of a data breach though the managers handled the incident quite loosely. It is reported that a hacker was able to breach the company and steal data of 57 million users. Some executives paid the hacker a significant amount of money to silence the hacker. In the end, this attempt to conceal the hacker rather than to deal with it came into the limelight and some executive employees were fired. The US White House has already banned the use of Kaspersky products on government computers after the popular antivirus maker was caught up within the traps of computer fraud. Kaspersky has been reported to have been hacked by Russian hackers to help them pull out data from a laptop owned by a contractor to the NSA that was using the antivirus. In this specialized attack, the hackers are said to have used the program's ability to access any file on a computer's hard drive to steal. This attacker showed the extent to which insecurity had gone to if an antivirus program could be used for data breaches. Another data breach that involved an unlikely perpetrator was that reported by WikiLeaks. According to the popular expose network, the US CIA had a database of exploits that it could use to track Windows users (Figure 5.3).

From all these attacks, it can be noted that there has been an increase in sophistication and effectiveness. One would think that big companies such as Yahoo would be invincible by attackers since they must have state-of-the-art security systems guarding their networks. However, it has been proven by hackers that data breaches can affect anyone and there are very many ways for them to conduct the breaches. This makes data breaches one of the most feared types of cybercrime and can affect just about anyone.

> WikiLeaks kicked off the year by dumping a slew of CIA secrets online, including the "Vault 7" database of exploits, some of which were marked Top Secret. One of the more interesting dumps detailed how the CIA can track Windows users using wi-fi signals and a process known as trilateration. There was also some interesting router hacking techniques disclosed in June.

Figure 5.3 An article on top data breaches of 2017.

Denial of Service

Denial-of-service (DoS) attacks are considered part of computer fraud since they are done to purposefully suppress or prevent normal processes or transactions, thereby leading to losses. DoS attacks involve the interruption of access to systems or networks due to an overwhelming amount of illegitimate requests being sent to servers. This type of an attack has become one of the most feared by organizations since it comes unannounced and is hard to stop once it has started. The main culprits behind the attack are botnets which have recruited thousands of devices that send huge amounts of requests to organizational servers. In 2016, an unlikely victim of distributed denial of service (DDoS) was a domain name resolving company called Dyn. The attack was executed by a botnet of 100,000 devices that continuously sent requests to the company at an estimated rate of 1 Tbps. The attack was a bold one since it was targeted at a company that directly influences internet performance since it is responsible for translating domain names into IP addresses (Figure 5.4).

With the attack on Dyn, several websites could not be accessed since their names were not able to be resolved. The attack served as a wakeup call to all other companies that had looked down upon the capabilities of determined attackers. Another DDoS attacker was against an investigative reporter called Brian Krebs whose website was taken down by a massive attack that peaked at 620 Gbps effectively putting the site offline. The significance of this attack was the sheer amount of force that was used against the investigative reporter. The attack was attributed to a Mirai botnet which had scanned devices connected to the web and infected thousands of them with malware to force them to participate in DDoS attacks. Lastly, for 2016 attacks, there was a wave of DDoS attacks against Russian banks whereby a botnet of approximately 24,000 computers was reported to be behind the attack. The attacks were targeted at five banks, and the attacks lasted over

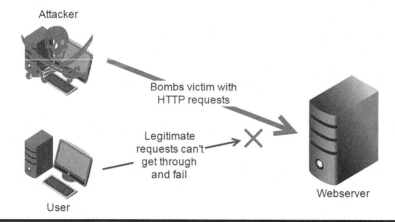

Figure 5.4   Depiction of a DoS attack.

- In Q3 2017, organizations experienced an average of 237 DDoS attack attempts per month, equal to eight per day. -Corero Network Security, 2017
- In Q3 2017, monthly DDoS attack attempts increased 35% over Q2, and 91% over Q1. -Corero Network Security, 2017
- The growing availability in DDoS-for-hire services and the proliferation of unsecured Internet of Things (IoT) devices has led to the increase in DDoS attacks in 2017. -Corero Network Security, 2017

Figure 5.5 Reports on DDoS prevalence. (https://techrepublic.com/article/ddos-attacks-increased-91-in-2017-thanks-to-iot/.)

2 days. However, it is reported that the attacking botnet was not able to take the websites offline. In 2017, there was a reported 915 increase in DDoS attacks. This was due to the increased adoption of Internet of Things (IoT) devices. IoT devices have been plagued with insufficient security, thus making them ideal targets for hackers wishing to get very many devices to recruit to their botnets. The attack on many organizations has been in an effort to either take them offline or to distract the organizations while a data breach takes place (Figure 5.5).

Email Account Compromise

This is quite similar to the discussed business email compromise. However, this type of an attack is not constrained to businesses only. It can be targeted at the general public and even to people that least expect to be targeted. Compromised email accounts belonging to professionals are used and the aim is to manipulate other people into sending money or sensitive information to the attackers. Individuals working in financial institutions, real estate, and law brokerage firms are likely targets by the attackers for the purpose of obtaining the email accounts. The attackers will pretend to be the professionals and continue on to engage with clients and request for payments or some favors. The accounts are compromised through password guessing or through social engineering techniques. The hacker can use the compromised email to target clients, friends, and relatives or perform transactions under the pretense of being the real owners of the account.

Malware

The malware was exhaustively covered in Chapter 4 where it was said to be malicious software that is broadly categorized into three classes: viruses, worms, and Trojans. These programs are created to alter, manipulate, or destroy systems and data. Some types of malware, especially the ones that are considered to be exploits, are used to open an avenue for attacks. Malware has increasingly been used at the core of most cybercrime activities. Malware can easily be installed onto unsecured devices and then be used to commit other crimes such as data theft. There are malware that automatically download onto a device once the user visits a certain page. It is difficult for the user to tell when his or her device has been infected without an antivirus program. Malware can not only steal data but can maintain an open communication channel between the hackers and the victim machine. The hackers can monitor everything that a user does for a long period before executing their attacks. In the previous chapter, there was a highlight on the new value chains of the underground malware economy. There was a particular value chain whereby when attackers were targeting businesses and financial institutions, they would compromise the machines and keep monitoring the infected devices for long. Once they were familiar with the systems that the targets were using, they would proceed to execute the last bit of the attack. This is the bit where they would use the systems on the infected devices to do either authorize transactions to their accounts or to create transactions to transfer money to their accounts.

Phishing

This is a form of computer fraud that involves the use of emails to manipulate people into sending money or sensitive information to cybercriminals. The normal phishing attack is hardly targeted at specific people since the same phishing email is sent to multiple recipients. The most common pattern of such attack is the claim by the sender to be from a legitimate company, and certain information or credentials are required from the recipient. Another variation of phishing attacks is where the recipients are deceived of having won lotteries or some competitions and they are required to give some information or part with a certain amount to claim their prize. A more advanced form of phishing is spear phishing which is quite different from normal phishing by the fact that the email is highly customized according to the recipient. The attacker will have some foreknowledge about the recipient and thus will know exactly where to target them. For instance, an attacker could create an email resembling that of the HR of a company and then use the email to manipulate the target into giving out their tax information or their sensitive information. It will not appear as inappropriate for the HR to request some personal information and so the target will most likely send it over. Phishing has been advancing with time and has incorporated technology into it. Whereas traditional phishing emails featured grammatical errors, spelling mistakes, and obviously faked emails, a new set of attackers has come up. These attackers create high-quality emails. There are tools that can clone websites, and all the attacker has to do is to play around with the domain name they will use to host the fake website. The attacker can then send a phishing email to the target informing them that there is a problem with their account with a certain company and they need to log in to solve the problem by clicking on a provided link. Upon clicking the link, the target will be directed to the clone website and will be prompted to log in using a similar interface as is on the legitimate website. When the target logs into the account, the credentials are sent to the attackers and the target will be taken round in circles being told to provide more personal information to authenticate himself or herself into the account (Figure 5.6).

Phishing has been a very effective attack of late with attackers duping many people with the new techniques that they are using. There have been PayPal phishing attacks where users are told that their PayPal accounts have a problem that needs to be resolved and thus they are required to immediately log in to through a provided link. The link would go to a cloned site, provide the targets with the normal PayPal login page and then they would enter their credentials. After doing so and submitting the information, the cloned website would take the user through a series of steps where they would continually be requested to give out a bit more of personal information. At the end of the attack, the target would have given out so much information such that they would be at the mercy of the attackers. PayPal acknowledged the attack and sent emails to all its users on how to prevent themselves from falling victim. Another successful wave of phishing attacks took place in the 2017 tax-filing season for US citizens. Hackers used the opportunity where people were in a rush to complete filing their taxes to defraud them. They would create emails purported to be from the Internal Revenue Service (IRS) requiring the recipients to either send out information or to send out some monies. The ring of phishers was, later on, tracked to India and the mastermind arrested. This was after Americans had lost millions of dollars to them. The same attack can be replicated just about anywhere else in the world using the same techniques and technologies that the attackers used.

The effectiveness of phishing attacks has definitely been noted by hackers. They are therefore capitalizing on this technique of reaching a large number of people

Figure 5.6 A depiction of phishing.

but using minimal resources. There have been many other attacks just as effective as the two described above. In Qatar, it was estimated that 1 of each 25 citizens had been hit by over 93,000 phishing attempts in just 3 months of 2017. In Czech, there was a fake campaign purporting to be by the country's postal service. The fake campaign urged people to download an app for their postal services. However, they were downloading a malicious app that turned out to steal their banking information. In the same year, companies in over 50 countries were fooled into downloading a pdf file on energy solutions. The pdf file had a malware injected into it and would infect any device that it was opened in. Amazon has seen the same fate as PayPal after hackers sent phishing emails claiming that there were some items on discount on the e-commerce site. When they clicked on items in the email, they would proceed to log into a clone site, but when they clicked on the discounted products, they would be told that the items were no longer available. However, the information that they would have already given the hackers would be used to attack them in future. There were very many other phishing attempts sent to organizational employees. From a security survey done to a sample of organizations worldwide, it was estimated that 75% of all organizations had received phishing emails in 2017. This estimate shows that phishing is making a great come back and they were increasingly becoming successful. Moreover, the survey showed that the impacts of phishing were malware infections, compromised accounts, and data loss.

Ransomware

This is a unique type of malware that uses cryptography for illegal purposes. Once the malware has infected a device, it will encrypt the files in the computer effectively making it unusable. One will not be able to open any file or program that is encrypted. This, therefore, affects the availability of the infected machine for any task. Ransomware are commonly distributed through phishing. End users get emails with malicious attachments, and when they open them, their computers get infected. Some types of ransomware will go on to infect all the other computers in the network that they are in. They can rapidly encrypt files, and therefore, users hardly have a chance to stop the attack once it starts. After the encryption process, the malware will display a warning that the computer has been encrypted and the victim needs to pay a certain amount in order for a decryption key to be provided, thus allowing the victim to locally decrypt the computer. In some cases, the attackers will give the victim a program that can do the decryption. Payment is mostly sent via Bitcoin to make it harder to trace.

The year 2017 saw quite a number of ransomware attacks, some of which were felt worldwide proving that many people are still to grasp the new reality of cybercrime. It is becoming indiscriminate and very effective. The biggest attack of the year was WannaCry, a ransomware that has ever since been tied to North Korea. The ransomware claimed victims in over 150 countries, thus receiving a lot of publicity. For each encrypted machine, the hackers would demand a ransom of $300 in Bitcoin. There were reportedly 150,000 reported cases all over the world within a short span of days. It was confirmed that the ransomware was so effective since it targeted an exploit called EternalBlue in Microsoft. The exploit had been patched 2 months earlier, but there were quite a number of people that had not updated their computers. EternalBlue is said to be among the exploits in possession of the National Security Agency; thus, the agency received condemnation after the attack. It is only after a static analysis of WannaCry's code that a weakness was revealed leading to the shutdown of the whole attack. However, it was already too late for the thousands of already encrypted machines. In unfortunate circumstances, the ransomware-encrypted computers in hospitals used to offer critical services. Not only did this lead to the unavailability of such computers, there were a number of deaths due to the stoppage of the services that those computers were offering.

NotPetya

This ransomware was reported almost a month after WannaCry. It started off by affecting power companies in both the Netherlands and Ukraine. Britain and Spain, later on, reported similar incidents of the ransomware. In a few days, NotPetya had spread to over 100 countries. The ransomware encrypted the MBR (Master Boot Record) thus was a level deeper than WannaCry. However, the ransomware still used the EternalBlue exploited that WannaCry used. NotPetya was named so to prevent people from confusing it with a much less prolific ransomware called Petya. The real impact of the ransomware was felt by the corporates, some of which reported $300 million in losses.

BadRabbit

It was a less successful ransomware that claimed hundreds of companies in Russia and Ukraine as victims. Some of these victims included Russia media outlets, a metro system used by Kiev, and an airport. There were scarce reports of the malware in South Korea, United States, and Poland. The BadRabbit malware did not exploit vulnerabilities in the Microsoft Windows OS like both WannaCry and Petya. Once the malware encrypted the computers, it demanded a ransom of 0.5 Bitcoin.

Locky

This was a malware that was first discovered in February 2016 but has ever since been going dark and resurfacing. It has been identified to rely on botnets that spew out multiple spam emails for its distribution. Particularly, it has been associated with Necurs. In August 2017, it was distributed through 23 million emails within a day. The emails had been written exciting subjects such as pictures and the body had downloadable attachments. The attachments were zipped and contained a Visual Basic Script. This is the script that would activate the ransomware once opened.

Cyberterrorism

A new type of terrorism that governments all over the world are having to face is cyberterrorism. There has been growing concern on agencies such as the FBI on the increased level of terrorism both on the surface web and the dark net. Cyberterrorists are a group of attackers that intimidate or coerce governments and organizations into adhering to the terrorists' propaganda through computer attacks. It, therefore, becomes terrorism targeted at computers and committed through computers or networks. The list is long of what can be considered as cyberterrorism. If a blogger publishes an article and spreads it on social media claiming that there are bombs planted at certain places and will be exploded on a certain day, this can be regarded as cyberterrorism. Terrorism propaganda spread through social media platforms aimed at causing distress to the citizens of a particular country is also cyberterrorism. Hacking government websites with the aim of causing fear or to demonstrate power and subversion of a country is also cyberterrorism.

Countries have increasingly digitized some of their systems. There are countries that rely on smart grids for electricity. In other countries or major cities, there are a lot more digitized basic services. Industries such as those that produce power from nuclear reactors also rely on information systems to keep going. However, there is a threat in that cyberterrorists can target these critical infrastructures through the computer systems used to control them. The United States and Israel are accused of taking down Iran's nuclear plant using a malware called Stuxnet. The malware infected the computers that had systems to control the nuclear reaction process and caused the plant to self-destruct. Investigations after the attack pointed out that it must have been state-sponsored.

This type of an attack can be replicated but by a more barbaric actor such as the Islamic State or Al Qaeda. With a large-enough team of experienced hackers, these terrorist groups could bring entire cities to their knees by interrupting the provision of sensitive services such as electricity and water. Fortunately, the famous terrorist groups lack members that have such skillset. Most of them prefer physical combat rather than a cyber-based one. There have only been isolated cases ever since Stuxnet to show deliberate cyberterrorism attempts. For instance, there were attacks on Ukraine's energy provider systems which led to blackouts. The United States has also been a victim once when a researcher took control of traffic systems merely by exploiting a vulnerability in the system used to control the lights. There have been a few other attacks that can be categorized as cyberterrorism in different countries.

One of the countries that have faced a full-scale attack that crippled all online services was Estonia. In 2007, Estonia was targeted with a DDoS attack that led to the shutdown of the internet. The country crept back to the dark days without any access to infrastructure dependent on the internet such as online banking, phone carrier networks, and online access to government services. The culprit was suspected to be Russia since the two countries had been in dispute after the removal of a Soviet statue in Tallinn. The attack on Estonia highlighted the increasing dependence of states on technology and thus their vulnerability to cyberterrorism.

Based on the few highlighted incidents, the number of cyberterrorism attacks is still low. However, it might not remain so in the next few years. The cyberspace is soon going to be the frontline where terrorism will be fought. The adoption of the IoT in many industries and infrastructure is on the rise. They are a necessary convenience for many. However, these devices are particularly vulnerable to attackers. Many of the available devices have been made without appropriate or adequate security controls; thus, they are vulnerable to many cyberattacks. Cyberterrorists might begin targeting infrastructure or industries that have integrated IoT in their processes. The lack of members of terrorist groups that have expertise in hacking is no longer an assurance that these groups cannot commit such attacks. The underground malware market has given an opportunity to hire skilled professionals that could be instructed to sabotage computer systems and networks in a certain country for political reasons. There are already pointers that terrorists will be headed in that direction in the future. One of key Jihad proponents, Mohammad Bin Ahmad wrote a piece on the ways that one could participate in Jihad. One of the ways was through disrupting western states by attacking their websites and other resources.

Globally, there are already preparations to deal with this type of threat. There are already formed institutions to aid in preventing cyberterrorism. The United States has already formed joint task forces in its military that are responsible for preventing and also responding to any cyberterrorism incidents. North Atlantic Treaty Organization (NATO) has a cyber defense unit that also responds to cyberterrorism attacks in member countries. South Korea, being considered as a hyperconnected society, is among the countries at the highest risk of cyberattacks. This is because the country's cutting-edge technology, though fascinating, is said to be weak in regards to its security. The country has already suffered some attacks that have proven this. The country has increasingly put efforts at securing critical organizations such as is National Intelligence Agency. China has a controversial defense unit called the Blue Army that is said to be purposefully for cyber defense thus can also handle cases of cyberterrorism. The Blue Army is controversial because it has also been associated with penetrating the systems used by other governments hence being a threat to other governments. More countries are recognizing the threat that is cyberterrorism and are mounting defenses for such attacks.

Cyber Extortion

This is a new type of threat where organizational servers are threatened with incessant DoS attacks if the organization does not pay a certain amount to hackers. The hackers assure that if the demanded amount is paid, they will not attack the servers. In another version of the attack, the hackers attack the servers with repeated DoS attacks just to prove their abilities and then request the organization to pay a certain amount for the attack to stop. Corporates have been facing this type of cyberattack, and they have mostly agreed to pay instead of watching as their systems and networks are crippled by the attackers. The FBI said that there are approximately 20 reported cases in a month but many go unreported especially by corporates that want to save face and also not to expose their vulnerabilities to the public.

Cyberwarfare

This is a politically motivated war between groups, states, or countries that is fought in the cyberspace. The states attack each other's computer systems and networks for the purpose of disrupting normal activities in organizations, industrial espionage, and also to obtain data that can be used for strategic military purposes. Cyberwarfare can take several forms. It could be in the form of malware spread to government institutions, infrastructure, or organizations in a certain country. The aim of the malware will be to take down normal operations, key infrastructure, and even military systems. The Stuxnet attack against Iran's nuclear facility was an act of cyberwarfare if the culprits could be positively confirmed to be the United States and Israel. Another form of cyberwarfare is the execution of DoS attacks on government computing systems or key industries in a given country with the purpose of preventing the legitimate users from accessing such systems. DoS attacks could cripple operations that are transacted or processed online. Some DoS attacks are so strong that they can shut off the entire internet connectivity of a country as is the case with Estonia. Hacking and theft of data on key government institutions and a country's industries are also considered to be a form of cyberwarfare. Many countries have accused Russia, China, and North Korea of hacking units in their governments or funded by governments to hack and steal data from foreign countries. Even though many cases have not been proven, there is tension being created and an actual cyberwarfare might take place in the near future. Countries have been arming themselves for such attacks too. Lastly, ransomware can be used in cyberwarfare where a country could target key government institutions with spam containing ransomware. The ransomware could encrypt computers used for vital services, thereby making them unavailable.

The motives of cyberwarfare are many, but they are aimed at attacking countries through their critical infrastructure or their key industries and institutions. Most countries are at the risk of falling victim to cyberwarfare attacks due to the increasingly inevitable need to automate services and to stay connected to the internet. Even with secured systems, there are specialist hackers that can be paid by enemy countries to find weaknesses in a country's systems so that they can be exploited. Key infrastructure are the most common targets. For instance, if an attack is made on a nation's power distribution network, there would be widespread blackouts. Sensitive services that rely on electricity to run would be brought to a halt. Some countries use hydroelectric power plants to generate power while others rely on nuclear reactors. When these plants are attacked, the production of electricity in the country could be affected. Systems used to control hydroelectric power plants could be attacked and the controls manipulated to cause flooding.

Computer systems used by government agencies and institutions could also be attacked. The data stored in these systems could be stolen and used by enemy states for political reasons. Identities of secret agents, spies, and even a government's secrets could be put into the public domain. The systems could also be made unusable by ransomware. Communication channels can be hacked to prevent further communication between government agencies or officials. Messages exchanged on the communication channels could be stolen and sensitive information could be obtained from them. Hacks to sensitive institutions could lead to the release of personal data the citizens of a country. Lastly, military databases could be attacked by enemy states to expose troop locations, the equipment they have, and the types of weapons they are using. Communication channels used to give orders to the military could be infiltrated to give the enemy state access to a backdoor to all communications.

Cybercriminal Activities through the Dark Net

Chapter 2 highlighted most of the cybercriminal activates that are carried out on the dark net. This section will just recap some of these activities.

Drugs

The sale of drugs is done in many dark net markets. The sellers list their products on some of the dark net markets. Buyers pay via Bitcoin and have their drug shipped to them. Since there are hardly any regulations, buyers rely on sellers that are proven to be reliable. Some websites will have a trust score that is updated by the buyers based on their experiences with different sellers. However, legal agencies have been taking down most markets. If previous patterns were anything to go by, new markets are being formed to absorb the demand from the sellers and buyers that used the markets that have been taken down.

Human Trafficking, Sex Trade, and Pornography

There was a time when 17% of all the dark net sites on Tor were adult websites. These sites provided access to porn but also to human trafficking and sex trade. Even though it might seem that sex trade and human trafficking are a thing of the past, in 2014, there were reports of 2.5 million people trafficked through the dark net and surface web. This means that the illegal business of selling humans might still be ongoing on the dark net. This has prompted US Defense Advanced Research Projects Agency (DARPA) to create a program called Memex that can search the dark net and follow up on possible human traffic activities being carried out on the dark net.

Child pornography was a disturbing issue on the dark net that showed the depths of human degradation. However, almost all the dark net sites that had been offering child porn were taken down by the FBI and their founders tracked down. Many sites on the dark net also prohibited the listing of child pornography material on their markets. For instance, among the things that were banned from Silk Road 2.0 was child porn. It is fortunate that there are hardly any sites left offering this type of obscene content.

Weapons

There are sites on the dark net that have been used for the purpose of buying and selling weapons. The weapons include guns, explosives, and their ammunition. These sites are a threat to security since the weapons are sold to many people that have malicious intentions. Terrorists have used the dark net to acquire weapons and use them in attacks. Terror activities such as the Paris attacks were carried out using weapons that were bought on the dark net. The Charlie Hebdo attack led to 130 deaths and 350 injuries. The weapons were military grade and they still landed in the hands of ISIS terrorists. Weapons are in plenty and not so expensive on these underground markets on Tor. There has been a notable increase in demand for deadlier weapons by terrorists. They are willing to pay more to get the coveted military equipment that outperforms their normal arsenal. Self-radicalized individuals are also getting access to weapons without much of a hustle through these markets (Figure 5.7).

Figure 5.7   Weapon on sale on the dark net.

Figure 5.8 UK passport on sale on the dark net.

Fake Documents

For a few hundreds of dollars, one can get fake citizenship. This is done through the issuing of fake passports. Alongside the fake passports are fake driving licenses. The fake documents are offered to immigrants, terrorists, and people that wish to leave or enter the country without putting their real identities at risk. Some of the offered passports are high quality and hardly can a layman tell apart the fake from the real passports. There is an excellent delivery network for these documents such that people can get them from their own countries if they wish to use the documents as they enter foreign countries (Figure 5.8).

ATM PIN Pad Skimmers and ATM Malware

There are reports of ATM fraud where users complain that their accounts have been withdrawn shortly after using ATM machines. One of the ways attackers use to get money out of other people's ATM cards is through ATM PIN pad skimmers. These can be fit on ATM machines to enable the attackers to collect data keyed in by the users of the machines. Even though banks might catch up with the perpetrators of the crime after some time, money will already have been stolen. ATM PIN pad skimmers are sold on the dark net markets to criminals.

ATM malware are malicious programs that are used to illegally withdraw money from ATM machines. The malware can be installed by third parties inside ATM computers. The attackers will then be able to send instructions to the ATM machines to cash out their cassettes. The money will be emptied to the waiting hands of the attackers.

Counterfeit Currency

The dark net has markets that people can find counterfeit currency of high quality. This currency can be used to do normal transactions in stores, restaurants, or other business premises without the owners knowing that they are receiving illegitimate currency. Such currency can lead to lots of losses especially to small businesses that lack the tools to check for the authenticity of currency. Even then, there are some sellers of the counterfeit currency that assure that the currency can pass the common UV light test.

Data Dumps

There are markets on the dark net where one can buy data dumps of stolen data. The data could include personal information such as names, age, physical address, phone number, email address, and login credentials to some websites. Some data dumps contain encrypted data, and it is the burden of the buyer to find out how they can decrypt it. The data dumps are sold according to the value of the data contained and size.

Exploit Kits

Cybercriminals can buy exploit kits that they can use for attacks on the dark net. Exploit kits have been sold on the dark net for a long period now. They have a regular demand since not many cybercriminals are good at programming, and thus, they cannot write their own exploits. Exploit writers are the ones that study different systems, find vulnerabilities, and then create exploits that can be used against these systems.

Fake Websites

Modern phishing attacks are advanced and have many things that can trick cautious users into falling into the traps. There are lots of efforts being put in modern-day phishing attacks to make them more believable. Traditional phishing emails only relied on the content to trick users into performing some actions. However, today's phishing emails do not just rely on content, they rely on trust. They try to make targets believe that they have actually been sent by legitimate people. They give their targets links to login to the purported companies that the emails claim to be sent from. The links will open identical sites to the legitimate one. Every part of the website will look real and the target will not have doubts about the legitimacy of the site that they are on. This is because there are dark net markets selling cloned copies of commonly used websites that are relevant for hacks. They have cloned online banking websites, cloned government institutions websites, and many other fake but high-quality clone websites (Figure 5.9).

Data Exfiltration

There are very many attacks today that are aimed at stealing data rather than money. In some cases, data is more valuable than money and is also less risky to

The fear and confusion after January's *Charlie Hebdo* attacks over how military-grade weapons made their way into the French capital has only worsened since the massacre on Nov. 13 carried out by ISIS supporters, which left 130 dead and injured some 350 more. In the wake of the latest attacks, fear only intensified—speaking to the French Parliament on Nov.19, Prime Minister Manuel Valls also warned that ISIS could use biological or chemical weapons to attack France. "We must not rule anything out."

Figure 5.9 A news article on the Charlie Hebdo attack. (http://time.com/ how-europes-terrorists-get-their-guns/.)

steal. When one steals money, there could be money trails left behind that could be used to track them. Data is, however, easier to handle. Data exfiltration is the process of transferring data from a storage medium to another. In the world of cybercrime, it refers to the theft process of data where hackers copy data from compromised servers to their own storage devices. Data exfiltration occurs at the last stages of an attack where a hacker has already been able to gain access to a network and then to storage servers in the network. A number of companies have had this befall them. Yahoo was a victim when records belonging to approximately 2 billion people were stolen. Most exfiltration attempts end with the placement of the data on dark net markets for sale. Here, there are markets that allow sellers to list data dumps where interested parties can buy. The data is mostly bought by advertising companies and other hackers. Advertising companies will use the data to profile users and send advertisements to them through any available communication media. Cybercriminals will use the data to conduct further attacks against the people whose personal information is in the stolen data. They could, for instance, use it to send spear phishing emails to these people. With the available information, they will be able to craft more convincing emails to trap the targets.

There are some exfiltration attempts where the hackers end up with encrypted data. There are two options when this happens. The first option is for the hackers to sell the data for cheap on the dark net and make the meager profits they can from the sale. The second option is to try and decrypt the data. Sometimes, decryption attempts work, especially for weak encryption algorithms. It was reported that hackers initially stole user data from Yahoo in encrypted formats. However, the encryption algorithm that was used was MD5 which is in the least of weak encryption algorithms. After several attempts, hackers were able to decrypt the data and thus get access to information on over 2 billion user accounts. Therefore, even if data exfiltration ends in a seemingly useless data that has been encrypted, attackers will still try to decrypt it.

There is a new security measure where organizations can hire professionals to scout through the surface and dark net to search for stolen data. This is done after the organizations have confirmed that they were hacked and data stolen from them. These can find such data and begin investigations into the culprits responsible for putting the stolen data online. There are also services that have made it easier for organizations to monitor data leaks. One of these is PwnedList.com. The service continually searches for new data posted on the dark web and indexes it. One can tell whether organizational data has been stolen by running a sample search using PwnedList, and if there are any hits, the organization will know that its data has been listed on the dark net. It can then follow up with authorities and try to find the culprits behind that. An alternative to PwnedList is Hold Security. Hold Security offers a similar service where it scans the dark webs for data and indexes it. The index can then be searched against by a company to determine whether its stolen data has been listed on the dark web. However, the challenge for these services is that when stolen data is posted on the dark net, it is normally for sale. Also, hackers will not display a whole data set. They may only describe the type of data that they are selling.

Monetization of Cybercrime

At the initial stages of hacking, the motivation was hardly financial. It was just a way of proving that one could do certain things. Moreover, most attacks involved the use of scripts either copy-pasted from the internet or simple software available on some forums. It was hardly a financial undertaking and the motives were only to cause problems and become famous. With time, however, hackers started to improve and with that, they wanted to leverage their skills for financial incentives. At that time, there was not a proven way to make them become elite out of cybercrime. Therefore, they started creating a market for hacking services and tools which could be monetized.

In 2006, the first exploit kits surfaced on Russian markets on the dark web. They marked a beginning of the monetization of cybercrime. More kits were listed on the underground markets. Some came with more features such as a graphical user interface that one would use to launch an attack from. These kits got buyers who sold them to crime groups that would find targets to exploit. At that time, the same exploit kit would be used over and over against different targets. Therefore, a hacker only needed to buy the kit once. However, it is no longer viable to use the same exploit many times today due to the nature of the cybersecurity products available. Once they determine a threat signature, the same threat can hardly be used again to attack secured systems.

Hackers have, however, come up with more techniques to generate revenue from cybercrime. These are as follows.

Extortion

The first option is through extortion. Extortion has gained popularity as a common money mincing technique since the victims hardly have a walk around ransomware

Figure 5.10 A depiction of extortion.

have been used to encrypt computer devices, thus requiring users to pay a certain amount to get their files decrypted. Traditionally, such an attack would only be for fun and the threat actors would hardly request anything from the victims. Today, ransomware attacks are spanning the whole continent, and the attackers are requesting significant amounts as ransom. For instance, the WannaCry ransomware used to demand for $300 to be paid in Bitcoin within a week. If the amount was not paid within that time, the price would go up to $600. If the victim never paid, the computer would be encrypted permanently. There have been similarly high charges from other malware, some that have gone as high as demand for 0.5 Bitcoin. To add seriousness to their threats, some ransomware display warning messages claiming to be from the FBI. They mostly say that one's computer has been locked due to either accessing illegal content or downloading pirated content. The ransom amount is said to be the fine, and there is always a stern warning that the failure to pay the stated amount could lead to the permanent lock of their computers or even arrests (Figure 5.10).

Phishing

Another monetization method of cybercrime is through phishing. The new techniques used in phishing have seen victims lose millions of dollars to hackers through fake messages. The traditional phishing attacks were a bit easy to tell since they did not feature the use of much technology. There was the widespread phishing email of the Nigerian prince. The email required a user to assist a Nigerian Prince to get inherited a fortune, and in the end, the assistance would be highly rewarded. When one opted to offer the assistance, they would be told to pay some clearance charges to facilitate the transfer of the money. However, the charges would seemingly never end because after paying a certain amount, there would be another request to pay more. It is only until too late that one would realize that it was a con game. Many people, however, came to know of this and avoided it. However, phishing has been advancing and now features well-laid traps to get people to give out money and their personal information to hackers. During the tax season in the United States, there is a group of phishers that comes up and starts sending messages to US citizens that they are required to pay some fines and penalties since they failed to file their returns in the right way. These emails are formatted with the font colors and styles of the real IRS that processes tax filings. Sometimes, they can even recreate the IRS website so appear to be more authentic. Similarly, PayPal phishers are on the rise, and they have been using an effective way of getting login credentials that they can use to hack users' accounts and steal their money. The PayPal phishers craft an email that features the same styling and layout as the real ones from PayPal. They then explain that one's account has been limited due to certain reasons. As per PayPal terms, when an account is limited, it cannot be withdrawn from or money deposited to till the limitation is removed. It is therefore plausible that a user will want to resolve the limitation within the shortest time. The phishers have clone sites that look and feel like the normal PayPal site. The site is used to harvest a user's login credentials and personal information.

Adverts

Another type of monetization of cybercrime is through adverts. There are cyber-criminals that get revenue from forcefully showing adverts to users. They infect many computing devices with adware. The adware will be displaying adverts in pop-ups. This might not be so harmful, but it is annoying to users since their browsing activities keep on getting interrupted by the adverts. The cybercriminals depend on payments from advertising companies either through the impressions the ad received or the number of clicks the ad got (Figure 5.11).

Figure 5.11   A depiction of ad pop-ups.

Theft of Login Details

There is an underground market for cybercriminals that has buyers willing to pay for stolen login information. The login credentials could be for online banks, social media websites, email accounts, or just normal websites. There is malware that is purposefully used for stealing credentials. Since many users store login credentials on their browsers, the malware automatically downloads onto a user's machine when certain websites are visited. The malware will steal the stored login information and send it back to the attackers. These logins could be used for extortion or direct theft through money withdrawal.

Premium Rate SMSs

This was a threat that surfaced on both Android and iOS play stores. Malicious apps that claimed to offer certain functionalities were found to be sending messages to premium rate numbers. The effect was that phone users would lose a lot of money without knowing that their apps were the culprits. This led to major improvements in Android and iOS. Android became more strict on the permissions that apps requested to have when installed. Both the platforms also instituted thorough checks on the apps that had been published in their app markets. However, there still are premium rate SMS attacks that are taking place. This is being carried out through surveys. Users are instructed to give out their numbers during surveys and send a certain code that they receive on their phones. When they send back the code, they are charged at premium rates.

Banking malware—a few years back, there were concerns over key loggers capturing the username–password combination one used to log into websites. There then came to the concerns of login information being sniffed from packets when entered into unsecured websites. Currently, there are Trojans that can infect phones and computers and record incoming messages and record one's screen. These can harvest a lot of information that can be used by hackers to get access to one's account.

Malware-as-a-Service and Money Laundering

Malware-as-a-service is one of the new value chains that attackers are using in their underground economies. Here, an attacker does not go through the trouble of creating a malware. Malware can be rented or bought from other specialists in the dark net. The following are some of the specialists in the malware-as-a-service delivery module (Figure 5.12).

Exploit Writers

These are the hackers that discover new vulnerabilities in systems and then create exploits for them. Exploits will be targeted at one or several vulnerabilities in a

Figure 5.12 A depiction of malware-as-a-service. Malware is bought by the cybercriminal from the cloud and then used to infect different devices.

system. For example, EternalBlue was an exploit written to target a vulnerability in Windows. The exploit has been used repeatedly in ransomware attacks such as WannaCry and NotPetya. When exploit writers create an exploit, they will sell it to other cybercriminals that do not have the coding expertise to make exploits. An exploit writer may never come to the frontline of an attack since they make their money through the sale or renting of the exploits. Exploits are sold differently based on their complexity and effectiveness. The most expensive category of exploits are zero-day exploits. These are exploits that target vulnerabilities that system owners have not yet detected. Therefore, their effectiveness is high. Stuxnet is said to have used a number of zero-day exploits. This added to the speculation that the attack was state-sponsored. Several zero-day exploits would be too expensive for the common cybercriminals to waste in a single attack that did not attract any financial rewards. There are other low-quality exploits which fetch less on black markets but can still be harmful to a target.

Bot Herders

There has been an increase in the number and sophistication of DDoS attackers. Big companies have fallen victim to these attacks, temporarily being put offline by the

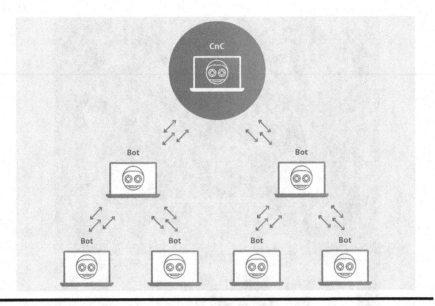

Figure 5.13   A botnet setup.

overwhelming number of illegitimate requests send to their servers. The infrastructure for conducting these types of attacks is sold on the dark net. There are specialist hackers whose sole purpose is to recruit computers to botnets. They infect zombie computers with a client version of a malware allowing them to control the activities of the infected computer. Bot herders maintain a program that allows all the zombie computers to be directed to send illegitimate traffic to certain addresses (Figure 5.13).

Malware Writers

Viruses, worms, and Trojans are coded by malware writers. These writers have the expertise of compromising browsers, operating systems, file systems, and networks. Malware writers can code different behaviors into malware to prevent their easy detection. They can also make them polymorphic hence can assume different behaviors. This makes it hard for them to be detected. Malware writers are always in a constant competition with antivirus systems. Since antivirus systems will index malware signatures rendering the malware no longer usable, malware writers have to keep releasing new variants of the malicious programs. Malware are sold on the dark net markets.

Money Laundering

When cybercriminals make money, they try as much as possible to reduce the traceability of the money. Money transfer leaves trails, and these can be used by law enforcement agencies to arrest the cybercriminals. To prevent this from happening, there are specialists on the dark net that offer money-muling services. Money mules

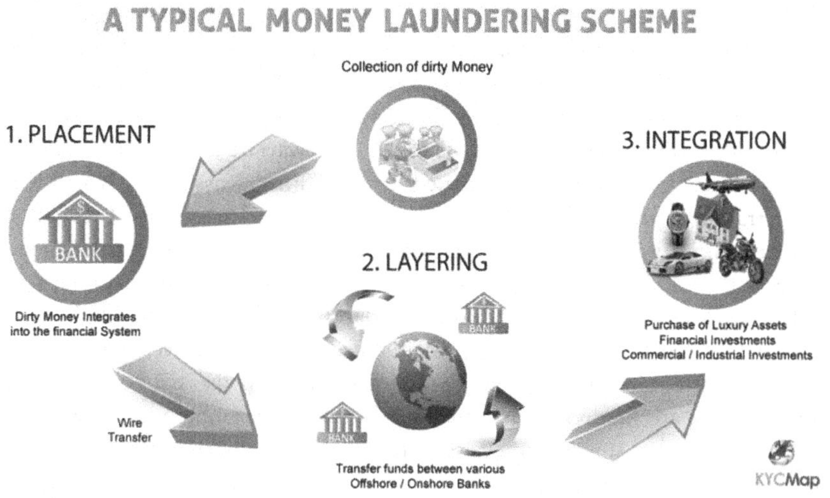

A TYPICAL MONEY LAUNDERING SCHEME

Collection of dirty Money

1. PLACEMENT

3. INTEGRATION

2. LAYERING

Dirty Money Integrates
into the financial System

Purchase of Luxury Assets
Financial Investments
Commercial / Industrial Investments

Wire
Transfer

Transfer funds between various
Offshore / Onshore Banks

KYCMap

Figure 5.14 Money laundering.

arguably play the most important role in the cybercrime chain. A cybercriminal cannot go to a bank account to cash out money that they have stolen from a victim. It is the money mule that will facilitate the movement of the money from where it is deposited by the hackers to cleansing platforms and then to the hackers. The cleansing services are those that make trails leading to the money disappear or at least difficult to trace. Cryptocurrencies are commonly used and a money mule may convert the stolen money back and forth from one cryptocurrency to another. The money mules can also buy products with the money and resale them to get clean money that can be given to the cybercriminals. This is why it is normally hard for money stolen by cybercriminals to be recovered. The money mules will be waiting for the cybercriminals to give them the go ahead to cleanse the money once it enters into bank accounts or Bitcoin address (Figure 5.14).

Summary of the Chapter

This chapter has discussed the cybercriminal activities on the dark net. It has first given the categories of cybercrime. The first category is that of computer fraud. Under this category are data breaches, DoS attacks, business email compromise, email account compromise, phishing, and ransomware. The second category that the chapter has looked at is cyberterrorism. Here, it has highlighted the increasing threat of critical services and infrastructure being taken down by terrorists through hacking. An explanation has been given on how different countries have prepared themselves to this threat. According to the current reports, there have not been many cyberterrorism incidents, but the chapter explains why countries need to prepare themselves for a future with such kinds of attacks. The next category of cybercriminal activities is cyber extortion. The paper has highlighted that there are attackers extorting money from organizations by threatening to hack them or attack them with DDoS. Lastly, the paper has looked into the category of cyberwarfare. Based on the research, there have been multiple confrontations between nations on the cyberspace, thus showing clear signs that a cyberwarfare is not far from happening. The isolated confrontations discussed feature China, Russia, and North Korea as perpetrators of attacks that could easily translate to cyberwarfare. These attacks range from shutting down the internet of other countries to industrial espionage and election meddling. The chapter has also gone through the cybercriminal activities that have been taking place through the dark net. These were highlights of the exhaustive list provided in Chapter 3 where most of the attacks were covered. Data exfiltration was discussed, and there was an explanation of what happens when huge chunks of data are finally stolen from companies. An example was given of how data from Yahoo was stolen, and even though it was initially encrypted, the hackers were able to decrypt it due to the use of a weak encryption algorithm. The chapter has delved into the monetization of cybercrime. A brief history has been given on how monetization of cybercrime began. The chapter has then looked at the current techniques of monetizing cybercrime. The discussion has looked at exploit kits, extortion, adverts, theft of login details, premium rate SMSs, and banking malware. Lastly, the chapter has looked at two important components of today's cybercrime market: malware-as-a-service and money laundering. Since not all cybercriminals are programmers, they have been relying on the services of experts to make the malware that they will use in attacks. Money laundering services offered by money mules have also been discussed. The techniques that are used by the money mules to eliminate trails behind the illegal proceeds of cybercrime have been highlighted.

Questions

1. Explain the business email compromise attack.
2. Give three categories of cybercrime.
3. Explain the difference between cyberterrorism and cyberwarfare.
4. What are premium rate SMSs?
5. Who are exploit writers?
6. Who are bot herders?
7. What do money mules do?

Further Reading

The following are resources that can be used to gain more knowledge on this chapter:

https://acorn.gov.au/learn-about-cybercrime.
https://interpol.int/Crime-areas/Cybercrime/Cybercrime.

Chapter 6

Evolution of the Web and Its Hidden Data

Introduction

The hallmark of man's revolutions in communication is the internet. It came in to fill a void in the interconnection of other inventions such as telegraphs, telephones, radios, and computers. The internet has created a worldwide network for information dissemination, collaboration, and interaction. It is a global interconnection of networks used by devices to communicate with each other. For devices to communicate on the internet, they have to connect individually and independently to it. Currently, the connection is done through Internet Protocol (IP) addresses whereby each device is given a unique address that can be used to identify it as a sender or receiver of the communication. Communication on the internet takes place through languages known as protocols.

The internet is currently made up of an assortment of networks. There are private networks, public networks, business networks, government networks, and even academic networks, among others. Special electronic devices and technologies are used to link these networks in a wired, wireless, or optical medium. Governments, businesses, and academic institutions cooperated to deploy and build up the internet. In this chapter, a discussion will be done on the history and development of the internet and its hidden data. The discussion will be done on the following topics:

It will cover this in the following topics:

- Origins of the internet
- Internet characteristics
- Evolution of the hidden web
- Deep web information retrieval process.

Terminologies and Explanations

The internet refers to a global system of interconnect IP networks. It is also referred to as the net, an acronym for network. However, there are some misunderstandings about the internet. Some people use the phrase World Wide Web to refer to the internet. However, there is a distinct difference between these two. The World Wide Web, also known as web, is only one of the components of the internet. The web is an information-sharing component that runs on the internet. It uses the Hypertext Transfer Protocol, commonly known as HTTP. This is just one of the many languages that are used by devices to communicate and share data on the internet. The web uses browsers which access documents published on the internet called web pages. These documents are normally linked with one another thus allowing one to jump from one web page to another through hyperlinks. The documents can contain text, graphics, audio, and video. The web supports specially formatted documents. The documents have to be written in a markup language such as HTML that can support the hyperlinking of documents. There are very many browsers that have been released to date to enable internet users to access the World Wide Web.

It might appear challenging as why the internet is not the web. Outside the World Wide Web are other components of the internet. These components do not communicate using HTTP. For example, emailing services rely on Simple Mail Transfer Protocol (SMTP) to send data and messages and this is another different part of the internet. There are others that are smaller compared to the internet but are not part of the World Wide Web. The dark net is part of the World Wide Web. This is because it also relies on HTTP and is composed of specially formatted documents as well. Hyperlinks allow one to easily jump from one of these documents to another. The only difference between the dark net and the surface web is that the dark net requires a certain type of browsers to access. These are browsers that can enter special networks on the internet that are highly encrypted to prevent outside parties from knowing the identities of communicating parties in the network. In a previous chapter, there was a discussion on how these networks are formed and operate. There are many "proxy" computers in the network that are used to bounce the transmission of data back and forth across the globe to make it hard for anyone to trail back the parties involved in communication. The special packets used to transmit the data on the World Wide Web are encrypted when it comes to the dark net for the purposes of security of the communicating parties.

Origins of the Internet

The concept of this global network was envisioned by J.C.R. Licklider, head of research at DARPA 1962, who described a galactic network that would interconnect computers globally. In his description, this network would give to the masses quick access to information and also programs on different web pages. After his term, Licklider convinced those who succeeded him in the post to focus on the global networking concept. An interest followed and in 1965, there was a project to connect a TX-2 computer in Mass to a Q-32 computer in California (Figures 6.1–6.3).

The interconnection was done through a dial-up telephone line. This inadvertently created the first wide area network. From this project, it was realized that computers could run well together. The computers connected were able to run programs and retrieve data from each other. The need for a network to support this on a large scale then arose.

In 1966, there was the introduction of a computer network called ARPANET in DARPA. This was followed by the development of the ARPANET network

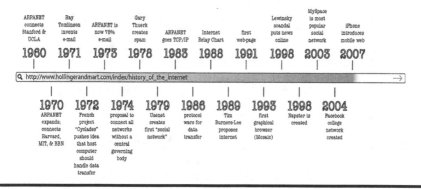

Figure 6.1   A timeline of the internet. (https://thinglink.com/scene/53320813764 6211072.)

Figure 6.2   A picture of part of the TX-2 computer. (http://gordonbell.azurewebsites. net/computer_engineering/00000149.htm.)

Figure 6.3 A section of the Q-32 computer. (https://sutori.com/item/q-32-computer.)

topology and optimization of its economics in 1968. There were some developments on a theory on packet switching that would be the basis of the communication between networked computers. In 1969, the first host was connected to the ARPANET in September 1969. By the end of the year, there were four host computers on the ARPANET. Over the following years, more computers were being connected to the ARPANET. A host-to-host protocol had been developed in 1970 and named the Network Control Protocol (NCP). Sites on the ARPANET started implementing the NCP. The ARPANET was then demonstrated to the public in 1972. An electronic messaging software that could write, send, and receive messages on the ARPANET was also launched. This gave ARPANET users an easy communication and coordination mechanism.

There was, however, a challenge with the mechanism of interconnecting computers on the ARPANET. A circuit switching method was used where networks would be connected at a circuitry level. Bits would be transmitted individually synchronously through an end-to-end circuit. The theory on packet switching was seen to be a welcome solution that would be efficient to the ARPANET. Computers had been functioning as components of each other on the network, and this was not efficient. There was a push to make them peers and also to ensure that they were independent. An open-network architecture was suggested. The open-network architecture would allow individual networks to be designed independent of each other and have their own unique features depending on the users. These individual networks would then be connected to the global network but they would not be enslaved to it.

The NCP was brought under review, and it was seen that it could not address the new needs of networks. A change to it was necessary. The NCP lacked basic error control mechanism, and if some data was lost in transit, the global network would first come to a halt. The NCP was not so reliable since it was created with the thought that the ARPANET would be the only network. With other small networks being created, there were major problems, especially with error control. Therefore, another protocol was developed. The Transmission Control Protocol/Internet Protocol, commonly known as TCP/IP came into being. It succeeded the NCP although the NCP was more of a device driver and TCP/IP a communication protocol.

The following are the four rules that were passed concerning the setup of networks:

- Each network would be independent of others. No changes would also be required for a network to be connected to the ARPANET.
- For error control, if a packet did not reach a destination, it would be retransmitted.
- There would be special black boxes used to connect networks. These are what are called gateways and routers. The devices would not, however, retain the flow of data passing through them to avoid complications and recovery from failure.
- There would not be global control of the network.

Four ground rules were critical to Kahn's early thinking:

- Each distinct network would have to stand on its own, and no internal changes could be required to any such network to connect it to the internet.
- Communications would be on a best effort basis. If a packet didn't make it to the final destination, it would shortly be retransmitted from the source.
- Black boxes would be used to connect the networks; these would later be called gateways and routers. There would be no information retained by the gateways about the individual flows of packets passing through them, thereby

keeping them simple and avoiding complicated adaptation and recovery from various failure modes.
■ There would be no global control at the operations level.

These rules became the foundation of a more reliable and efficient global network. However, there still were some challenges that needed to be addressed. To begin with, there needs to be an algorithm to identify lost packets and request their retransmission. There was also a need for host-to-host pipelining. This would allow for multiple packets to be sent to a single destination from different sources. With the introduction of gateways, there was a need for them to have functions that would enable them to forward packets correctly to their networks. They needed to read information in IP headers to use it for routing packets. In response to these and other concerns, some basic approaches were formed. Communication was to be done into streams of bytes, every flow of bytes would be done through sliding windows with acknowledgments, and then IP addresses were formed to identify hosts within the network. These basic approaches strengthened and improved the efficiency of the global network.

With these improvements, TCP/IP was being adopted. Initially, it was thought that TCP/IP would be too complex for personal computers. However, using early versions of the Xerox Alto personal computer and IBM PC, the practicality of TCP/IP was proven. In the 1980s, there had been developments in the computing world with many personal computers, workstations, and small networks between a few computers (local area networks). To accommodate the new increasing number of hosts that would be eventually connected to the global network, some changes were done to IP addressing. Three network classes were introduced: A, B, and C. Class A were for national scale networks, class B for regional scale, and class C for local area networks. Due to the increase in the number of hosts on the global network, there arose a need to make it easier for hosts on it to be accessed. Initially, since there were a few hosts, it was feasible for people to use their numeric IP addresses to access them. However, with so many networks and computers, it was no longer feasible. Therefore, the Domain Name System (DNS) was introduced. This would allow for computers to access hosts using their hostnames. The DNS would resolve the hostnames into the IP addresses (Figure 6.4).

In 1980, TCP/IP had been adopted as a defense standard by the military. In 3 years, the ARPANET was used mostly by defense forces, research and development, and operational institutions. By 1985, there were more users. The global network was being used for daily communications between people through email (Figure 6.5).

This then led to the worldwide adoption of the global network, and it was referred to as the internet. The internet grew beyond the normal usage to become exploited for commercial purposes. In the early 1990s, Tim Berners Lee invented the World Wide Web. This allowed for documents on the internet to be identified using Unique Resource Locators (URLs). The World Wide Web enabled users on

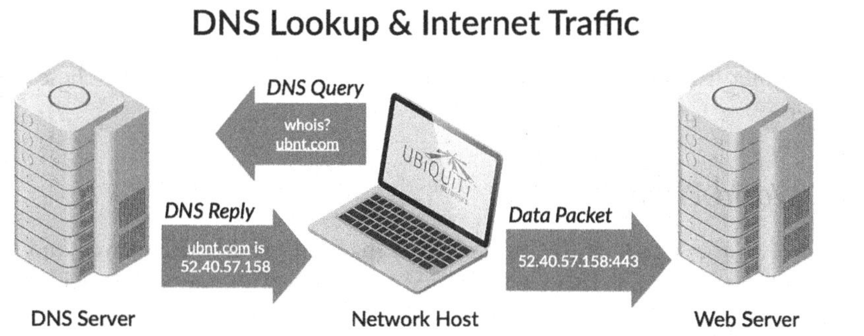

DNS Lookup & Internet Traffic

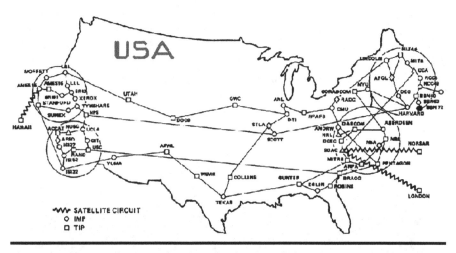

Figure 6.4   An illustration of how the DNS system works. A user sends a domain name to the DNS server which replies with a numeric address that the browser then uses to access the web servers of the website.

Figure 6.5   An early map showing the layout of the ARPANET in the United States. (http://djo.ca/cbbz00.html.)

the internet to access information that had been linked to the internet anywhere in the globe.

The internet has for two decades been in existence and has supported many technologies. It has survived through the introduction of many personal computers and client–server and peer-to-peer computing models. It has also seen commercial success with billions of dollars invested annually through it. The internet is still changing though. For example, there are still discussions on the next generation of IP addresses that will be able to handle the increasing number of users. More discussions are still ongoing about the desired direction that the internet must follow to survive to the future.

Internet Characteristics

The internet is made up of different components as explained earlier. These are as follows.

The World Wide Web

This is the largest part of the internet. It is made up of the surface web and deep web. The surface web is that part of the World Wide Web that is indexed by standard search engines. In the discussion of the development of the internet, there was a highlight that Tim Berners Lee invented the World Wide Web. It is estimated that only 5% of this web is visible to everyone (Figure 6.6).

Although it might seem small, this is where most news websites, e-commerce stores, social media platforms, chat forums, institutional websites, and government sites are found. The surface web is estimated to have over a billion documents on it. These are best known as websites and web pages. The deep web is the part of the World Wide Web that is not indexed by normal search engines. However, it can still be accessed by the public, just that different methods are used to access it. The deep web contains the dark web. The dark web is made up of dark nets. These dark nets are isolated networks that run on top of the internet. These networks, such as Tor, tend to be highly encrypted and feature more security characteristics than the normal internet. They are accessed only using browsers that can connect to their networks. Another portion of the deep web is the side of websites that is kept away

Figure 6.6   A 2014 illustration of the percentage of the visible and deep World Wide Web.

from the public eyes. This includes medical records, social media files, government files, and other secret information that needs to be kept secure. In recent times, there have been data breaches that have revealed some of these sensitive files that are normally hidden in the deep web. Some of these breaches have been done by hackers, but others have been as a result of careless behaviors.

The biggest data breach to date is the one that happened at Yahoo. It is estimated that the records of close to 3 billion users were stolen by hackers in 2014. This breach greatly impacted Yahoo which had earlier claimed that it had encrypted all the user records. The algorithm used to encrypt the records was later identified to be a weak one that allowed hackers to decrypt the records. The same organization had been attacked in 2013 where the data belonging to close to 1 billion user accounts was stolen. This data included names, dates of birth, secret questions, and passwords. Another large-scale breach was one on Adult Friend Finder in 2016 where the records of close to 412 million users were stolen. This is after the hackers accessed six databases that had been used over 20 years. Even though these records were said to be encrypted, it was later found out that this had been done using a weak encryption algorithm and most of the records had already been cracked.

An example of data exposure that was done non-maliciously was one that happened to the Australian Red Cross. The data exposure that happened in 2016 saw the release of information relating to close to 550 million blood donors that had been stored on the organizational website. The data exposure happened because a third party contracted to maintain the website moved a backup file and left it in an unsecured location on the web servers. In a web setup, there are folders that can be accessed by the public and those that cannot. Sensitive files that are to be buried in the deep web are kept in folders that cannot be accessed by the public. In the scenario of the Red Cross data exposure, the backup file was copied to a folder that was accessible to the public. The human error led to the sensitive file being downloaded and accessed by persons outside the Red Cross.

The discussed data breaches show the importance of the Deep Web. It houses secrets that should not be exposed to the general public. This is why hackers are always after this data. When sensitive data is moved from the deep web to the surface web, there are several consequences. This is why organizations invest a lot in protecting the back-end access to their systems. It is through this access that people can normally access their data stored on the deep web. It is also the common way through which hackers get access to this highly valued data. In summary, the following are the characteristics of the three parts of the World Wide Web.

Surface Web Characteristics

The surface web is accessible to the public. It can be accessed using normal browsers and is not restrictive to who can access it (Figure 6.7).

The surface web is indexed by search engines. Search engines rank websites based on the keywords that they match to users' search queries.

Figure 6.7 An illustration of the surface web vs the deep web. (https:// dreammarketdrugs.com/the-deep-web-dark-web-and-the-darknet-marketplaces/.)

The surface web sees little illegal activity. This is because it is easy to trace back actions to their actors. If someone publishes an inflammatory post on a blog, he or she can be tracked down easily. It is also easier to monitor activities on the surface web. However, users that are growing concerned with their privacy have been using VPNs. These software programs make it harder but not impossible to track down a user's activities such as the websites they visit.

The surface web is also small in size. As said before, the surface web is only about 5% of the entire World Wide Web.

Deep Web

This is the chunk of the web that is not indexed by search engines. The contents are at times too sensitive such that it would be a catastrophe if search engines were to index them. Google hacking is a technique that is intended at exposing sensitive data by using special operators in search queries that can retrieve sensitive information from web servers. The technique is normally used against improperly configured servers. It can expose databases, sensitive files, and even live camera footage. Some of the search operators used include

- Filetype: this operator limits a query to a specific filetype such as sql, docx, or pdf
- Intitle: this operator searches for a certain text in the title of web pages
- Inurl: this operator limits search to particular text in the URL of a page.

Some part of the deep web can be accessed using passwords or other forms of authentication. One has to be authenticated and authorized to access the content.

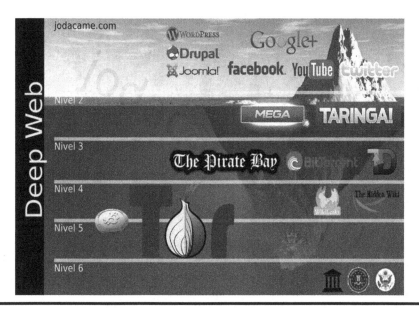

Figure 6.8 An illustration of the deep web and different services that run on different layers of it. (http://evil.wikia.com/wiki/Deep_Web_Conspiracy.)

Therefore, most content ranging from email accounts to website accounts is stored in the deep web. Banks also store their records on this part of the web (Figure 6.8).

Dark Net

This is highly confused with the deep web. The dark web is a subset of the deep web that is entirely made up of dark nets. The most common dark net is Tor. Dark nets run on top of the internet and feature encryption that makes it hard for other parties to monitor the interactions of users or their activities. Unlike the deep web, the dark web is only accessible through special browsers. The most common browser used to enter one of the dark nets on the deep web is the Tor browser. Normal browsers such as Google Chrome can only enter the dark web using special plugins. Without these special add-ons, the browser will be unable to access the dark net sites. Dark net websites are not indexed by search engines. Even though there are special search engines that run on dark nets such as Tor, they too cannot index dark net sites (Figure 6.9).

Dark web sites are known for their large-scale criminal and terrorist activity. These sites are used to sell drugs, weapons, ammunition, fake citizenship, malware-as-a-service, assassinations, hacking services, and fake currency. Legal agencies have been clamping down on some sites and taking down their founders due to their involvement in criminal or terrorist activity. Most of the sites that were famous for selling drugs have already been eliminated. However, it is believed that

Figure 6.9 Some of the services available on the dark net. (http://007hacker. com/darknet-access-dark-net-websites/.)

the solution will only be temporary since the demand from buyers and sellers leads to the creation of a new black market. Lastly, the dark net is said to be immeasurable. There are special properties about it that make it hard to know just how big it is. There are some sites that are yet to be discovered. People that have tried to index it have only been able to identify a small portion of the sites that have many visitors. It cannot, therefore, be accurately said as to how many dark net sites exist on different dark nets.

Internet Relay Chat

This is a chat system that is built on the internet. It runs on the application layer and facilitates the chat process using a client–server model. The clients are the programs that users either install on their devices or systems that they access on the internet that can access servers. The servers handle the exchange of messages between clients. The IRC (internet relay chat) allows group and one-on-one communication. IRC chat rooms can be connected to simply by getting access to the server supporting the chat rooms. Access is obtained by visiting the IRC server using the format irc+servername+.com/.org/.net. Most chat rooms do not require users to register so as to chat. They can engage in chats if they have just a username. However, there are more restrictions that can be applied to IRC chat rooms. These include the kicking out of users from chat rooms for inappropriate behavior, making a channel a secret channel, making a channel private, preventing messages from being forwarded outside the chatroom, restricting access to users that have invites, and limiting the number of users that can access the channel (Figure 6.10).

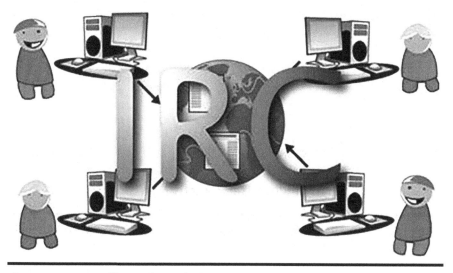

Figure 6.10 An illustration of the IRC. (https://esds.co.in/blog/what-is-irc-internet-relay-chat/#sthash.9eV4LitQ.dpbs.)

The challenges that IRC has met have mostly been cyberattacks. It has greatly been affected by denial-of-service (DoS) attacks. Servers offering the message exchange service have been subjected to DoS attacks where they have been bombarded with too much traffic to make them unavailable for some time. Hackers have also tried packet sniffing on IRC networks. This has been in an effort to try and read the messages being exchanged by users. In response to these, the IRC has been improving its security. Most networks use SSL connections. This secure connection between clients and servers has been effective at beating packet sniffers. In addition, some channels are implementing end-to-end encryption of the messages exchanged on their networks.

Usenet

This is a global network that acts as a discussion system. It can be used to send and receive messages or files. Messages on this network are called news. Each category of news is termed as a newsgroup. Unlike web forums, the Usenet does not have a central server and an administrator. It is distributed over many servers in the world that are used to store and forward messages to each other called newsfeeds. A user can read and post news if they can access a Usenet provider (Figure 6.11).

Email

Emails are electronic messages that can be sent over the internet. Emails use different protocols such as SMTP, IMAP (Internet Message Access Protocol), and Post

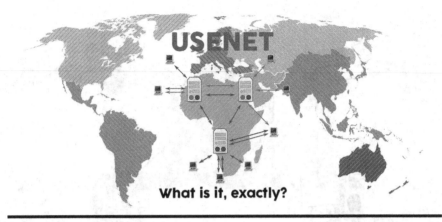

Figure 6.11 An illustration of Usenet. (https://addictivetips.com/usenet/understand-usenet-is-it-legal/.)

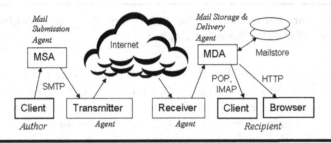

Figure 6.12 An illustration of the emailing process. (http://en.citizendium.org/wiki/Email_system.)

Office Protocol (POP) to enable the sending and receiving of messages. Emails are sent to mail servers who then forward them to the correct destinations. Today, anyone with a registered domain name is in most cases offered email services free of charge (Figure 6.12).

Hosting

The documents or web pages on the World Wide Web have to exist on a storage space on the internet for them to be accessed by other computers. The process of keeping these documents on the internet-accessible storage space is called hosting. There are very many hosting companies in the world, and tech-savvy internet users can even host their own documents on the internet. Hosting companies work closely with DNS companies. The host gives a domain name to a website and provides the numerical address for the domain name. The DNS companies simply resolve the domain names to the numerical addresses when internet users wish to visit certain websites (Figure 6.13).

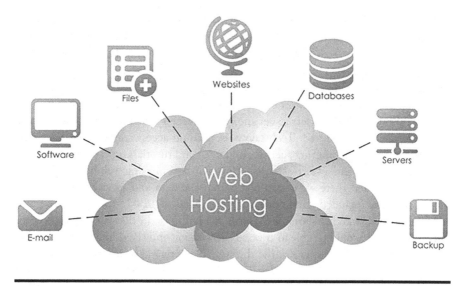

Figure 6.13 An illustration of the features available through web hosts. (https://programage.com/blog/The_web_developer_guide_to_web_hosting_profitability_101.html.)

Evolution of the Hidden Web

As has been explained in previous sections, beyond the surface web is the part of the internet that is hidden. It is not indexed by browsers and can only be accessed using special browsers. Dark nets do not normally answer to pings or inquiries from search engines, thus, they remain hidden. They can only be visited directly from their URLs. For instance, if one wants to access a dark net marketplace such as Silk Road 2.0, searching for this marketplace on Google will not yield a result that gives one a direct link. It is not the same as searching for a website such as Facebook that will give back results showing the URLs that can be used to access Facebook. This section will discuss how dark nets came into being.

In 1969, when the internet was still ARPANET and still a work in progress, there were a few networks that run alongside it. Most of these networks would be connected to the ARPANET thus continue to create a vast worldwide network. However, there were some networks that were not getting connected to the internet for different purposes. These networks were growing alongside the ARPANET and were isolated. In the 1980s, most of the groundwork had been laid and the internet was going mainstream. There was also the adoption of personal computers, and people were excited to use the internet for purposes such as sending emails or visiting the web pages that were available then. The dark net was also growing but in a physical form. Dark nets were offering data havens, gambling operations, and pornography. These, deemed as illegal, were not being linked to the global internet.

In the 1990s, the internet was going mainstream and many people had adopted it. Storage costs were falling, and there were technological advancements that allowed for the compression of files. These served as triggers for the dark net activity. There soon came peer-to-peer data transmission which gave rise to piracy. Instead of users buying content, they were getting it from others that had already bought it. In March 2000, a software developer called Ian Clarke released Freenet. This software allowed internet users to get anonymous access to dark parts of the internet that were not being indexed. Tech-savvy users could access content that had been hidden away from the internet such as child porn and tutorials on explosive making. In the mid of the year, a start-up called HavenCo was offering web hosting or dark net sites. However, there were restrictions that the data and services to be hosted should not have included child porn, spam, or fraud. In 2002, Tor was released by the US Naval Research Laboratory. This was a hallmark in the world of dark web. The Tor network would be able to conceal the location and IP addresses of users. The network would direct internet traffic through an overlay network that runs on volunteer servers from a source to a destination. The involvement of the United States in this dark net might seem puzzling since the network is currently associated with illegal activity such as terrorism and drug huddling. However, the United States at the time of launching the network had interests in protecting the identities of its operatives in countries that were repressive such as China. Since the network was highly encrypted, it would be hard for anyone to dig down and find out communicating parties in such an exchange. The network is still being used for such purposes. However, it is not as watertight as it used to be. This is because the US legal agencies have introduced loopholes that can lead to the identification of parties of interest on the network. This is a technique that they have used to apprehend some of the notable people behind successful black markets on the dark net.

In 2005, some of the negative impacts of dark nets were starting to be felt. The first industry that came to face these impacts was the entertainment industry. It was reported that the industry lost $34 billion within that year to software piracy. The dark net had a lot of bandwidth, and this was being used to distribute an estimated half million movies each day. Copyright infringement was also felt by software vendors especially those that sold productivity software such as the Microsoft Office Suite (Figure 6.14).

In 2009, a major development happened that led to the commercialization of activities on the dark net. An unknown person known as Satoshi Nakamoto invented Bitcoin. These were untraceable cryptocurrencies that were not subject to centralized or government control. Bitcoin was successful because it was stronger and more secure than earlier failed digital currencies that did not have mechanisms to prevent the money from being copied. Bitcoin used a public accounting ledger that made sure that there was no double spending of the same digital currencies due to the exploitation of delays in updating records. The concept of the public accounting ledger has been adopted by many other successful cryptocurrencies (Figure 6.15).

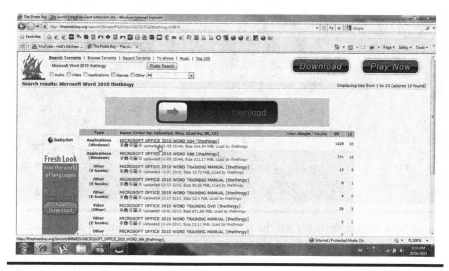

Figure 6.14 Pirated copies of Microsoft Office 2010 listed on a torrent site.

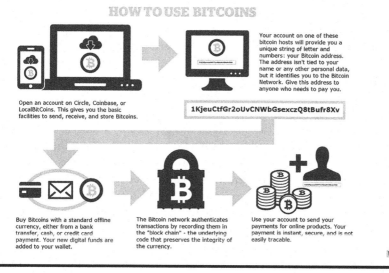

Figure 6.15 An infographic on how to use Bitcoin. (http://divinework.in/what-is-bitcoin.php.)

With the introduction of Bitcoin, dark net sites started offering commercial services. This is because it sorted out the anonymity challenge when it came to exchanging money. With Bitcoin, parties could transact without fearing that they would be discovered. Therefore, criminal activity went on the rise. New services were introduced. The sale of drugs, weapons, and ammunition gained traction. There was an increase in the number of buyers and sellers in dark net sites.

Figure 6.16   A terrorist site on the dark net requesting for Bitcoin donations.

In 2010, a new entrant came to be identified in the dark net. Terrorists had started using the same network used by US security operatives for highly encrypted and anonymous communication. It was discovered that there were over 50,000 terrorism-related sites (Figure 6.16).

There were also close to 300 chat forums that had been set up by terrorists. A form of financing was also discovered. The terrorists on the dark nets used to participate in the sale of pirated content. The proceeds from these sales were going towards funding terrorism. This was one of the notable negative impacts of the highly anonymous networks of dark nets (Figures 6.17 and 6.18).

In 2011, exposes of criminal activity taking place on the dark net started to surface on the surface web. The Silk Road was exposed by a blogger as a dark net marketplace that was being used for the buying and sale of drugs. The expose said that transacting parties only accepted Bitcoin. This led to the value of Bitcoin to jump from $10 to $30 due to its perceived usefulness by the general public.

In 2013, there was an outcry on the illegal and terrorist activities that were taking place on the internet due to the dark net. Particularly, child pornography was gaining an audience. Legal authorities started taking action and apprehending the suspects behind some of the dark net illegal activities. There was a crack by Irish authorities on an apartment where they apprehended Eric Eoin who was said to be a big facilitator of child porn. The FBI soon after descendent on many other people that were facilitators of child porn. They exploited a breach that was on the Firefox browser bundle that came with a certain version of Tor. This breach allowed the FBI to directly identify the users on the Tor network. They were able to isolate the ones that were engaging in child porn business. Later on, the US government started intercepting communication between suspected terrorist operatives. Communication between two Al Qaeda chiefs was intercepted, and the discoveries from their communication were significant since they lead to the United States shuttering its embassies in Islamic countries.

Figure 6.17   A screenshot of the ISIS website on the dark net.

"The site mirrors many of the other standard bulletin boards that the jihadi's have had over the years replete with videos and sections in all languages. Given that this site has popped up today in the Darknet just post the attacks in Paris, one has to assume that an all out media blitz is spinning up by Al-Hayat to capitalize on the situation," Terban wrote.

Figure 6.18   An article on the discovery of the ISIS website on the dark net. (https://csoonline.com/article/3004648/security-awareness/after-paris-isis-moves-propaganda-machine-to-darknet.html.)

In October 2013, the FBI shut down the most famous drug market by then that was called Silk Road. The alleged founder, Ross Ulbricht, was sentenced to life imprisonment. During the crackdown of the dark net site, the marketplace had accumulated over \$1.2 billion from the sale of drugs, weapons, and fake documents among other things (Figure 6.19).

A report by The Guardian showed that the NSA was targeting people that were using Tor. The report claimed that the NSA had exploits for the software on computers that would allow the agency to determine their actual identities. Between 2013 and 2015, there was an upsurge in the number of visitors on the dark net. This was due to the popularity that dark net marketplaces were getting. Even after legal

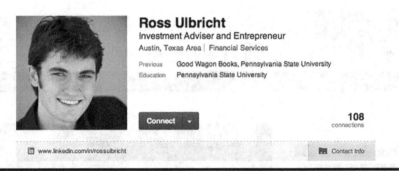

Figure 6.19   Ross Ulbricht's LinkedIn account.

agencies took down a famous marketplace, another one would come right back to absorb the growing demand from buyers and sellers.

As from 2016, the war against illegal activities on the dark net intensified. Legal agencies had come up with newer techniques that would be used to identify users on the dark net. Major black markets were taken down during this time. Raids became common occurrences. Apart from law enforcement agencies, rogue users and vigilantes also participated in the takedown of sites. Some extortionists took advantage of the situation and started demanding for some money to give away the details of administrators of different marketplaces to authorities.

An example of a vigilante attack was witnessed in February 2017. A vigilante hacker brought down an estimated 10,000 sites that were running on a host called Freedom Hosting 2. This was one of the largest hosts on the dark web. The vigilante is said to have taken the action to take down all the sites on the host after it was discovered that the host had also been hosting child pornography. In addition to taking down Freedom Hosting 2, the vigilante leaked databases gotten from the hack and also released some private keys that were used for decryption of data on the host (Figure 6.20).

The takedown of Freedom Hosting 2 had some major similarities with the takedown of its earlier version, Freedom Hosting 1. The predecessor was taken down by the FBI in 2013 due to reports that it was hosting child pornography.

In July, a joint operation involving different government agencies took down Alpha Bay and Hansa marketplaces. Alpha Bay was the market that had absorbed most of the demand from the fall of Silk Road 2 after Ross Ulbricht was arrested. The takedown followed a familiar pattern where the legal agencies first got access to the site, and they started collecting information that they would use to build a case against the founders or participants of the marketplace (Figure 6.21).

The takedown of Alpha Bay preceded that of Hansa. Shortly after Alpha Bay was taken down, sellers were advertising their services on the surface web that they had moved to Hansa. Hansa had already been seized by law enforcement agencies, and soon after, it was taken down as well (Figure 6.22).

MOTHERBOARD

TOR NETWORK

We Talked to the Hacker Who Took Down a Fifth of the Dark Web

 Joseph Cox
Feb 4 2017, 7:37pm

"This is in fact my first hack ever."

On Friday, a hacker took down a huge chunk of the dark web. Visitors to over 10,000 Tor hidden services running on Freedom Hosting II—a hosting provider for dark web sites—were greeted with a perhaps surprising message, The Verge reported.

"Hello, Freedom Hosting II, you have been hacked," the message read. According to a report from independent security researcher Sarah Jamie Lewis, Freedom Hosting II ran around 20 percent of all dark web sites.

Figure 6.20 An article about an interview with the vigilante that took down Freedom Hosting 2.

Figure 6.21 A screenshot of the taken down Alpha Bay.

Figure 6.22   A screenshot of the taken down Hansa marketplace.

The takedowns and apprehending of people that were behind these dark net marketplaces served as a warning to other users. It was proof that the dark net was not a place to hide with sinister motives. People have used it for illegal purposes and have ended up in jail. The takedowns are supported by the legitimate users of Tor. This is the concerned group that wants networks such as Tor to be used for their intended purposes and that is to protect one's identity (Figure 6.23).

From another viewpoint, agencies are starting the cobra effect in the dark net landscape. The cobra effect is whereby a solution to a problem ends up making it worse such as the attempted control of cobras in India that ended up increasing the snake population. With these takedowns, vendors and operators are going to

A report yesterday by Onionscan—a series of probes into the health of the Tor network—queried a database of 30,000 Tor sites, doing so over several days as onions tend to have much less reliable uptime than websites on the "clearnet" you're reading this on now. The report found about 4,400 were online—just under 15 percent. It's impossible to claim these findings are ironclad, but they're at least indicative of a larger downward trend.

Figure 6.23   An article on the disappearance of the major part of the dark web. (https://gizmodo.com/the-dark-web-is-disappearing-1793037736.)

be motivated to create other marketplaces that are even harder to access. These marketplaces will be thoroughly tested to ensure that it is hard for authorities to crack them open. Since the dark net black markets have proven to be profitable to the traders and buyers, it is only with time that they will be back. Therefore, authorities are going to be facing more resilient hidden services. There will be many checks to prevent authorities from gaining access to these marketplaces.

As has been the pattern, there is an anticipation that another marketplace will rise and grow significantly bigger than any of the previously taken down markets. Through trial and error, the marketplace will be evolved to make sure that law enforcement agencies cannot use the same techniques they have used in the past to get access to the sites, obtain data to charge the admins, and then shut down the marketplace. However, the new marketplace will not just be meeting resistance from law enforcement agencies. There are vigilantes and extortionists that will also be against be the administrators of these sites. The vigilantes will want to take down sites that engage in some type of illegal business. Extortionists will be looking to making money from site administrators not to give up their real details to law enforcement agencies.

Deep Web Information Retrieval Process

As has been stated before, most search engines do not index contents of the deep web. However, it is not very different in terms of structure from the surface web. Since it is part of the World Wide Web, it is also made up of well-formatted documents that can be accessed through hyperlinks. Since it is bigger than the surface web, it has billions of HTML pages, several times more than those available on the surface web. However, there are even more dynamic pages that form the back end of websites. This makes it hard for an internet user to find out the URLs of deep web and dark net sites. It is not a major concern since most of these pages are supposed to be kept away from the public. Normal search engines cannot also crawl the deep web since it also contains sensitive data items such as databases.

However, there are some special search techniques that can be used to crawl the dark net. It is not a small fete to crawl the dark net. This is because of the heterogeneity of the contents which make it hard to generate the queries to be The surface web is composed of almost homogeneous contents thus it is easy for search engines such as Google and Bing to index it. The process of crawling the deep web is known as deep web surfacing. It aims at harvesting records from the deep net and indexing them at an affordable cost. The biggest challenge is generating the right queries. There are two crawling methods that are used to index the deep web. The first one is using prior knowledge-based methods and the second is using non-prior knowledge methods. Prior knowledge-based methods rely on some knowledge being passed to search queries to help with the web crawling process. The challenges with this are that one is required to have sufficient knowledge of the deep web and that the process of filling the prior knowledge in forms reduces the number of possible hits for the query. Non-prior knowledge-based methods have been developed to overcome these deficiencies. The non-prior knowledge-based methods generate new queries based on the results of previous search queries. Therefore, no prior knowledge is required in order to crawl the deep web. An advancement of this is a technique that was introduced by a researcher called Ntoulas. The technique involved the use of a greedy query that focuses on harvest rates. Queries with different keywords are run and the ones that return the maximum harvest rates are used for the next query. A combination of these methods often leads to the indexing of the deep web. Legal agencies have used these methods to index up to about 20,000 dark net websites. The indexing of the deep web helps in the identification of sites on the deep web. Also, when data is stolen from companies during breaches, these indexing techniques are used to locate it on the deep web and thus point investigative bodies on the direction to take to try and retrieve it.

Summary of the Chapter

This chapter has looked at the background of the internet and the deep web. It has examined critical events that led to the establishment of the internet from a global network that was known as ARPANET. The rules that led to the coordinated development of the ARPANET alongside other networks have also been discussed. The characteristics of the internet have been discussed in depth. It has been broken down into its components and their characteristics described. From the discussion, the World Wide Web has been discussed as the largest part of the internet. The World Wide Web has two subsets, the surface net and the deep web. The surface web is the indexed part of the web, while the deep web is the dark unindexed part. The surface web has been said to be close to 5% of the World Wide Web, features little illegal activity, and is accessible to the public. The deep web has been said to be large, a container of all dark nets, and the back ends of websites. A subset of the deep web called the dark net has also been explained. Other components of the internet such as IRC, Usenet, email, and hosting have been discussed. The chapter has then looked at the evolution of the hidden web. The role of the NSA in its development has been highlighted. The rise and fall of illegal activity on the deep web has been explained. Lastly, the chapter has looked at the ways used to index the deep web.

Questions

1. What was the ARPANET?
2. Give the four rules that were passed to ensure the development of the ARPANET collaboratively with other networks.

3. Differentiate between the surface web, deep web, and dark web?
4. Why is it correct to say that the deep web sees little illegal activity?
5. Research to find out and explain another dark net other than Tor.
6. Explain the basics of the internet relay chat.
7. What was the main impact of Bitcoin to dark nets?
8. Why are normal search engines unable to index the deep web?
9. Explain two techniques that are used to index the deep web.

Further Reading

The following are resources that can be used to gain more knowledge on this chapter:

Liu J., Jiang L., Wu Z., Zheng Q., Deep web adaptive crawling based on minimum executable pattern, *Journal of Intelligent Information Systems*, 36, 197–215, 2011.
https://cdn.prod.internetsociety.org/wp-content/uploads/2017/09/ISOC-History-of-the-Internet_1997.pdf.

Chapter 7

Dark Web Content Analyzing Techniques

Introduction

The dark web is home to content that is hidden from normal search engines. It can only be accessed through special software, and even then, it is not exactly given where one should begin looking for content. There are isolated listings of some of the websites that one can access on the dark net. These listings are commonly found on surface websites such as The Hidden Wiki and popular social networks such as Reddit. Even then, the listings are limited, and with time, most of the sites listed have either changed their hosting, been shut down by law enforcement officers, or ceased operating altogether. To the ordinary person, these listings are everything that the dark net has to offer. However, technical users and law enforcement agencies have special techniques that they use to analyze the content on dark nets. To analyze content on these dark nets, special tools and techniques are combined. The normal search engines using traditional crawling techniques cannot find the content on the dark web. They rely on web pages being hyperlinked with each other in order to be effectively crawled. This makes them unable to crawl the dark net which lacks hyperlinking and typically discourages indexing. This chapter will focus on the techniques that can be used to analyze the contents of the dark web.

It will cover this in the following topics:

- Surface web versus deep web
- Traditional web crawlers mechanism

- Surfacing deep web content
- Analysis of deep web sites.

Surface Web versus Deep Web

To understand how web content analysis is done, it is good to take the familiar example of how surface web indexing engines work. Their workings are normally through creating indexes of web pages that they have crawled. Web crawling is done through robots that have special automated scripts that browse the World Wide Web in a systematic way. Search engines continue to crawl the internet in order to grow or update their indices. This happens without much restrictions on the surface web. Since crawling takes some of the resources on the sites being crawled, there are some surface web sites that will discourage search engines from crawling them. They can do so by including some commands in the robot.txt file on the root folders of their websites. Due to the huge amounts of information being released to the internet today, it is increasingly challenging for search engines to crawl. Engines such as Google are yet to create a complete index of the surface web.

However, these search engines cannot crawl or analyze the deep web as they do the surface web. Crawling is most effective where web pages are hyperlinked. When the crawler gets to an external link to another page, it associates it with the page it is on. It will also jump to the linked websites creating a spider-like web of how the pages are linked. The crawler requires that the pages be static. This means that the content should not be dynamically generated. However, much of the internet is made up of hidden data that cannot be indexed by normal crawlers. Therefore, search engines do not have any data about them. The following are the characteristics that make much of the deep web data.

- Dynamic—this is content generated as a response to queries. It is dependent on the inputs a user provides to specify some of the attributes of the data that they wish to view. When an input is given, there is an HTML page that is generated dynamically which is then returned as output.
- Unlinked—the pages on the deep web are not hyperlinked to each other.
- Non-textual content—these are contents particularly hard to index as they include multimedia files and non-HTML contents.

It is estimated that the deep web is close to 500 times of the total size of the surface web. Over 200,000 websites are said to exist on dark nets on the deep web. Their contents cannot be accessed since the normal search engines are not capable of crawling them (Figure 7.1).

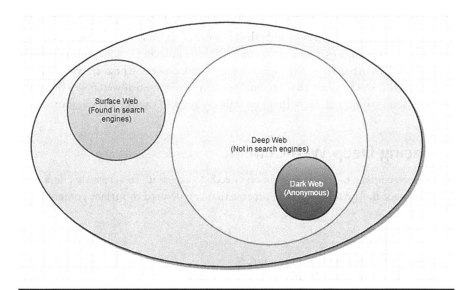

Figure 7.1   Illustration of the surface and deep web. (Source: https://cambiare-search.com/articles/85/surface-web-deep-web-dark-web----whats-the-difference.)

Traditional Web Crawlers Mechanism

Traditional crawlers are the ones that are used to index surface websites. These include Yahoo Search, Google, and Bing. Their working is as shown in the figure below.

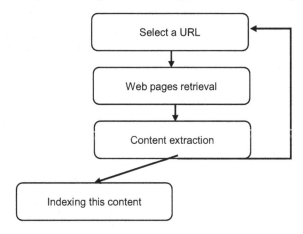

The crawler starts with a URL. This URL could have been found on another website that was being crawled. The crawler will retrieve all the web pages in that URL. The retrieved web pages will be used for the extraction of content and hyperlinks that they contain. The extracted data are sent to an indexer which indexes them based on certain categories. These may include the keywords they contain, the pages that they are linked to, the authors, and much more. After the indexing is done, the hyperlinks from the URLs are used as the inputs for a similar process. These crawlers are not equipped with mechanisms that can enable them to distinguish web pages that have forms or semi-structured data. They can only do loops to capture data in forms.

Surfacing Deep Web Content

To analyze content in the deep web, one needs to access it. To access this data, one has to surface it. The following is a process that can be used to surface content from the dark net:

1. Finding the sources
2. Selecting the data from the sources
3. Sending the selected data to an analysis system.

The data in the dark net includes content from databases, servers on the internet, and dynamic websites. In the process of analyzing information from the dark net, data sources may be integrated or bundled together. However, this integration might not be effective in some cases due to four reasons. The first one is that there may be the addition of redundant data. The second reason why the integration might be bad is that irrelevant data may be added to the data repository by the integration system. This, in turn, will reduce the quality of the results returned by the data integration system. The third reason is that adding more data to the integration system may lead to the inclusion of low-quality data. Lastly, there is a high cost of including data to the integration system. These costs are associated with sourcing the data and processing it so that it can be included in the repository and the integration system.

Schema Matching for Sources

With the completion of the previous step, the data is surfaced and the analysis process begins. Schema matching is whereby the extracted data is matched for relevance to a search keyword or phrase. A schema is developed with the required data, and the dark net sites that return data relevant to the schema are the ones retrieved. This eases the burden and reduces the cost of extracting web pages from the dark net just to process them. The schemas ensure that processing efforts are concentrated on data sources that have relevant data.

Data Extraction

Once the schema match is done and the relevant data source has been identified, it is time for the data to be retrieved. Different techniques are used to retrieve data from the deep web. For the convenience of costs and time, entire websites are not extracted. Only sections that contain data that is of interest are extracted.

Data Selection

Even in the normal surface web searches, there are hundreds or thousands of results of pages that can be retrieved from the internet. All these have relevant data based on the keywords used in the search operation. However, not all of these search results are of high relevance. Some may also be of low quality. The same is observed in the deep web. When a search is done based on some keywords, there may be hundreds or thousands of deep web sources that have been found to have related data. However, they also differ in quality. Therefore, they need to be ranked. On the surface web, the ranking is done on a rather competitive basis and that is why many websites invest in search engine optimization. However, the deep web does not have SEO (search engine optimization) since website owners do not expect that their websites will be found using search engines. Therefore, it is the burden of the search engine or search technique to find out how to index the extracted data. The following is a set of steps used to do a basic ranking:

- Defining quality dimensions—the quality parameters for relevance of a search action are defined. They may be keywords, phrases, headings, or size of content, among other things. This helps filter out low-quality results from search operations.
- Defining the quality assessment model—other criteria for defining quality sources are designed here.
- Ranking the sources on quality basis depending on a certain threshold—based on the quality dimensions and assessment model, the retrieved sources are ranked.

Analysis of Deep Web Sites

Analysis of the deep web is complex and tiresome. It involves the following separate processes.

Qualification of a Deep Web Site Search Analysis

The surface web has a familiar problem of content replication and duplicate sites. These can severely affect the quality of search results since the same content can be listed over and over in repeating search results. The approach by surface web search engines is to punish websites that have identical content. Therefore, if a search engine has a near match of all the content that is in a certain website, the new content is ranked lower. The deep web has a similar problem when it comes to content analysis after searching the servers of this part of the web. There may be tens of thousands of results but a fraction of those may be duplicate listings. Therefore, an inspection needs to be done so that the duplicates are removed from the search results. The unique sources are then to be passed for the next stage of analysis. The next stage is a check to determine whether the listings are actually sites.

Unlike most results on the surface web, some part of the results from the deep web are filled with non-HTML content. The deep web is a stash of lots of content kept out of the public. Most of them are not websites, and some of these contents have to be filtered out. Ultimately, one ends up with actual websites that are hits of search queries. This analysis is not simple and not very accurate; thus, the algorithms used keep on being updated on what qualifies a search result as relevant.

Analysis of the Number of Deep Web Websites

It is important for some people and institutions such as law agencies to keep abreast with the sites that are on the deep web. If new drug marketplaces or child porn websites are opened, it ultimately falls down to the law enforcement agencies to find out these sites deep in the darkness of the dark net. Monitoring the number of dark net websites, therefore, helps to note when there are new sites that have to be inspected. When an overall number of deep web sites is mentioned, it is not from a wild guess. It is due to a special type of analysis that can be used to determine the number of websites that are in this part of the internet. One of the techniques used to estimate the number of active websites on the deep web is called overlap analysis. Overlap analysis is based on search engines that already exist on the deep web or custom-built search engines for crawling the deep web.

The technique does analysis based on the coverage of the search engines. Pairwise comparisons are done based on the number of search results retrieved from two sources and the number of shared results that overlap (Figure 7.2).

In the figure above, n_a and n_b are the listings from two sources. N is the estimated total size of the population, that is, the number of websites. N_0 is the degree

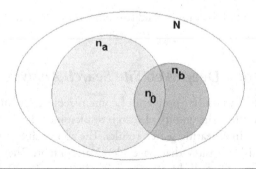

Figure 7.2 A diagrammatic representation of overlap analysis.

of overlap between the listings of the search results. An estimation of the total population of the deep web can, therefore, be arrived at by dividing $n_a/(n_0/n_b)$. This might be seen as vague; thus, we might have to consider a simpler explanation. For instance, assume that the total population is known to be 100, and let us see whether overlap analysis will give us the same figure. If the search listings from two sources show that they both contain 50 items in the total population and that an average of 25 items is shared by these sources, hence are unique, it follows that 25 items should not be listed by either. Therefore, they should have 25 unique items. To get to the total population we have to perform the following: 50/(25/50). The end result here is 100 which is the total population we had earlier said. The division from the overlap analysis has arrived at the same figure. However, it is more complex in the actual deep web to do this due to the procedures involved in determining the listings from two sources and the number of listings that are shared or unshared by them.

There are two considerations that are made during this type of analysis. The first one is that there should be accuracy in the determination of the number of listings from a source. The success of the whole analysis is pegged on this. If the number of listings is not arrived at correctly, the accuracy of the whole analysis procedure dips. The second consideration is how the listings are to be arrived at. They should be arrived at independently. In our example, our analysis violates the second rule; thus, the end result is on the lower side. This is because the listings used are search engine listings, and this should not be taken to mean independence. Searchable databases are in most cases linked to each other; thus, the independence of dark web search engines is questionable. However, when the two considerations are taken care of in a real scenario and with multiple pairwise comparisons, a more accurate number can be arrived at to show the number of sites on the deep web.

Deep Web Size Analysis

It might sound strange why there are estimates on the size of the deep web belittling the size of the surface web. It is said that 95% of the whole internet is the deep web while just a mere 5% is the surface web. The actual size of the deep web must, therefore, be very big. This is because surface web search engines such as Google already index billions of documents on the internet (web pages are documents too), and this is said to only be 5% of the internet. A common figure thrown around as the said size of the deep web is 3.4 TB. However, it is interesting to know how this estimation was arrived at owing to the fact that it is already a challenge to find the number of documents on the deep web. There is a type of analysis that is done to arrive at such figures which are mostly estimations.

To arrive at the estimated total size of this part of the internet, averages are used. The average sizes of the documents and data storage are used. A multiplier is then applied to come up with the estimated size of the deep web. Since the figures are enormous and the process of obtaining the average sizes is not simple, a lengthy process is used during the evaluation of the sizes of sample sites. In our previous example, there were 100 sites in the total population. To find out the total size of the population, we can first arrive at the average size of a sample of these sites and then apply a multiplier to arrive at a figure that we can say to be the total size of all our 100 sites.

In a real-world scenario, if there are 17,000 sites identified to be the population of the dark net, we can come up with the size of the whole dark net using this process. To begin with, we have to identify sample sites. With a 10% confidence interval and 95% confidence level, we can randomly select 100 websites. For the 100 samples, we can analyze the record count or document count of all these sites. For these sites, the total number of documents and their sizes could be used to get the average size of each page. When the average size of a page in one site is determined, the average could be used to determine the full size of the dark net site. When the full size of each dark net site is determined, an average can be calculated to show the average size of a dark net site. Using this figure, the full size of the dark net can be reached. All it takes is multiplying the average size of a site on the dark net with the total number of dark net sites.

Dark net size = Average site size*no. of dark net sites

Content Type Analysis

The media has been blamed for presenting a jaundiced view of the deep web. They often cover it as a dangerous part of the internet where all manner of crimes take place. From their perspective, it is the part of the internet where no one should try visiting or else they are hacked or their IP addresses are tracked and kidnappers send to them. Their uninformed view of this type of the web comes from the fact that they only cover it when law enforcement agencies have taken down drug black markets, arrested founders of illegal activity-related dark net sites, or taken down weapon-selling sites. Rarely will they cover this part of the internet in any other light. The fact is that the dark net is a vast space and has different types of contents. It would be unfair to demonize it based on media opinion. The dark net is a facilitator of many things, some of which the media is either unaware of or chooses to ignore when reporting about this hidden part of the internet.

However, it is a task to find out the types of content that exist on the dark net. This is because the content is purposefully meant to be hidden. To determine the type of content in the dark net, it is necessary for some analysis to be done. Since the dark net is big and there is not an exact number that can give the actual size, some cost-effective mechanisms have to be used to find the types of data and services available. The least costly way of analyzing the types of content on the deep web is through sampling. If there are presumed 17,000 dark net websites, an evaluation can be done on a sample of 700 sites. Through the samples, the type of data on each site can be analyzed and thus be used to categorize the dark net.

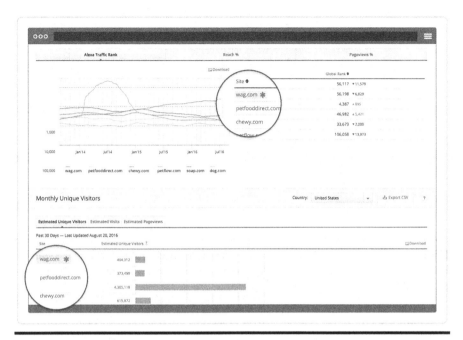

Figure 7.3   Alexa's interface.

Site Popularity Analysis

It is possible to analyze the popularity of dark net websites based on the number of visitors, page views, and references that the site has. Alexa is a web-based system that keeps records of page visits, and up to date, it keeps analyzing sites on the dark net. Up to 71% of deep web sites are analyzed by Alexa, and it keeps updating their popularity. This is made possible by a universal power function that it runs on the internet that can record page views (Figure 7.3).

Log Analysis

However, analysis of the deep web is not only during the data retrieval process. The analysis is also done for malicious purposes such as to compromise the communication channels. Unlike the surface web, the connection between Tor clients and dark net servers is not convincingly safe. Traffic originating or destined to the dark web can be analyzed. There have been conceptual developments on how logs can be exploited to help analyze the deep web.

Theoretically, it is possible to analyze the dark web using the NetFlow protocol. An attacker can analyze NetFlow records stored on routers that act as direct Tor nodes or are close to such nodes. These logs which may be retrieved from inside the Tor network and contain lots of information can be used to analyze the dark net. NetFlow records store the following data (Figure 7.4):

- Protocol version number;
- Record number;
- Inbound and outgoing network interface;
- Time of stream head and stream end;
- Number of bytes and packets in the stream;
- Address of source and destination;
- Port of source and destination;
- IP protocol number;
- The value of Type of Service;
- All flags observed during TCP connections;
- Gateway address;
- Masks of the source and destination subnets.

Figure 7.4 Types of data that can be retrieved from NetFlow. (Source: https://securelist.com/uncovering-tor-users-where-anonymity-ends-in-the-darknet/70673/.)

Netflow analysis has been said to be capable of analyzing traffic to and from Tor that can lead to the deanonymization of 81% of the dark net's users. Netflow technology is commonly used by Cisco, which is the leading company in networking products and services. Netflow is used in Cisco routers, and it is used to collect the IP addresses of network traffic entering and exiting a router. Netflow is used primarily for admins to monitor congestion in routers. Apart from Cisco, Netflow is a standard that is run by many other manufacturers of networking devices. Therefore, the chances of coming across this technology in a dark net traffic flow are high.

In a research by Chakravarty, Netflow was used for active traffic analysis on the dark net in laboratory and real-world environments. The research, first of its kind, used an analysis method to find information about users accessing certain content on the dark net. The research created a perturbation on the server side of Tor and then observed where a similar perturbation would be observed at the client side. The observation was done through statistical correlation. The research came to a 100% success rate in laboratory environment, and when they applied the same analysis technique in the real world, the success rate was at 81%. The research was a demonstration that the dark net is not fully secure since it can be analyzed to deanonymize the users and content that they are accessing. The research showed that a persistent attacker on the Tor network could perform unlimited runs of traffic analysis through the creation of perturbation and observation of traffic at entry and exit routers, respectively. Figure 7.5 shows this traffic analysis technique.

The research was done with a setup of a server and website on the deep web. Visitors to the website downloaded a large file from the server. The server had an injected code that would allow the researcher to access the NetFlow of routers that it passed through. When the fetching of the NetFlow logs was happening, the

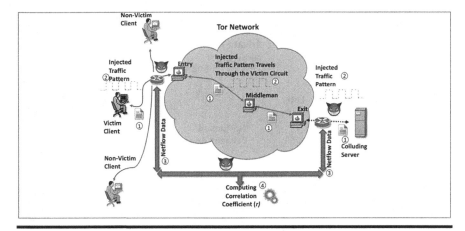

Figure 7.5 NetFlow-based traffic analysis against Tor: The client is forced to download a file from the server ①, while the server induces a characteristic traffic pattern ②. After the connection is terminated, the adversary obtains flow data corresponding to the server-to-client traffic ③ and computes their coefficient ④.

server on the dark net was sending data through Tor's anonymous network. This is where correlation analysis would come in. The end user would continue receiving data through the Tor network from the server for several minutes, and within this time, the NetFlow records of the router where the data was passing would be analyzed. The researcher would then be able to correlate the traffic flowing to an anonymous client with the logs of a certain router read from the Netflow. Not only would this reveal the client's exit node, it would also reveal the type of content that they were accessing. The following is another representation of how this dark net analysis is done.

This analysis method threatens the anonymity of the dark web in future. If 81% of the users could be identified, Tor is, therefore, going to be insecure. A legal agency such as the FBI could set up servers on the dark net with catchy websites that have rigged content. If a user visits the site and downloads the Netflow malware file, their identity could be discovered within minutes (Figures 7.6 and 7.7).

Summary of the Chapter

This chapter has looked at how the deep web can be analyzed. It has given the difference between the surface and deep web that makes the deep web so difficult to index and analyze. The chapter has gone through the workings of a traditional web crawler, that is, the normal web crawler used by surface web search engines. It has shown that the simplistic nature of the surface web websites and their hyperlinked structure makes them easy to be crawled. When the crawler starts crawling a website, it will identify the linked pages and jump to them after it is done crawling the

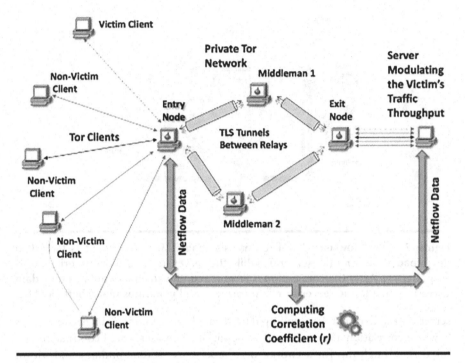

Figure 7.6 Diagrammatic representation of log analysis.

"In our attack model, we assume that the victim is lured to access a particular server through Tor, while the adversary collects NetFlow data corresponding to the traffic between the exit node and the server, as well as between Tor clients and victim's entry node. The adversary has control of the particular server (and potentially many others, which victims may visit), and thus knows which exit node the victim traffic originates from."

Figure 7.7 Part of the paper by Chakravarty. (https://motherboard.vice.com/ en_us/article/4x3qnj/how-the-nsa-or-anyone-else-can-crack-tors-anonymity.)

contents of the page that it is on. However, the deep web does not have this type of hyperlinking. It is therefore almost impossible for normal search engines to analyze and index the dark net sites. Analysis is therefore done systematically. The first step is to surface the deep web content. To surface it, a search has to be done, relevant data extracted, and then the essential data selected for analysis. The chapter has looked into the different types of analysis that can be done on deep web sites. These include content type analysis, site popularity analysis, size analysis, analysis of the number of websites, and finally log analysis. Log analysis has been covered differently since it is not a typical analysis technique. It is a technique used purposefully to compromise dark net websites. The analysis is done using log files retrieved from the NetFlow of compromised routers. The analysis finds out the users of the anonymous network and the types of content that they are accessing. The discussed types of analysis are the most common ones on the dark net.

Questions

1. What are the characteristics of the surface web that make it easy to index?
2. Explain the mechanism used by traditional web crawlers to crawl the internet.
3. Explain the three steps used to surface content from the deep web.
4. Log analysis is a technique used to compromise dark nets, which networking equipment does it target to infiltrate the communication channel?
5. What is NetFlow?
6. Give two rivals of Cisco that also produce switches and routers.
7. How can an attacker find out the exit node being used by a Tor user during log analysis?
8. What is the current real-life success rate of log analysis?

Further Reading

The following are resources that can be used to gain more knowledge on this chapter:

https://brightplanet.com/wp-content/uploads/ 2012/03/12550176481-deepwebwhitepaper1. pdf.

https://cambiaresearch.com/articles/85/surface-web-deep-web-dark-web----whats-the- difference.

Chapter 8

Extracting Information from Dark Web Contents/Logs

Introduction

The dark web is filled with unstructured and semi-structured data which is complex to analyze. Traditional systems used for analysis cannot handle unstructured data, and it has previously been impossible to automatically extract information from this type of data. However, evolution in technology has brought up tools that are able to perform analysis to extract useful information from unstructured data. This chapter will go through these technologies and their guidelines in the following topics:

- Analyzing the web contents/logs
- Policy guidelines for log analysis
- Log analysis tools
- Analyzing files
- Extracting information from unstructured data.

Analyzing the Web Contents/Logs

The deep web has been of key interest to many following the overexcitement peddled that it is the place where just about anything wrong takes place. The general public is now more interested than ever to learn more about the contents of the deep web, especially after the media coverage on dark net sites that were taken down by security agencies for selling illegal products. Security agencies have dedicated resources to prevent the coming up of notorious illegal sites on the dark web to fill the voids left by sites that have been taken down. Researchers are also increasingly attempting to demystify the dark web; hence, they have been playing part in analyzing the web content it contains. Content analysis is a commonly used methodology in both the surface and deep web that can be focused at analyzing the structure and meaning of data. This data can be text, images, sounds, and video clips. The information obtained from this analysis is not only usable by researchers but also by legal agencies. It also helps to identify the political, academic, legal, security, social, and economic significance of this part of the web (Figure 8.1).

Content on the deep web varies, and there is more diversity than on the surface web. Content analysis of data extracted from the deep web helps categorize all the data into specific categories for further analysis or use. Content analysis can identify repeating patterns, usability, and credibility of the data among other characteristics.

Content analysis can be done through different methods, which are either manual or involve the use of specific tools. Deeper in this chapter, we will take a look at the tools that are used for content and log analysis of the deep web. We are now going to look at the types of analysis that can be done on extracted deep web data.

Web Content Analysis

When data is extracted from the dark web, there is an overload of information and thus not easy to find what is relevant or what is not. The dark web suffers from the

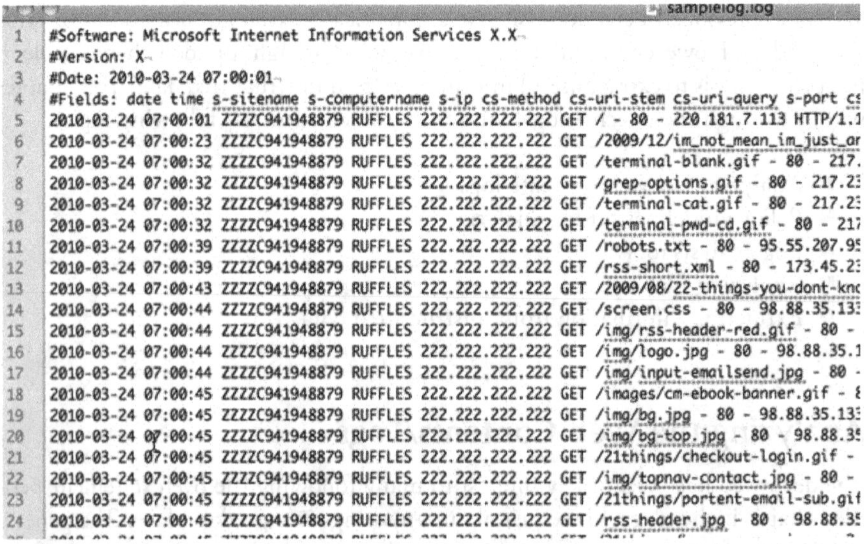

```
                                                              sampielog.iog
1   #Software: Microsoft Internet Information Services X.X
2   #Version: X
3   #Date: 2010-03-24 07:00:01
4   #Fields: date time s-sitename s-computername s-ip cs-method cs-uri-stem cs-uri-query s-port cs
5   2010-03-24 07:00:01 ZZZZC941948879 RUFFLES 222.222.222.222 GET / - 80 - 220.181.7.113 HTTP/1.1
6   2010-03-24 07:00:23 ZZZZC941948879 RUFFLES 222.222.222.222 GET /2009/12/im_not_mean_im_just_ar
7   2010-03-24 07:00:32 ZZZZC941948879 RUFFLES 222.222.222.222 GET /terminal-blank.gif - 80 - 217.
8   2010-03-24 07:00:32 ZZZZC941948879 RUFFLES 222.222.222.222 GET /grep-options.gif - 80 - 217.23
9   2010-03-24 07:00:32 ZZZZC941948879 RUFFLES 222.222.222.222 GET /terminal-cat.gif - 80 - 217.23
10  2010-03-24 07:00:32 ZZZZC941948879 RUFFLES 222.222.222.222 GET /terminal-pwd-cd.gif - 80 - 217
11  2010-03-24 07:00:39 ZZZZC941948879 RUFFLES 222.222.222.222 GET /robots.txt - 80 - 95.55.207.95
12  2010-03-24 07:00:39 ZZZZC941948879 RUFFLES 222.222.222.222 GET /rss-short.xml - 80 - 173.45.23
13  2010-03-24 07:00:43 ZZZZC941948879 RUFFLES 222.222.222.222 GET /2009/08/22-things-you-dont-knc
14  2010-03-24 07:00:44 ZZZZC941948879 RUFFLES 222.222.222.222 GET /screen.css - 80 - 98.88.35.133
15  2010-03-24 07:00:44 ZZZZC941948879 RUFFLES 222.222.222.222 GET /img/rss-header-red.gif - 80 -
16  2010-03-24 07:00:44 ZZZZC941948879 RUFFLES 222.222.222.222 GET /img/logo.jpg - 80 - 98.88.35.1
17  2010-03-24 07:00:44 ZZZZC941948879 RUFFLES 222.222.222.222 GET /img/input-emailsend.gif - 80 -
18  2010-03-24 07:00:45 ZZZZC941948879 RUFFLES 222.222.222.222 GET /images/cm-ebook-banner.gif - 8
19  2010-03-24 07:00:45 ZZZZC941948879 RUFFLES 222.222.222.222 GET /img/bg.jpg - 80 - 98.88.35.133
20  2010-03-24 07:00:45 ZZZZC941948879 RUFFLES 222.222.222.222 GET /img/bg-top.jpg - 80 - 98.88.35
21  2010-03-24 07:00:45 ZZZZC941948879 RUFFLES 222.222.222.222 GET /21things/checkout-login.gif -
22  2010-03-24 07:00:45 ZZZZC941948879 RUFFLES 222.222.222.222 GET /img/topnav-contact.jpg - 80 -
23  2010-03-24 07:00:45 ZZZZC941948879 RUFFLES 222.222.222.222 GET /21things/portent-email-sub.gif
24  2010-03-24 07:00:45 ZZZZC941948879 RUFFLES 222.222.222.222 GET /rss-header.jpg - 80 - 98.88.35
```

Figure 8.1 An example of a website log file.

deficiency of search engines, which are particularly helpful in analyzing different types of web contents. Even with the existing techniques for crawling content, it is impossible to get an extensive analysis of the dark web solely through search engines. The mix of the types of data that is stored on the internet, specifically the dark web, prompts for the use of more advanced tools for analyzing the content.

Intelligent tools will analyze specific information of content on the dark web such as the domains, user statistics, and then further interpret this data for research or legal purposes. For instance, useful information can be collected from collected dark web data if user statistics are located. Users tend to flock around sites that have appealing content, and this is an indicative sign that there is something of interest in the sites that they visit on the dark web. Further analysis of the sites whose logs have most visitors could lead to the classification of the types of websites that most users visit while on the dark web. This shows that analysis is not merely crawling the deep web but extracting information from extracted data such as documents, web pages, and user stats. Analysis can help in the organization of unstructured data into structured data. Data dumps can be extracted from the deep web and while they may not immediately hold much value, analysis helps to make them more structured and useful.

Another aspect of web content analysis on the deep web is usage. As highlighted before, users will visit certain sites that are of interest more. If a new site opens up and starts selling illegal drugs, legal agencies can come to know of it by looking at usage stats from tools that record site visits. Even though analysis may not directly point out the individual locations of the users visiting a dark net site, it is useful for further action. For instance, if legal agencies discover that there is heavy traffic to a malware-selling site, they can initiate the process of compromising it so as to arrest the site admins and some users. Usage analysis is also helpful for people that wish to put up sites on the dark web. There are very many services offered on the dark web, and since more people wish to add on to these services, they may want to visit sites that have most visitors. They can capture design elements of these websites so as to attract their own customers. For instance, one of the successful drug stores on the dark web had a fully customized interface of an e-commerce store such as Amazon. Due to the sudden adoption of the site by users, other sites came up featuring similar aesthetics. Even though these sites no longer exist due to legal agencies taking them down, this is a good example of how usage analysis is put into practical use on the dark web.

Other than content and usage analysis, web structure may also be analyzed in deep web analysis. Web structure analysis is focused on the link structure on a site that enables retrieval of more information or jumping from one web document to the other. It can discover similarities in data through link analysis.

Benefits of Content Analysis

Content analysis is commonly done for the purposes of aiding in making certain decisions. The analysis is done by interest groups such as law enforcement agencies and researchers. When analysis is complete, useful patterns may be discovered and interpreted. These can be used for decision-making such as to tell legal agencies the dark net domain names that they should concentrate investigations on. Analysis can help identify fraudulent contents, terrorism propaganda, illegal online shops, virus peddlers, child pornography sites, and internet fraud sites. Further action on such data could be used to reveal the identities of the sellers' and buyers' illegal substances and items on these sites, those that engage in cyber terrorism, the sellers of malware, and many other interest groups. Web content analysis is best suited for identifying the illegal content while web structure analysis is good for discovering the communication networks used by interest groups on the dark web. If these communication networks are discovered, legal agencies can listen in or try to intercept communication that could lead to the arrest of individual actors in either terrorism, drug sale, or those that engage in other illegal activities.

Researchers can also find out unexplored parts of the dark web that may be of significant interest from web content analysis. Content analysis may also help find out stolen data that is dumped on the dark web. There are hackers that put stolen data for sale or release it on the dark web for purchase or use by other users. Content analysis of the deep web can help identify stolen data and thus help with investigations. There are companies already offering this service whereby they scan the deep web for stolen data of companies that have contracted them. Early finding of this data may help solve much larger problems such as sensitive data being sold to extremely malicious people. One example of a company that has gone into the business of offering this service is News Monitors, Sweden. The company uses Artificial Intelligence (AI)technology to monitor and analyze contents on the dark web searching for signs of data that has been stolen and offered for sale on this part of the internet. When it comes to a match, the company alerts its clients that they might have been victims of a data breach and should commence investigations. The use of AI makes monitoring and analysis easier than using conventional analysis technologies (Figures 8.2 and 8.3).

Therefore, deep web content and log analysis is very useful at helping curtail the misuse of the dark web for illegal purposes and also helping in the discovery of other services on the deep web. Search engines can only crawl a small portion of the deep web, but in-depth analysis is good at uncovering what lies deeper in this part of the internet.

Policy Guidelines for Log Analysis

Log analysis involves critical evaluation of content collected, processed, and stored within information systems. In this case, the information is collected from the dark web for a myriad of reasons. Some of them include educational purposes, security reasons as well as informational reasons. Web content and log analysis is essential because the information collected for the abovementioned reasons has to

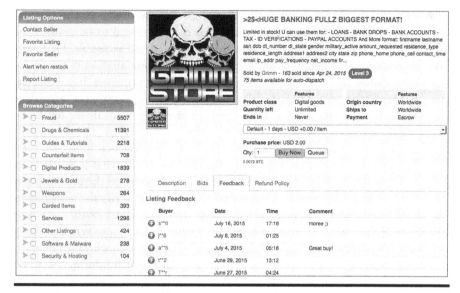

Figure 8.2 Stolen bank database for sale on a dark net site.

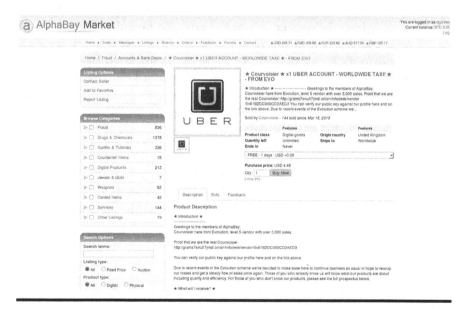

Figure 8.3 Alleged stolen Uber records for sale on the dark web.

be fit for use. The fairness is determined from the availability, accuracy, integrity, authenticity, reliability, and usability of this information. Each of this property is described briefly below.

■ Availability and reliability: these two properties are similar in this context and are therefore grouped together. Web content is said to be available of reliable when it refers to a resource that is updated and accessible. Dark web content is highly dynamic, and most logging solutions fall short of this property because they are rarely designed to update their databases. It is, however, hard to keep updated copies of dynamic content using automated tools. Most of this logged content has to be maintained manually to ensure the reliability of this information to which these logs refer.

■ Authenticity: this property refers to logs of web content that have been verified and ascertained to be or represent content that is what it purports to be. This feature is least prevalent within the dark web and therefore is often hard to design designs systems or tools that can easily verify the authenticity of the web content mined from the deep web. The nature of the deep web is such that the authenticity of the web content is lost. However, some content is specifically created and shared within the dark web with the intention of informing the users and the public. In order for such information to be usable, the source needs to be verified for authenticity to whichever extent that the system allows.

■ Accuracy and integrity: this property refers to the extent to which the correctness and completeness of a web record, log, or content is presented. Weblogs especially from the content collected or extracted from the dark web would be expected to be full of integrity issues and unfilled gaps in information due to the dynamic nature of the space. However, a capable weblogging strategy should be able to keep logs of accessed and collected information with the highest accuracy level possible.

■ Usability: usable logs and web content refer to information that is collected, analyzed, and interpreted for a specified function. Mining and analyzing web content from the dark web would majorly serve the purpose of informing and aiding in the creation of sound security strategies for system protection. Careful observation and analysis of website content logs should be able to enable the decision makers to better protect systems and make investment decisions that will ensure that the body corporate achieve or maintain competitive advantage in the industry.

Risk Assessment

Risk analysis and mitigation are essential especially when accessing, mining, and logging website content from the dark web. Risk in the dark web context refers to the use of potentially outdated, incomplete, inaccurate, and incorrect information. It also involves the study of new landscapes when the management is seeking to venture into a new product or service line. Through risk analysis, the management is better prepared for any uncertain eventualities. Most of the information that could be collected from the dark web is valuable, and therefore, before the organization undertakes any measures to secure such information, they would have to undertake a risk analysis and mitigation process to ensure that they protect the systems that will be used to mine, process, and store the information.

The following are some of the risks that are inherent when collecting and analyzing information from the dark web:

- Legality of collection and use of the data.
- Collection of false or untrustworthy information.
- Collection of corrupt and potentially malware attached content that could destroy the systems processing the data.
- Financial losses from attacks due to malware injection into the system.
- Fallout and loss of support from the critical shareholders.
- Negative media attention.

Duties and Responsibilities on Risk Assessment and Mitigation

The following are some of the strategies that should be used when carrying out analysis of deep web content:

- Accurate description of the web content information collected and stored in the organizational network—the users of this information should be correctly identified and properly trained to handle web content scrapped from the dark web.
- Site maintenance—this entails who is responsible for site updates, content deletion as well as ensuring the accuracy of the content collected. More often than not, this is the information systems staff under guidance of the chief information officer. This is the individual responsible for the systems that control all the informational needs of the organization. The security of the information collected from the dark web is solely her responsibility.
- Legal requirements of the organizations are the responsibility of the legal department. In this case, the legal department should have a team of professionals that is especially trained to handle information systems legal matters.

Risk Mitigation

This procedure involves the taking of the necessary steps to ensure that identified risks are addressed and the eventual happening of these events is avoided. The risk mitigation techniques outlined below address some of the important risks that have been identified in the previous section.

- Proper documentation of the logs and website content scrapped and held for storage on the organizational systems. Most information on the dark web is dynamic and on display temporarily available. Therefore, to ensure that the company does not hold information that is illegal and suspect, the individuals responsible for the data collection should be required to take snapshots of the websites that they scrap the information from as legal proof of the information they hold. The time stamp should be especially important and this information stored with the collected data for easier retrieval.
- Having in place legally sound procedures for the scrapping, collection, processing, and storage of this information accessed from the dark web. Consequently, the systems used to access these dark websites should be properly secured and their securities should be updated regularly to patch up any loopholes and avoid the collection of malware and other malicious tools when scouring the space.
- A regularly updated database is highly encouraged due to the high dynamism of the industry. A retention schedule would be appropriate which dictates how often the database should be updated and new content collected. This should be fairly regular to ensure that the system has very accurate and updated information.
- Staff training to ensure that the individuals responsible for the collection of information from the dark web are properly equipped to handle the procedures necessary when collecting and storing the information.

Responsibility for Maintenance of Web Content Logs

Access and usage of content from the dark web have several risks that will have to be handled with care and diligence. If the information needed to be accessed is expected to be positive information that will be beneficial to the organization, then a special team of authorized individuals is supposed to be selected to carry out this process. The individuals will undergo special training that is customized to the needs of the organization. To reduce risk of exposure when using the dark web, these individuals will be required to use the tools that they will be provided by the chief information officer. The tools will be preapproved and vetted to be ideal and able to carry out the tasks of accessing the information needed and transmitting it to the storage systems safely. This team will be responsible for educating the rest of the staff outside the direct responsibility of collecting this information from the dark web.

The chosen team will be responsible for updating the databases and ensuring the accuracy and integrity of the information. More appropriately, this team needs to comprise of the individuals in the information technology department and more specifically, the security officials. By reducing the number of people allowed to access the dark web on behalf of the organization, the strategist has reduced the attack vectors and consequently the risk factors.

Log Analysis Tools

Weblog analysis is the process of gaining insight from weblogs such as clickstream data, IP addresses of users, resources that reside in the deep web, and user profiles that can be used to understand user behavior and discover hidden patterns. It is challenging to access various types of logs that can support reliable analysis in the deep web. This is because the level of anonymity offered to users in the deep web makes it challenging to access the logs and analyze them. However, one can examine the content and popularity of a given deep web resource to gain some insight such as its user base. In addition, one can collect a reasonable sample of deep web resources and analyze them, for example, based on language, to get a glimpse of where users of a given deep web resource could be located. One can also use the data available in websites that specialize in tracking activities in the deep web such as https://dnstats.net/. This information can then be analyzed to determine popular resources or activities in the deep web. It is also possible to collect the domains of various resources in the deep web and examine their associated protocols to know the kind of resources they host.

The deep web is made up of huge volumes of heterogeneous data that cannot be processed and analyzed using the traditional database and data analysis systems. This is mainly because the data found in deep web is of huge quantities and heterogeneous. As a result, new data analysis tools are required to handle the data. The new data-processing tools should be able to support concurrent access, allow loading and querying large heterogeneous data sets, dynamic aligning of data schema for specific data sets, and continuous integration of new data into existing data sets. In addition, the tools should allow users to drill down into the source details so as to get insight that can be used in decision-making.

There are several tools in the market that can be used to analyze huge volumes of heterogeneous and unstructured or semi-structured weblogs. Some of the tools include Apache Pig and Hive, Apache Hadoop framework, MapReduce, Apache Flume, and Apache Flink. To begin with, Hadoop is a software framework that can be installed on a certain hardware to perform large-scale distributed data analysis (Figure 8.4).

Apache Hadoop is an open source software framework for storage and large scale processing of data-sets on clusters of commodity hardware. Hadoop is an Apache top-level project being built and used by a global community of contributors and users. It is licensed under the Apache License 2.0

Figure 8.4 Information about Apache Hadoop. (*Source:* https://opensource. com/life/14/8/intro-apache-hadoop-big-data.)

The framework is made up of Hadoop MapReduce tools such as Pig, Flume, Hive, and Hadoop Distributed File System (HDFS). The HDFS component offers the underlying support for distributed storage. It supports two types of nodes. These are the Name Node that is used to provide data services and the Data Node that provides the actual storage services for files. HDFS is thus used in the Hadoop framework to support parallel processing across nodes using the MapReduce paradigm. HDFS works by taking a given file of data and breaking it into smaller pieces. The small pieces of data are then distributed to different nodes within a cluster. In addition, HDFS file system copies the data to individual nodes and ensures that at least one copy of the data is placed on a different server for redundancy in case of failure. Therefore, in case of failure in one server, the data that it holds can still be found elsewhere and processed.

Hive is a data warehouse framework that is built on top of Hadoop to support ad hoc querying using a query language known as Hive QL that resembles SQL query although it supports more complex analysis. Pig, on the other hand, is a framework that is made up of high-level scripting and a run-time environment that enable users to run MapReduce programs within Hadoop.

MapReduce is a large-scale data-processing platform that can be used in distributed environments. Implementations of MapReduce support common data analysis and calculations on computing clusters. MapReduce data analysis model is commonly used in conjunction with Hadoop. The model utilizes mappers and reducers to analyze unstructured data. Mappers are responsible for collecting and analyzing data. The Mappers then produce intermediate data that passed to reducers where the data is aggregated before the results are produced in a format that can be understood.

MapReduce can be described as a processing technique and program model that supports distributed computing using the Java programming language. The algorithm used in MapReduce has two main tasks. The first task is the map which takes a set of data files and converts each data file into another set of data whose individual elements are divided into tuples made up of key/value pairings. The second task, which is referred to as the reduce job, entails taking the output from the map as input and combining the data tuples into a smaller set of tuples (Figure 8.5).

The main advantage of using the MapReduce to process large volumes of heterogeneous data is that it is easy to scale data processing using multiple computing nodes. This can enhance the efficiency of data processing and analysis.

There are also several technologies that are built on top of Hadoop that can be used to support processing and analysis of huge volumes of unstructured or structured data in the deep web. These technologies include Apache Pig, Apache Hive, Apache Flink, Jaql, Zookeeper, and Apache Flume. Apache Pig is a big data-processing tool that supports distributed data analysis. This tool uses a programming language known as Pig Latin that makes it easier to implement parallel programming, optimization, and extensibility. Pig Latin is also operating system

The term MapReduce actually refers to two separate and distinct tasks that Hadoop programs perform. The first is the map job, which takes a set of data and converts it into another set of data, where individual elements are broken down into tuples (key/value pairs).

The reduce job takes the output from a map as input and combines those data tuples into a smaller set of tuples. As the sequence of the name MapReduce implies, the reduce job is always performed after the map job.

Figure 8.5 Explanation of MapReduce. (https://ibm.com/analytics/hadoop/mapreduce.)

independent. Apache Pig, therefore, provides the Hadoop ecosystem with a high-level language that makes it easier to use the MapReduce library. Apache Hive, on the other hand, provides data warehousing services in Hadoop ecosystem. It thus allows huge volumes of heterogeneous data to be stored, queried, and managed. This is achieved using a querying language that is similar to SQL known as HiveQL. Apache Hive is therefore used in the Hadoop ecosystem to turn Hadoop into a data warehouse that can process SQL-like queries.

Apache Flink is a streaming data flow engine. The tool can be used to perform distributed operations on a stream of data. Flink is made up of several Application Programming Interfaces (APIs) that enable it to communicate with various data sources. In addition, Flick has its own machine learning and graph libraries that enable it to work with stream flows. Apache Flume is a distributed and reliable system for collecting large amounts of log data from applications before delivering the data into a centralized data space within the Hadoop ecosystem. Flume is thus used as a tool for harvesting, aggregating, and moving large amounts of log data in and out of Hadoop (Figures 8.6 and 8.7).

Jaql is the component of the Hadoop framework that provides a functional, declarative language. The language is in Hadoop framework to facilitate processing of large data sets faster. Moreover, the language is used in the framework to convert high-level queries into low-level queries that comprise of MapReduce tasks so as to enable parallel processing of huge volumes of heterogeneous data. The final component of the Hadoop framework that will be examined in this section

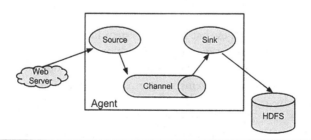

Figure 8.6 A depiction of Apache Flume.

> Flume is a distributed, reliable, and available service for efficiently collecting, aggregating, and moving large amounts of log data. It has a simple and flexible architecture based on streaming data flows. It is robust and fault tolerant with tunable reliability mechanisms and many failover and recovery mechanisms. It uses a simple extensible data model that allows for online analytic application.

Figure 8.7   Explanation of Apache Flume. (*Source:* https://flume.apache.org/.)

is the Zookeeper. This component is used in the framework to offer a centralized infrastructure that comprises of many services that enable synchronization across a cluster of servers. The services offered by the Zookeeper are important because they coordinate parallel processing across a big cluster of servers.

Advantages of Using Hadoop Framework

There are several advantages of using Hadoop ecosystem to process and analyze data in the deep web. Hadoop is run on a cluster of servers. This allows servers to be added or deleted at any given time. As a result, the framework can detect and compensate any hardware failure or system problem making it reliable and efficient in processing and analyzing huge volumes of heterogeneous data. Furthermore, Hadoop can be used in conjunction with existing data-processing systems to enhance their data-processing powers. This is because Hadoop is capable of resolving a number of problems associated with big data. Existing systems in an organization such as relational databases can thus be used to perform the tasks they were designed to focus on like transaction processing, while Hadoop systems are used to absorb any type of data from any number of data sources. This is possible because Hadoop can handle either structured data or unstructured data by combining and aggregating data from various sources to support in-depth analysis. Finally, Hadoop systems can interact with existing systems in an organization to support efficient and cost-effective data storage and support data processing in any possible way since Hadoop does not handle indexing and relationships. As such, when a given set of data is stored in Hadoop system, the issue of how the data will be analyzed later is not a consideration since the system can handle any type of data.

In spite of the advantages that Hadoop system has as far as handling bid data is concerned, Hadoop system is usually difficult to install, configure, and administer. It is also challenging to find the right people with Hadoop skills in the labor market. Moreover, Hadoop systems mostly require a lot of computing resources particularly hardware-like servers. Finally, Hadoop systems suffer from high computational overheads. This is due to the fact that the systems have to support a large amount of internode communication and synchronization that are critical to support big data processing and analysis.

Analyzing Files

Weblogs generated from the deep web can be used by entities such as law enforcement agencies to make strategic decisions. The main challenge is however how to process the huge amount of unstructured or semi-structured data efficiently for analysis. Log files, blogs, chats, social media feeds, and text files from the deep web are unstructured or semi-structured. There are several Hadoop distributions that can be used to analyze this type of data. After accessing the data from the deep web, one can use Apache Flume to harvest, aggregate, and move them in and out of a given Hadoop distribution for processing and analysis. Some of the Hadoop distributions that are available in the market and can be used to analyze weblogs from the deep web are Amazon that offers the Amazon Elastic MapReduce data analytics platform and the Hortonworks Data Platform (HDP).

Most of the Hadoop distributions like HDP come with Apache Flume that is used to collect log data from various applications and deliver the data into Hadoop framework. Flume is used in most Hadoop distributions because it is robust and fault tolerant. In addition, the system can be used in major operating systems such as Linux, Windows, and OSX. Apache Flume is made up of three main components.

Amazon offers the Amazon Elastic MapReduce data analytics platform. The platform is based on the HDFS architecture and is effective for handling the MapReduce queries. The data analytics tool can be used handle big data uses such as web indexing, scientific simulation, log analysis, bioinformatics, machine learning, and data warehousing. The main advantage of using Amazon Elastic MapReduce is that users are given the option of renting servers from the cloud. As such, the tool can be easy to implement and use. In addition, by renting the tool, an organization is relieved from the cost associated with acquiring fixed information technology assets.

HDP is a secure Hadoop distribution that is based on YARN's centralized architecture. The data analytics platform can be used on data-at-rest or real-time applications to deliver big data analytics. One can use HDP to deploy, integrate, and work with large volumes of structured or unstructured data that have been harvested from the deep web. The main advantage of using the HDP platform is that it uses an open approach to software development. As such, users can modify some components of the platform to meet their unique needs. The data analysis platform is also interoperable with common data ecosystems both within data centers and on the cloud. The main components of the HDP are the YARN and HDFS. The YARN is used in the platform to provide a centralized architecture that enables users to process multiple workloads simultaneously. In addition, the YARN component is used to manage resources and support a pluggable architecture that can handle various data access methods. HDFS, on the other hand, is used in the platform to provide data storage services in a manner that is scalable, fault-tolerant, and cost-effective storage.

The figure below shows the process of analyzing weblogs using a Hadoop-based commercial tool known as Teradata Aster. According to the figure, Hadoop component called Apache Flume is used to collect various types of data such as emails and weblogs from the deep web. Flume is capable of collecting the data from applications like email systems before the data is stored in a centralized data space within the Hadoop ecosystem. After collecting the data and storing it in centralized space, the data is then prepared for analysis. Data preparation is important because it will allow one to select the essential features and clean data to remove irrelevant records that will not add any value to the analysis. After cleaning the data, one will end up with data that can be exploited successfully. Feature selection is also important because log files usually contain nonessential information as far as analysis is concerned. This process will involve selecting the required features and reducing the number of features so that one is only left with important features. This will ensure efficiency in the analysis process since log files usually contain huge information that may require a lot of computational resources.

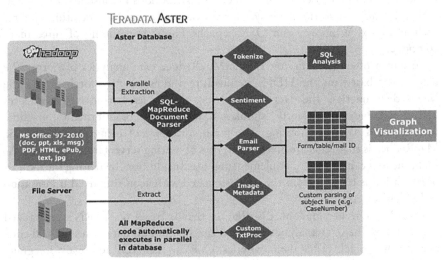

Hadoop's component known as Hadoop Distributed File System (HDFS) is then used to quickly load and store any type of file in its native format. HDFS will, therefore, provide the underlying support for storing the files in a distributed manner. This is done using two types of nodes which are Name Node and Data Node. The Name Node is used to provide data services to the collected data which in this case includes log files, blogs, chats, social media feeds, and text files, while the Data Node is used to provide distributed storage for the files. HDFS is used to support parallel processing which is essential for processing and analyzing big data. HDFS file system works by taking the files that need to be analyzed and breaking them into smaller pieces. The small pieces of data are then distributed to different nodes within a cluster. The files are then copied to individual nodes, and the system ensures that at least one copy of the data is placed on a different server to offer redundancy in case of failure.

Once stored in a distributed manner, the files are processed to extract the relevant data and structure for analysis. This is achieved using the SQL–MapReduce functions that support tokenization, email parsing, text analysis, and other types of processing. MapReduce component is thus used to identify trends, correlations, or associations within the files under consideration. MapReduce works by sending computers where data is stored in distributed storage systems. The data is then executed in three stages which as the map, shuffle, and reduce. In the map stage, mappers are used to process the data. The data is then stored in the HDFS. It is noteworthy that the input files in this stage are passed by mapper function line by line before the data is broken into smaller chunks.

In the reduce stage, the input files are processed further to produce a new set of output which is then stored in the HDFS. During the MapReduce process, Hadoop is used to send various MapReduce tasks to appropriate servers within the cluster. In addition, Hadoop is used to manage various tasks involved in data passing such as allocating tasks to servers, verifying that various tasks are completed effectively, and copying data around server clusters and nodes. After completing various data passing tasks, the data is collected and reduced to form an appropriate result before it is sent to the Hadoop server. The data analysis, therefore, relies heavily on the MapReduce component of the Hadoop ecosystem to extract text from files to support in-depth analysis.

Extracting Information from Unstructured Data

Unstructured data is the type of data that does not generally conform to specific formats. The deep web is filled with this type of data which ranges from log data, documents, pictures, and videos in different repositories stored on this part of the internet. Some of the unstructured data on the internet is machine generated, and thus, it is enormous. Collectively, it is said that organizations only have access to 20% structured data. The rest of the data available on the internet is unstructured. Till recently, there had not been technology that was supportive of analyzing unstructured data. The only way that it could be analyzed was manually, which was not very viable due to the limitations of humans in terms of speed and processing ability.

However, technology has evolved, and today, it is possible to transform unstructured data into structured data. When it is in the form of structured data, it can be easily leveraged for other purposes. The ability to extract value from the chaos of unstructured data is important not only for legal agencies but also researchers and even business organizations. There are different techniques that are used in the extraction of information, and all have a varying degree of success. One of these methods is called text analytics. It is focused on unstructured text since most value can be derived from textual data.

Text analytics is possible due to the progress that has been made in computing enabling the use of natural language processing (NLP). As said before, since prior technology could not extract information from data that was unstructured, humans were often put to that task. The main reason why they could get some value from this type of data is due to their ability to understand and synthesize natural language. Therefore, even if data were of different formats and lengths, they could still understand what it meant. With NLP, computers have gained this ability. Therefore, some tasks that required a human to perform can now be computerized, such as analyzing unstructured data. NLP was developed with a focus of making computers derive meaning from natural language. Today, NLP is extensively used as it has seen the creation of many voice assistants. Text analysis uses NLP and statistical techniques during the extraction of information from unstructured data. NLP can help a computer understand the who, what, when, where, why, and how of data.

Text analytics can analyze different and seemingly unrelated pieces of information and find a connection between them. For instance, in real life, NLP is used for marketing purposes for software and hardware. If, for instance, the sales of a certain program go down and user feedback has been collected, NLP can be used to find the connection between the user feedback and the number of sales. Even if the two data sets are presented from different sources and without a direct tie to each other, the NLP will be able to pick negative comments from customers and relate them with error reports and declining sales. When it comes to the deep web, text analytics can match different types of data from unstructured data dumps thus coming up with a structured and useful piece of data.

Even though NLP is marvelous at analyzing unstructured data, it relies on some level of human input. It cannot therefore work entirely on its own since there are some processes that require actual human intelligence. For instance, a human needs to set up the parameters for characterization of unstructured data. In other cases, a human needs to specify the relationships that NLP will be looking for. Text analytics comes with an inbuilt taxonomy. It acts like a dictionary of words that help the NLP understand better words in chunks of data. The taxonomy can be customized to add some terms, phrases, or words that can be used for analysis. For instance, if some contents of an unstructured data dump contain names of drugs as well as comments from buyers, the NLP can be given a taxonomy with a list of the known drugs as well as some expected comments such as "this is good stuff," "I trust this seller," "they are conmen," and others. These and many others can help the NLP analyze the data dump and churn out the parts that contain words within the taxonomy and also show their relationship. Metadata about a comment can point to the buyer and the seller, for instance.

After analysis is done by NLP or using equally capable tools, it comes back to human intelligence to interpret the results. It is said that the results from analysis of unstructured data should not be considered to be 100% correct. Even though there might be accuracy issues, NLP is able to give significantly accurate results that can be used for decision-making. However, the provided results of structured data can be refined by a human to improve on accuracy. There are some things that humans understand best such as negative sarcasm whereby there is a hidden negative meaning behind a rather humorous comment.

Outside the deep web, text analytics is widely applied. It has been used heavily by companies that mine data from social media networks. The stream of data from social media platforms both from posts or comments of users that mention a company's name is captured and analyzed by this tool. The real-time capturing and analysis is good for a company that wants to maintain a good brand name. When there are negative comments, the company can follow-up with the individual customer's concerns. Apart from companies, politicians might also want to mine social media channels especially during campaigns. There are companies that offer social media analytics and they can gauge the general feel of social media users about a politician's candidature and chances of success. Text analytics is also used to process feedback left by customers on large websites. Since it may not be humanly possible for a human to go through all the comments, NLP is commonly used to go through the comments and categorize positive and negative comments. When there are negative comments, the company can look at the possible ways that they can improve customer satisfaction. Text analytics has also been used by companies that settle claims, especially insurance companies, to detect fraud. When analysis is done focusing on text given by the claimant third party and from other sources, it is possible for NLP to identify potential fraud. NLP will give a score based on the analysis of data collected that will help the insurance company either settle a claim or investigate a potential fraud. From these real-world applications, it can be seen that NLP is instrumental in the analysis of unstructured data. Streams from social media networks are not structured. Feedback from customers left on websites are also not structured. Information from different sources collected by insurance companies is also semi-structured or unstructured. However, NLP is able to make sense out of all this chaos of information. It shows that it can be applied in analyzing unstructured deep web content.

The continued need to analyze unstructured data means that tools such as text analytics will continue to grow. Even though accuracy levels might be at the lows of 80%, analysis of unstructured data can yield very useful information. The introduction of new technologies such as cloud computing is also promising to improve the performance of tools such as text analytics. It can be expected that with time, analyzing unstructured data from the deep web will only be easier. It is no longer impossible as it was previously to get out useful information from unstructured data. All that is left is the improvement of performance in terms of accuracy and analysis time. The underlying algorithms in NLP are continuously undergoing improvement to help them overcome obstacles that have plagued them. One of these obstacles is the ability to develop their taxonomies. Machine learning and artificial intelligence are getting better and soon it will not be necessary for humans to give their inputs so that analysis can be done for unstructured data.

Summary of the Chapter

This chapter has focused on the extraction of valuable information from unstructured data that makes up much of the content on the deep web. A background has been given explaining why traditional analysis methods were not effective at analyzing the unstructured contents of the dark web. The chapter has looked how web content analysis is being done using NLP tools. These are tools that are capable of synthesizing text at the level of a human. They can therefore make connections between disparate sets of data that have some similarities. The aspects of concern in web content analysis that have been discussed include deep web usage, web content, and web structure and their different areas of concern have also been explained. The chapter has also looked at the policy guidelines for extracting and analyzing unstructured content from the deep web. Data stored on dark webs is meant to be kept out of the public eye, and therefore, there might be some legalities into how it should be extracted and analyzed. The chapter has looked at the risks that go with handling data from the deep web and has given mitigations for these. Log analysis tools have been delved into and the chapter has looked at some of the most powerful systems that are used in analysis of huge chunks of information such as big data. Big data tends to have a mix of structured, semi-structured, and unstructured data. Therefore, tools that can handle big data can handle unstructured data as well. An exhaustive explanation has been given detailing how the analysis process takes place to churn out meaningful information from unstructured data. Finally, the chapter has looked at the analysis of unstructured web content through a tool called text analytics. The NLP-based tool has been used in analyzing huge amounts of data and thus is highly applicable to the deep web. The next chapter will go into deep web forensics and look at the different ways through which forensics is done on the deep web.

Questions

1. What is the difference between unstructured, semi-structured, and structured data?
2. Analysis can be done with respect to deep web usage, content, and structure. Explain what is sought after in the three aspects of analysis.
3. What are some of the risks that are associated with collecting and analyzing deep web data?
4. Explain how one can mitigate the risks they are exposed to when doing deep web data collection and analysis.
5. At a basic level, explain the Hadoop framework.
6. When extracting information from unstructured data, NLP is used. Explain what NLP is.
7. Before technology evolved, how was unstructured data analyzed?

8. Explain any new technology that can be leveraged for better performance in NLP.
9. Explain why human inputs are still required even when using NLP to analyze unstructured data.

Further Reading

The following are resources that can be used to gain more knowledge on this chapter:

https://docs.hortonworks.com/HDPDocuments/HDP2/HDP-2.6.4/bk_data-access/content/ch_using-hive.html.

https://opensource.com/life/14/8/intro-apache-hadoop-big-data.

https://datacrops.com/blogs/7-steps-extract-insights-unstructured-data/.

https://analyticsvidhya.com/blog/2014/08/step-step-guide-extract-inforation-free-text-unstructured-data/.

Chapter 9

Dark Web Forensics

Introduction

The dark web has been associated with all manner of criminal and terrorist activity. It is obvious that cybercriminals will choose it as a base of operation and communication given its rather strongly anonymous structure. The dark web has seen the sale of drugs, weapons, hitmen for hire, hackers for hire, malware, stolen data, and terrorist communication. The main belief by many has been that the illegal activities taking place on the dark web are not traceable by law enforcement agencies. The dark web does not have any oversight authorities to prevent crime from taking place or the purchase of illegal items from occurring. The existence of this part of the internet still presents a threat to organizations who fear that their sensitive information could be stolen and listed for sale on markets on the dark web.

However, it is not 100% accurate to say that the dark web is completely out of reach for the law. It is similarly inaccurate to say that the dark web is 100% anonymous. From recent events such as the shutdown of many illegal marketplaces on the dark web, it can be seen that the law still catches up with perpetrators of crime on the dark net. A good example is Ross Ulbricht who was the alleged founder of the Silk Road 2 marketplace. Ross Ulbricht was sentenced to a life imprisonment for his alleged activities on the dark web. This is a testament that there is no such a thing as complete anonymity or absolute lack of accountability in this part of the internet. This chapter will focus on the forensic investigation aspects of the dark web and methods designed to beat them. It will do so in the following topics:

- Forensic introduction
- Crypto market and Cryptocurrencies in the dark web

- Forensic investigation scope and models
- Forensic toolkits (FTKs)
- Anti-forensic techniques

Introduction to Forensics

With all the illegal activities that take place on the dark web, it may seem that it is unwatched by legal agencies. While this is partially true, law enforcement agencies have increasingly been successfully carrying out investigations and apprehending the chief suspects behind the illegal goods and services offered on the dark web. By mid-2015, 312 people had been arrested by legal agencies for participating in illegal activities on dark net markets. These activities included the sale of drugs, weapons, child porn, and malware sale, among others. The following is a breakdown of these arrests as per the individual markets (Table 9.1).

Of the total number of arrests, 162 were buyers and sellers were 116. Additionally, the black market staff arrested were ten in number and the market owners were four. The arrest of buyers shows that the law enforcement agencies were not just targeting the people listing illegal items on the dark web but also those that were buying these items. In Australia, there were four buyers arrested while trying to obtain weapons from the dark net marketplaces through a seller based in the United States. In Denmark, officers reported having arrested two notorious drug sellers on the dark web. It is believed that these sellers are the ones that had listed their drugs on Silk Road 1 and 2, Agora and Evolution. The European Union reported the arrest of about ten weapon buyers in the region. In Uganda, an American was arrested for counterfeiting and selling fake currencies. He had

Table 9.1 Users Arrested on the Dark Web

Marketplace	No. of Arrests
Silk Road 1	138
Silk Road 2	85
Evolution	27
BMR	9
Agora	6
Utopia	5
Sheep	3
Hydra	1

relocated to the African country where an undercover sting operation led to his arrest and deportation to face charges in the United States.

In the United States, there were more prolific arrests of the leading sellers. One of the sellers that were famed for selling weapons was known as *weaponsguy*, and in mid-2014, many customers were complaining of their packages not arriving. It was later alleged that the law enforcement agencies in the United States had managed to arrest him and use his account for investigations to arrest other sellers and buyers. Most of the weapon-related arrests were successful after the law enforcement agencies successfully set up traps using his account. In May 2015, a college student was arrested for buying drugs on the dark web and reselling them. His arrest came after banks reported suspicious activity in his accounts where he was mostly using his deposits to purchase cryptocurrency.

There have been more arrests that have been covered here. This means that it has been possible to bring to justice crooks hiding under the anonymity of dark nets. It is also a clear show that forensics work too on the dark web to successfully make arrests and charge people in court. Dark web forensics involve more complex operations than normal forensics in order to gather evidence or track crooks. The way that most dark nets were designed was such that it would be hard to tell the users on the networks and the sites that they were visiting. The advent of cryptocurrency also made it harder for criminals to be tracked using money trails. Therefore, investigators normally have to use more resources if they are to be able to catch or track the criminals hiding in the dark web.

The difficulty in carrying out forensics on the dark web is that there is a challenge in both finding the users and tracking their activities on dark nets. Even though not 100%, the dark web will still remain to be anonymous. Therefore, this anonymity barrier has to be taken down one way or another in order to get to the targets. With this cloak on, the location and internet activity of any seller, buyer, terrorist, or black market owner will remain anonymous. Without the location of a target, legal agencies find challenges in their investigations since they first need to establish jurisdiction, something merely possible without a physical location. Therefore, even if law enforcement agencies know the pseudonyms of the targets on dark net markets and also know the crimes that they commit, it is still a challenge to start acting on them if they do not know where they are.

Over time, legal enforcement agencies such as the NSA and Federal Bureau of Investigation (FBI) have been finding vulnerabilities deep within the architecture of the dark web to help them get the necessary information about dark net users for forensic investigations. Although this has caused an uproar from the user community of the dark web, it can only be explained as a necessary evil to ensure that the law takes its course even when culprits try to hide from it. There have been several vulnerabilities within browsers used to access dark nets that have been exploited by the FBI and NSA to collect evidence and arrest suspected criminals. Legal agencies have also devised ways to do special analysis and correlation of traffic entering and exiting dark networks via entry and exit nodes to collect data about individual users and the type of traffic that was flowing to their computers. Rogue entry and exit nodes have also been set up by security agencies on dark nets to collect data about the traffic getting in and out of the dark nets. Therefore, it is possible today for law enforcement agencies to find out the locations of criminals on the dark net based on these techniques and many more. It is no longer safe for one to assume that because they are on the dark web, everything they do will remain anonymous and that they will not face the law.

Even when law enforcement agencies lack the techniques to find out the identities of crooks on the dark net, they can still hire digital forensic professionals to help them. They have the resources to do that and there are professionals willing to expose criminals on the dark net to the real-world security agencies and get paid while doing it. There are also individual groups that hack into dark net websites that they presume to be engaging in illegal activity. For instance, recently all the websites hosted by freedom hosting were hacked by a vigilante because the hosting companies allowed sites that had child pornography to host their services there. Therefore, it is easy to find willing hands to do digital forensics to either capture or collect evidence about criminals on the dark net.

Crypto Market and Cryptocurrencies in the Dark Web

A basis of operations for law enforcement agencies has been to follow the money and it will lead to the criminal. This was particularly effective when the main way that money could change hands was through banks. Since banks are governed and controlled, law enforcement agencies court just come with court orders requesting to see more details about the accounts that received some money in a money trail. Therefore, the task was to find out who was paid the money, and this would bring up many more details about a crime (Figure 9.1).

However, in 2009, the digital currency called Bitcoin was invented and this coin made significant changes to crime. It was a cryptocurrency that ensured the anonymity of the transacting parties. Therefore, if money was converted to Bitcoin and exchanged, no one would tell who the transacting parties were since the transaction would not leave any trails. Therefore, money could vanish from paper trails and safely make its way back to the criminals. It came as such a relief and was adopted as the cryptocurrency of choice on the dark web. This is when there was a proliferation of websites offering illegal services and products and accepting payment via Bitcoin only. Today much has not changed as the dark web relies on cryptocurrencies for financial purposes. There have been global-scale demonstrations on the practicality of using cryptocurrency in any attack. In 2017, there was a ransomware that caused devastation across the globe by encrypting victim computers and demanding a ransom to be paid. The ransom was to be paid to a Bitcoin address. There have also been incidents of other ransomware types that have encrypted computers and demanded payment via Bitcoin or other cryptocurrencies.

Figure 9.1   Bitcoin logo.

On the dark web, cryptocurrencies are the only acceptable payment options in many illegal black markets. For instance, to buy fake IDs and passports, the buyer will have to pay a certain amount to the seller via Bitcoin. So many other transactions take place in the same manner. No one wants to transact using cash in these markets and run the risk of being identified by law enforcement agencies (Figure 9.2).

There are many reasons that make cryptocurrencies the ideal medium of value exchange on the dark web. The first one is anonymity. Cryptocurrencies run on the Blockchain technology which uses an open ledger to conduct transactions to individual user wallets. The open ledger is not centrally stored; thus, the FBI cannot bust some servers and collect evidence to incriminate users that have sent or received money through cryptocurrencies. There are no details about the transacting parties kept. Money just gets deducted or added to one's cryptocurrency wallet without details of transacting parties being kept. Second, cryptocurrency money transfers cannot be reversed. Therefore, there is an added level of protection to a seller that a rogue buyer will not get a transaction to be reversed as could be the case with the transfer of actual money through services such as PayPal.

The third reason why cryptocurrencies are commonly used on dark net transactions is that they can easily be laundered. This will be covered in a later section. The fourth reason is that cryptocurrency transactions are not charged the same fees as bank transactions. The charges, if any, are minimal, and thus, customers are attracted to them. The last and least reason why sellers prefer cryptocurrencies over

Figure 9.2   Fake IDs and licenses on the dark web.

fiat currencies is because these currencies change value. Cryptocurrencies had been rising in value in 2017 such that ordinary people started to use them as investments. They could convert currency from fiat to cryptocurrency in anticipation of further price increments. In January, however, the value of most cryptocurrencies started dropping. Bitcoin, which was the preferred cryptocurrency on the dark web, fell in value from $20,000 to $9,000 and continued depreciating in value. However, the prospects of getting paid in an investment-like currency are definitely an appealing one especially for those doing dirty business.

Cryptocurrencies and Money Laundering

Money laundering is one of the effective ways used to conceal the traces of illegally acquired money. Traditionally, it involved the transfer of money to foreign banks or businesses and then reobtaining the cash. This made it not seem like obtaining money from the proceeds of crime. A common place where money laundering has been taking place is through Swiss banks. This is because Swiss banks have come to be known for their utmost secrecy and protection of foreign accounts. They have therefore been used as tax havens and money-laundering points over time. This is because the previous legislations made it illegal for banks to disclose information about their clients. There has been international pressure to get these banks to be more open and compliant with offering information about clients that are implicated in scandals or those that are being investigated. However, Swiss regulators have maintained the stand that foreign clients are to be afforded the highest levels of confidentiality. Therefore, very few questions are asked when foreign clients deposit huge sums of money into Swiss bank accounts. It is not a new trend since tax evasion through Swiss banks goes back to the 1900s. During the world wars when European companies raised taxes to source funds for the war, wealthy individuals decided to move their funds to Swiss bank accounts and avoid these taxes altogether. However, Swiss banking authorities have introduced hurdles to make it impossible or significantly harder for money laundering to take place (Figure 9.3).

This void has been filled by the best alternative that is now accessible to everyone. There are cryptocurrency money-laundering services offered on the dark web. These services serve the interests of criminals, terrorists, and dirty politicians and businesspeople. There are several types of money-laundering activities that this section will cover.

The first laundering service is offered to cybercriminals when collecting the proceeds of their crime. For instance, the makers of WannaCry ransomware received sums of money from individuals that had paid either the $300 or $600 ransoms to salvage their files. Out of caution, these hackers will not rush to directly withdraw the amounts paid to them in Bitcoin. Even though Bitcoin transactions are said to be anonymous, they are not really so in reality. It is only difficult to trace them. But, with all the attention that these hackers got from law enforcement agencies in the 150 countries that they attacked, there is the risk that they could be traced. Therefore, there definitely was a need for them to mask their trails further. There are dark net websites that offer money laundering as a service to cybercriminals. They are part of the underground economy that has enabled hackers to get more successful with their heists. Laundering as a service is the final service in the underground economy where the dirty money obtained from crime is sanitized and made usable without risks of arrest.

Laundering as a service can be offered by cashers. These are the individuals that exchange cryptocurrencies to fiat currencies on behalf of the holders of these

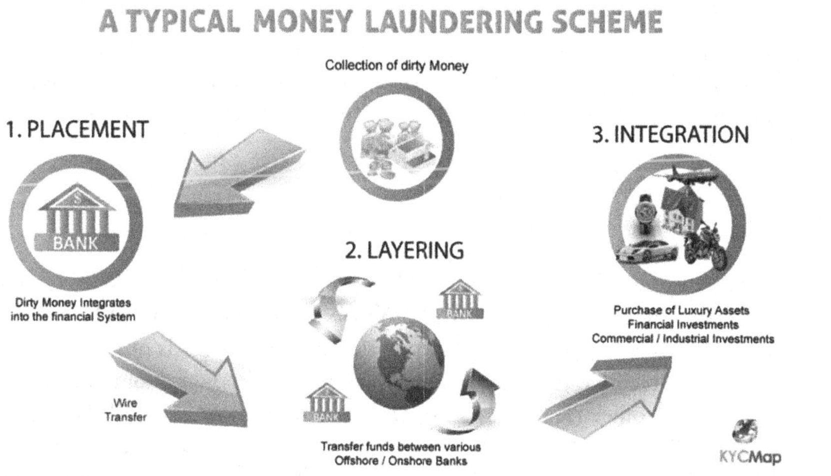

Figure 9.3 A traditional money-laundering scheme.

cryptocurrencies. It is believed that they have access to huge sums in cash and will send back to the holder of cryptocurrencies that are "dirty." Apart from offering cash, they can also give luxury cars and expensive items that can be resold in order to recover the cash. Casher's have secret avenues that they use to get huge amounts of clean money. For instance, they could have connections working in actual banks that can set up fake accounts that can be used to deposit and withdraw cash. They can also use fake identification documents to create fake accounts in banks themselves. Therefore, when they accept dirty cryptocurrencies, they can go to any site that converts cryptocurrency to actual currency and sends the amounts converted to the fake bank account. At the end of the day, if a trail is followed successfully from cryptocurrencies to the end, it is only the fake account that will turn up and everything else will be masked out.

The second laundering type is one where one can oversee everything themselves. However, it is riskier since one is closer to the money trail. This is whereby one uses a myriad of cryptocurrency converters and the resulting cryptocurrency is used to buy items anonymously on the dark web stores. Either these items bought will be resold on the cryptocurrency market using another account and wallet or they will be delivered and resold in the real world. For instance, if one received dirty money through a cryptocurrency wallet X, they can use the money to buy goods on the dark net or real world whereby Bitcoin is acceptable. Once they have done so, they can resale these items and get the money deposited into a cryptocurrency wallet Y that is not registered with the same details as X. Therefore, the path to trace the dirty money will be long and cumbersome. It is important to note that the records for such transactions are not easy to find due to their decentralized nature, and thus, there are some people that opt to just convert their cryptocurrencies in bits to fiat currency and they feel safe that they cannot be traced. However, those that launder money are very good at what they do and can hardly be found out unless they make mistakes.

There are a few other avenues that can be exploited by people seeking to get dirty money cleansed. However, since they could still be used by innocent cryptocurrency holders, we will not directly classify them as types of laundering. These include the following.

Bitcoin ATMs

These are privately owned Bitcoin ATMs that are preferred by holders of Bitcoin that wish to remain anonymous. These ATMs work like normal ATMs whereby they exchange Bitcoins with cash without asking for the details of the person converting. Their objective is to ensure that very little is known about the customer. Know Your Customer (KYC) laws are generally not followed to achieve this. The only catch is that these ATMs charge a lot more than other Bitcoin exchangers with prices averaging about 15% of the value being exchanged.

Bitcoin Mixers

One of the ways through which Bitcoin transactions can be tracked is by analyzing the transactions on the public ledger. If wallet X received $5,000 in Bitcoin and wallet Y was deducted $5,000 worth Bitcoin within a short time window, it could be said that the owners of these wallets were transacting. Therefore, further investigations can reveal the details of these transacting parties. Bitcoin mixers come to fill this vulnerable space. They are used to obfuscate transactions such that it is nearly impossible for any observer to tell who the transacting parties were. Therefore, if wallet X had $5,000 in Bitcoin, a receiving party may not receive this as a whole, the Bitcoin mixer can take the money through several splits, conversion to other currencies, purchase, and buying of new currencies before the amounts are finally slowly transferred to the account(s) of the receiver. Therefore, there is no direct link between the sender and receiver of this money. Bitcoin mixers are however costly as they can take up to 15% of the value being mixed.

Bitcoin Property Exchanges

With the increased public adoption of cryptocurrency, there are some business organizations that are now accepting Bitcoin as a form of payment. It was anticipated that Amazon.com would soon adopt Bitcoin, but hopes seem to have been lost due to the lack of confirmation from the giant e-commerce store. Those hopes were purely speculative, and it was hoped that such an adoption would lead to a big rise in the value of Bitcoin. However, there are other organizations that have not anticipated to adopt cryptocurrency as a form of payment. There is an online service called purse.io that facilitates people to exchange their Bitcoin for actual property. The online service accepts Bitcoins on behalf of stores like Amazon and complete purchases for anyone that intends to use Bitcoin for purchasing purposes. For instance, if a buyer wants a $2,000 Tv from Amazon but wants to use Bitcoin, it is impossible to purchase directly from Amazon. However, purse.io will accept the Bitcoin and transact with Amazon on one's behalf with actual money instead of Bitcoin. Once purse.io completes the purchase, the items are shipped or collected by the buyer. The buyer will not yet have sent the Bitcoin. Purse.io is still in the business of selling Bitcoins. Therefore, they will get an address or addresses of buyers that want Bitcoin and give the Amazon buyer these accounts to transfer the cryptocurrency to.

Therefore, once the customer that wanted merchandise from Amazon gets his or her product, purse.io will ensure that Bitcoins are sent to a willing buyer. The willing buyer will have to pay a certain fee for receiving the Bitcoin anonymously and without having to visit a Bitcoin exchange platform. This is an efficient business model that enables holders of Bitcoin to be able to make purchases without necessarily converting their Bitcoin to fiat. However, this could also be used by a money launderer. They could make a list of items they want, give the list to purse.io, and assure of payment. When the items are delivered and the money sent to buyers of cryptocurrencies, the laundering process is almost done. All one needs to do is to resell the items bought on Amazon through other avenues such as eBay.

Monero

After the arrest of Ross Ulbricht, the alleged founder of Silk Road 2, there were concerns about the anonymity of Bitcoin transactions and that of the distributed ledger technology. Therefore, money launderers searched for other cryptocurrencies that could offer more anonymity. There has been an uptake of Monero in the dark web mainly because the digital currency has an in-built tumbling/mixing technique. Therefore, any transaction made using Monero is more anonymous than any that is made using Bitcoin. Many marketplaces have been accepting Monero alongside Bitcoin. Due to this uptake, even more anonymous cryptocurrencies have been and are still being created. There are altcoins such as DASH and Cryptonite cryptos that are even more anonymous and can assure transactors of their security since it is hard for any observer to make any sensible money trail on them. These present a big challenge to forensic investigators especially when they are used for criminal purposes.

Exposed Cryptocurrency Laundering Schemes

Arrests of Bitcoin Laundering

In 2016, young men in their early twenties were apprehended for money laundering. Investigations pointed out that they had laundered up to $22 worth of Bitcoin that had been proceeds of drug deals on dark net websites. Therefore, it is likely that these were the cashers trusted by sellers on dark net sites to sanitize dirty money. During their arrests, law enforcement agencies seized high-end cars and loads of cash that they used for the laundering business. The more interesting bit is that they were discovered due to a mistake they made. They used to make huge cash deposits from online sources to their bank accounts and then very quickly withdraw the money. Therefore, it was not out of a cash trail that they were discovered, it was because they were not careful with their deposits and withdrawals. If, for instance, they had created fake bank accounts using fake identification documents, police would be called to arrest the account holders of the suspicious accounts, but it would all end there. There would be no one to arrest since the reportedly suspicious bank accounts would be found out to be registered under the names of nonexistent people. However, due to their careless mistakes, they were put behind bars at such young ages (Figure 9.4).

Dutch police have arrested 10 men believed to have used Bitcoin to launder proceeds from criminal sales in the Dark Web.

According to local media, the Dutch Fiscal Information and Investigation Service and public prosecution department raided 15 addresses across the country -- including homes in Rotterdam, Dordrecht, The Hague and Putten -- resulting in the arrest of 10 men in their early 20's.

Police seized cash, luxury cars and chemicals used to make the drug ecstasy after being tipped off by banks concerning large cash deposits which were then quickly withdrawn via ATMs.

Figure 9.4   A news article on the arrest of young men over Bitcoin-laundering scheme. (https://zdnet.com/article/arrests-made-over-bitcoin-laundering-scheme-dark-web-drug-deals/.)

BTC-e

A Russian that has been investigated of large-scale Bitcoin laundering was arrested and currently faces charges that amount to 55 years in prison if he is convicted. The Russian was found to be behind a successful Bitcoin-laundering scheme that had laundered $4 billion for people that had been engaging in computer hacking and drug sale activities mostly on the dark net. The man was arrested in Greece while staying at a beach hotel where he ran his services from. Since 2011, the Russian known as Vinnik created a site called BTC-e, and it grew to be a large Bitcoin trading platform. However, behind the scenes, BTC-e was doing money laundering for dark web clients. From one perspective, it was an ideal business since the exchange platform was a center stage for digital and fiat currencies exchanging hands. Therefore, there was an open avenue for the owner of this site to do the laundering services with the currencies that were already availed to him by the customers. It is said that most of the sites' revenues did not come from come from cryptocurrency exchanges, rather, from money laundering.

The laundering process was found out to be actually a two-step process to stifle authorities from directly associating BTC-e to money laundering. The two steps were to make BTC-e to appear as a victim instead of the perpetrator. The first step was where the funds for laundering were being obtained from the dark web. These came from drug dealers, child porn sellers, and stolen cryptocurrency coins from users. These were deposited to the account of Mt. Gox which was under the control of Mr. Vinnik. Mt. Gox was another exchange platform that had been hacked, possibly by Mr. Vinnik, who then took control of it and put it into the business of money laundering. Mt. Gox would make several transactions with BTC-e, and BTC-e would go on to cleanse the dirty money when exchanging cryptocurrencies with cash for BTC-e customers.

Forensic investigators were able to collect evidence against Mr. Vinnik before tracking him down and arresting him with the assistance of Greece authorities in

August 2017. Mr. Vinnik faces charges for money laundering and illegal money transactions. Prosecutors in court said that Mr. Vinnik's platform was one of the most preferred by cybercriminals for money-laundering services. The site was reported to have a chat platform where users would openly discuss profitable criminal activities and the customer service would offer advice on how they would launder the money. This is a relevant court case which shows the abilities of forensic investigations to get through pseudo websites and accounts and bring the real culprits to justice. Despite the general claim that cryptocurrencies are anonymous, such cases openly show that a dedicated forensics team can get through the anonymity and expose criminals.

Forensic Investigation Scope and Models

The most important aspect of forensics is the collection of evidence. This evidence could lead to the successful prosecution of a cybercriminal, child porn peddler, terrorist, or scammer hiding in the deep web. Unlike other environments, gathering evidence on the dark web is both complex and challenging. Even if law enforcement agencies know a particular notorious criminal on the dark web, they can simply do nothing until they verify who the person is in real life. They will also not rush to arrest the person before they acquire sufficient evidence to build a strong case that can lead to a conviction. This is the reason why, even when an illegal marketplace has been infiltrated by law enforcement agencies, they will not rush to shut it down. They can spend weeks or months trying to collect evidence or to reveal the identities of several users of the marketplace. They can even participate in selling the drugs just to get some of the sellers. They can spend a lot of resources just to collect some evidence such as the real name or location of a wanted suspect on the dark web.

For the purposes of context, let us look at the arrest of Ross Ulbricht, the famous founder of Silk Road 2 who was also called Dread Pirate Roberts. He was first connected to Dread Pirate Roberts by investigators working with the American Drug Enforcement Administration (DEA) on a Silk Road case. The forensic investigators wanted to find out the people behind this marketplace that had wildly grown out of control and supplied very many people with illegal drugs. However, connecting Ulbricht to Dread Pirate Roberts was not a cheap affair. Investigators had a hard time with the anonymity of Tor, the dark net where Silk Road was operating on. However, they had been able to find out a username called Altoid who announced the launch of Silk Road 2. There was therefore sufficient reason to follow up on who used this username. They searched around for this username until 1 day, the same username popped up on a programming forum asking for some help with coding. In this forum post, Altoid gave his email address which fortunately or unfortunately contained his real names. The investigators then started working out on who, Altoid, who had exposed himself as Ross Ulbricht, was. They observed his activity both on the real world and on the Silk Road website where he used to log in as the admin. There were concerns brought in court by Ulbricht's defense that the admin account of Dread Pirate Roberts was shared and it had been handed down by several people. If at all the investigators had not collected any other evidence, this claim could have dealt a big blow to the case. However, investigators had forensically collected digital evidence that tied Ulbricht squarely to Dread Pirate Roberts.

They had recorded the strange internet traffic associated with Tor from Ulbricht's computer. They had also collected evidence from the messages that Dread Pirate Roberts exchanged with other members of Silk Road. The FBI had also disguised themselves as members that had grown to be close confidants of Dread Pirate Roberts. At the time of his arrest, an officer that had masqueraded as a Silk Road loyal member and a close friend of Dread Pirate Roberts asked him to look into an account that had some issues. When Ulbricht stepped into a library and logged into the site as Dread Pirate Roberts, law enforcement agencies distracted him, and then arrested him. They also seized the most important thing, his laptop while logged in as Dread Pirate Roberts. This allowed them to collect more evidence against Ross which the court upheld and used to sentence Ross to life imprisonment (Figure 9.5).

The collection of evidence and prosecution of Ross Ulbricht lays some foundation on how forensic investigations are carried out to lead to the successful prosecution of offenders hiding in the dark web. The following are explanations of the forensic scope and steps followed.

Scope

The scope for the digital forensics on the dark web is a little bit broad. The forensics have to cover everything from policies and procedures, evidence acquisition, evidence assessment, evidence analysis, and then reporting. The scope therefore defines the steps that are followed during the process of conducting a forensic investigation. The following is a layout of these general steps that will be followed in any forensic investigation.

Federal agents swooped on Ross William Ulbricht in a San Francisco public library Tuesday afternoon, charging the 29-year-old American with narcotics trafficking, computer hacking and money laundering. They allege he is "the Dread Pirate Roberts," the Silk Road's mysterious founder, who drew his pseudonym from the feared, fictitious character in the film The Princess Bride.

Figure 9.5   A news article on the arrest of Ross Ulbricht. (https://edition.cnn. com/2013/10/04/world/americas/silk-road-ross-ulbricht/index.html.)

Policy and Procedure Development

The forensics exercise on the dark web is quite delicate, and highly sensitive data is involved. This is data that, if lost, it might never be recovered again. Therefore, each forensics exercise has to be treated in a special manner to ensure that crucial evidence that will be collected is handled in the right way. This is why most forensics will start by setting up detailed guidelines and procedures that investigators have to use when doing the investigations. These procedures could cover how certain evidence is to be recovered, how some evidence can be retrieved from devices, how evidence should be stored, and also how to document the activities involved to ensure the authenticity of the data. Law enforcement agencies working on deep web cases often have to rely on the assistance from seasoned cybersecurity experts. These experts can accompany them to collect the evidence or just give rigorous training on how such evidence can be and should be collected. This is especially helpful if the evidence will be collected from the field where it might be unsuitable to bring people without physical assault or defense training. The cybersecurity experts are still helpful when evidence is to be collected online. They can list the programs that can be used to collect the evidence.

A very important part of the policies and procedures is the codification of actions regarding the constitution of evidence, what should be looked for in it and how it should be safely handled once retrieved. Also, before the investigation begins, it is important for details available about the case to be understood and the allowable investigative actions to be stated. There are some types of evidence that require warrants and authorizations before they are collected. If such are not obtained, a defense team in court could make the judge throw away such evidence. As a matter of fact, the defense of Ross Ulbricht used a similar tactic when they appealed his case. They particularly argued that Ulbricht's internet traffic was seized without a warrant or probable cause which was in violation of the US constitution. Luckily, the appeal did not go through, but there were high hopes that it would from the defense side. Therefore, the understanding of warranties and authorizations must be ensured before the investigations begin to prevent key evidence from going to waste.

Evidence Assessment

It is important for any forensic investigation process to assess the potential evidence to be collected beforehand. It is important that these types of details about the case are understood. For example, if the goals of the investigations are to show that person X has committed crimes such as identity theft, the investigators need to know that they have to collect and go through evidence in hard disks, emails, social media, and other data collection spaces. They also need to understand that they will be required to assess whether the information they collect from such sources can be used for the particular crime. In another example, if person Y is being investigated for manipulating people to disclose their personal information, the investigators have to assess which type of evidence that they are seeking for. They also need to understand how such evidence has to be preserved. The integrity of these sources is also assessed to ensure that it will not be thrown out of court due to the incorrect collection or storage.

In the Ross Ulbricht's case, investigators had assessed that the evidence they much needed from him was on his laptop. They also wanted evidence from within the Silk Road site, and thus, they had to find him logged into the site. That is the reason why they masqueraded as members on the site and could request for some favors from him. During his arrest, they wanted to find the laptop logged in and that is why they called on him to look into a Silk Road member account, and while he was logged in, they pounced on him. They were then able to collect and preserve the evidence they needed. This was elaborate evidence assessment prior to the collection and they followed the assessment with surgical precision.

Evidence Acquisition

This is a very important step in the forensic exercise where the evidence being sought after is retrieved. A lot of resources are used alongside care to ensure that the evidence is not destroyed during acquisition. To add some perspective to this, let us relook at the Ulbricht's case evidence acquisition process. Investigators had already drawn him out into the open, in a library. He had logged into his computer and into the Silk Road website. It was a tense moment in which the investigators could capture all that they wanted or lose it. If they dashed at him, it is possible that he would set his laptop to auto-erase. They could also not use lethal methods since it would defeat the objectives of the investigations which were to bring him to face justice and serve as a lesson to others. They, therefore, used a ploy where secret agents inside the laboratory acted like a couple that was fighting. When Ulbricht tried to find out what was happening, it was only then that he was arrested. He was not in a position to rush back to his laptop and either destroy it or destroy the data it contained. The agents arrested him on the spot and used a data extraction software in a flash drive to start extracting data from Ulbricht's computer. That was a spectacular example of how evidence acquisition is done at times.

It is very critical for any case, and thus, the acquisition process follows a rigorously detailed plan. Alongside taking care of how the evidence is obtained, documentation is needed for court purposes. Therefore, documentation has to be done prior to, during, and after the evidence collection. The documentation should include the hardware and software used as well as details about the systems being investigated. Evidence acquisition has to follow the laid out plans to prevent destruction or loss of integrity of data as it is retrieved from sources. The guidelines relating to reservation of evidence should also be followed as soon as the evidence has been retrieved. Additional precautions such as copying and transferring evidence to the investigators should take place as soon to prevent cases where evidence is stolen after being retrieved.

Of utmost importance is to ensure that all the pieces of evidence collected are collected using legal means. For instance, a court will throw out data that was obtained through illegal means. This is why documentation is important to help explain to the court how every piece was retrieved.

Evidence Examination

To ensure that the investigations of potential evidence are effective, there are some procedures that have to be laid out for the retrieval, copying, and storage of evidence. During investigations, data is commonly stored in designated archives wherever possible. There is also a list of methods that are used to analyze the evidence. Some of these methods include the use of software. For instance, if Ross Ulbricht would have begun erasing files from his computer before his arrest, law enforcement agencies would have had to use special software to recover the deleted data. If he had locked his computer, there are software that they could have used to gain access to the computer even without having to use his password. Apart from software, there are techniques that the investigators can use to locate important data. They can use metadata on files such as authors and last modification dates to find recent data. Even though this case is not from the dark net, it is highly relevant to this discussion. In 2012, Mr. Higinio Ochoa was part of a hacker group known as anonymous. He used the name Cabin Cr3w and commonly hacked police databases. However, in one instance, he hacked a police database and to taunt the officers, he posted a bikini photo of his girlfriend telling them that he had pawned them. Unfortunately, he forgot to scrape metadata from the photo. Later, the police used this metadata to locate the hacker, Mr. Ochoa, and arrest him. Part of his parole agreement, he is up to date not allowed to connect to the internet. From this case, it can be noted that readily available data such as metadata on files can be collected as evidence. The chances of finding useful data from such sources are normally high since it is hard for culprits to keep their tracks 100% hidden.

Investigators can also use techniques to search for certain keywords in hard disks, files, posts on social media, or blog posts to find certain data. For instance, the only way Ross Ulbricht came to be linked to Dread Pirate Roberts was from the username Altoid. Investigators searched around where else on the internet that Altoid was used and they came to find that there was a post on a forum and disclosed his personal email that had his real names. There are special search techniques that can be used on Google to find out exact information. Investigators can also use some techniques to find out hidden files or programs that may be of importance to a case.

The analysis of file names is also useful in evidence examination. Files on the internet or dark web can be analyzed to determine the directories within which they are stored in servers. This helps investigators to find other related files that may be stored in the same folder. For instance, take a look at the following URL to a pdf file:

www.domainname.com/files/secret_files/hacking/stolen_passwords.pdf

By going in reverse order, investigators can find out more information contained in the hacking and secret files directories in the above domain name. For instance, in the hacking directory, they could find more files such as stolen credit cards, stolen identities, and stolen bank details among other things.

Downloaded files also give clues as to where they were downloaded from. Using this information, they can go to the source and find out what other pieces of information are available. Also, there are some cases where a suspect is alleged to be the distributor of some content. In this scenario, the investigators have to tie the suspect to files on a distribution medium such as a website. Therefore, they may have to match file names of files on a suspect's computer with those on the said website as verification.

During the analysis of evidence, investigators normally work with lawyers and other investigators to ensure that the evidence is handled in the right and permissible way. They can also be guided on how to prepare the evidence for a court case.

Documentation and Reporting

The end goal of the collection of forensic evidence is so that it can be used in court. Documentation and reporting are therefore the last steps in a forensic investigation exercise. Throughout the evidence collection process, there was much focus on the documentation of the exercise. This documentation has to be verified to be accurate and complete. All the methods used to retrieve, copy, and store evidence as well as examine and assess evidence afterward have to be recorded. This is very helpful when it comes to questions of integrity in court. Investigator's inability to document how they collected evidence has led to dismissals of serious cases after judges could not tell whether the evidence presented before them was factual or fabricated. It is easy to fabricate digital data and that is why there is an insistence on the documentation of every process. Documentation also allows courts to verify whether the data extraction and analysis techniques used were legal. The court can appoint its own experts to do that.

Cybersecurity experts are normally contracted by investigators to help with the preparation of data for reporting purposes. The data has to be kept in a readable format that judges and other laymen can understand. Some explanations have to be simplified by these experts such that the judge and jury can easily understand even without information security training.

Digital Forensic Models

It is of importance that digital forensic investigators conduct their investigations in the right way. It is very easy for a judge to dismiss digital evidence due to the ease at which it can be modified. Therefore, since as early as 1984, law enforcement agencies have developed processes and procedures for conducting digital forensic investigations. There have been models that have been developed to help investigators, and this section will take a look at some of them. Before then, it is good to take an overall look at the computer forensic investigation process. Models may differ on the individual processes, but the flow is all the same and all are based on a similar abstract frame. The first methodology on how digital evidence was to be acquired and made legally acceptable dates back to 1984. The methodology forms a basis of all the current digital forensic investigation models. The investigative process was outlined as being composed of the following processes.

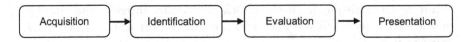

We have already looked all the above stages when covering the steps involved in digital forensics. Therefore, we are straight away going to look at the models used by law enforcement agencies in digital forensics. All these models are based on the four-step investigative process that has been diagrammatically illustrated above.

Digital Forensics Framework Investigative Model

This is the Digital Forensics Framework (DFRWS) that was developed in 2001. It has six phases as shown in the diagram below.

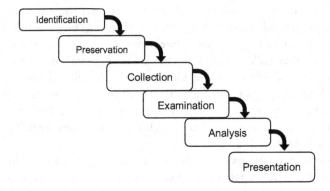

This model was the base of most digital forensic investigations. It was known to be standardized and consistent thus could easily be accepted in court. Each of the phases had laid out techniques that investigators could use. In the first phase of identification, there were techniques to prevent crime, resolve signatures, detect anomalies, monitor systems, do audit analysis, and many other things. It made the identification process very strict and watertight. This was followed by preservation where there was a case management guideline that helped investigators store different data formats. There were imaging technologies given to help the retention of accurate and acceptable evidence. In the collection phase, the model discussed the software and hardware tools that could be used to extract the fine details from the evidence. There were also recovery techniques for deleted data. After this were the examination and analysis phases. This is where tracking, pattern matching, and hidden data discovery were done. The last phase was the presentation which included documentation, clarifications, and recommendations from experts.

Abstract Digital Forensics Model

This forensic investigation model was derived from DFRWS above and enhanced so that it could include nine phases. The model is as shown in the diagram below.

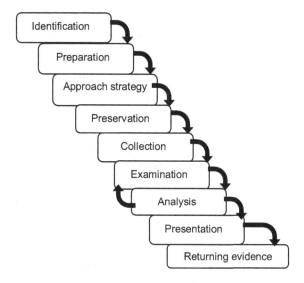

In this model, identification is still the first phase but it is followed by preparation. The preparation phase was introduced in this model to allow for some investigative procedures to take place. These include search warrants, acquisition of tools, authorizations to monitor a suspect, and management support. Following this is the Approach Strategy that is also a new introduction. Here, the model allows for further collection of evidence with minimal impacts to the victims. The phase allows for a defined strategy to be used. In the preservation phase, data is isolated and secured. In the collection phase, data is finally moved from the sources to the investigators. The phase encourages that the evidence should be duplicated. In the examination phases, an in-depth systematic analysis is done where the fine details are obtained from the evidence. The analysis phase helps to determine the value of the derived details in relation to the case at hand. This is followed by presentation where the processes used are summarized in a report form. The last phase is returning evidence whereby the withheld pieces of evidence such as laptops and servers are returned to their respective owners. The main advantage of this model is that it caters for pre- and post-investigation processes while DFRWS assumed them.

Integrated Digital Investigation Process

This model was proposed in 2003, and it sought to integrate the available models at the time. The goal was to come up with a model that integrated digital and physical investigations since these at times went together. It is a very big model which is composed of 17 phases broken down into 5 groups. The following are the five groups that make up the entire model.

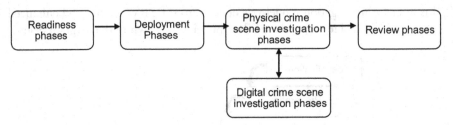

The model starts with a readiness phase which makes sure that investigators are ready with all the training and equipment for investigating a case. The readiness phase also includes the acquisition of any data required for the investigation. The next group is the deployment phase group. This is where the mechanisms for incident detection and confirmation are provided. The phase has phases related to detection, notifications, confirmations, and authorizations during the forensic investigation. The next group is the physical crime scene investigation phase group. As the name suggests, it is the phase in which physical evidence is collected and analyzed. It consists of the preservation of the scene, survey of the scene for evidence, documentation of the evidence, searching for more evidence with digital investigation phases, crime scene reconstruction, and then the presentation of the complete theory. This is as shown in the diagram below.

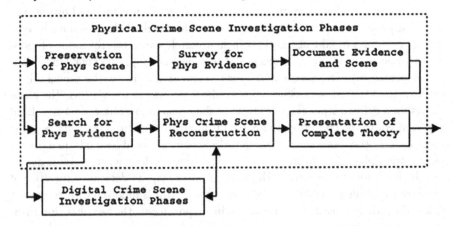

The last group of phases is the digital crime scene investigation. This phase is what is centered on the digital side of the investigation. It looks at every device in an investigation as a crime scene on its own and seeks to retrieve data from it. Like the physical phase, the digital phase has six phases as well. These are as shown in the diagram below.

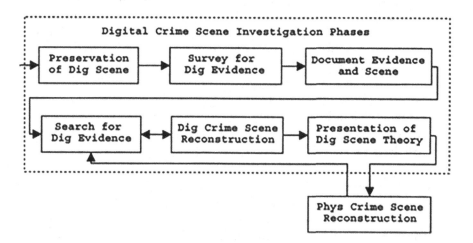

The last phase of the model is the review phase that seeks to enhance the model over time. The review phase includes the review of all the processes followed in the investigation process and finding points of improvement.

There are other models, but these are the main ones that have continually been used by law enforcement agencies. The newer models are specific to different types of technologies such as cloud, Internet of Things, and data mining. However, their applicability is only limited to the technologies that they cannot be used for other types of forensics.

Forensic Toolkit

To enhance the effectiveness of forensic investigations, investigators at times have to turn on some toolkits designed for this purpose. These toolkits enable them to gather evidence faster and automate some processes. There are a few tools that have been developed for this purpose. However, the one that stands out and is mostly applied by investigators is the FTK. The FTK is a software made by AccessData specifically for doing digital forensics.

FTK is said to be able to do fast searches on data and also to fasten the process of analyzing data sets. The main technique that allows this is the upfront indexing of data thus removing the delays occasioned by other searching tools and techniques. The tool can fetch out details from huge data sets quicker than any other tool according to the information provided by the creators. The following are the main selling points of the FTK for forensic investigations.

- Fast speeds with stability—the tool is greatly praised for being extremely fast. It is said to be the only forensic tool that can take advantage of multiple cores on a computer processor. Therefore, it is able to leverage all the available computer resources leading to a faster execution than other tools.
- Fast searches—with the upfront indexing of data, the tool can perform searches and filtering of data quickly. It also removes the need for having duplicate files since it can analyze files directly from their sources.
- Database driven—FTK uses a shared case database to store data in a central point. Therefore, when investigators are analyzing data, FTK will store it in a central point for quicker and easier analysis. This helps solve the issue of working with different data sets in the same investigation. It also helps investigators that are not working from the same place physically as all of them will have access to the same data.

FTK is not limited to searching through data, it comes with other capabilities. The tool can be used to crack passwords. If during investigations there are some locked files that bear essential data, investigators can use this tool to crack the password and open the file. This is very useful especially when a suspect is not cooperative and will not open files on his or her computer. The tool can also analyze emails. With access to the email dump, the tool will fish out details that one is searching for. If it is a word, a number, or a phrase, the tool will extract it from the data dump. The following are the components of the FTK:

- Email analysis—this toolkit is used when dealing with email data. As mentioned before, FTK will enable investigators to analyze volumes of emails and search for characters, phrases, or numbers that they seek for in emails. The tool is able to parse emails making it possible for analysis to be done even at an IP address level.
- File decryption—it is common for investigators to find encrypted files in the course of their investigations. The creators say that file decryption has come to be the most used functionality of the tool. FKT is able to decrypt files and also crack into password-protected files.
- Data carving—the FTK has an advanced system for searching through files. It can search through them based on different properties such as their sizes or even pixels.
- Web viewing—this component is mostly used for court purposes and to ensure that every legal aspect is followed. It grants a web-based view of evidence that is being analyzed to attorneys. If some operations are deemed illegal, attorneys can advise.
- Malware detection—FTK comes with a malware detection component called Cerberus. Some suspects may keep their laptops laden with malware such that when they are being analyzed or data is being retrieved from them, they

can derail the process by infecting files. Cerberus comes with the abilities to sniff out malware so that files are not destroyed.

- Imager—the FTK imager is a component that allows investigators to view and operate on image files retrieved from suspect devices. It is a normal practice for investigators to obtain image files of systems that they are investigating and run analysis on these images instead of running them directly on the device.

FTK is a premium tool that is sold by AccessData. However, the company gives a free trial for both the FTK toolkit and the FTK imager. The imager will work free for an unlimited amount of time, but the toolkit will expire if the user does not pay for a license key. It is a worthy buy for investigators, and it can make the forensic investigation exercise simpler.

Anti-Forensics Analysis

Digital forensic investigations can be hampered by some techniques designed to make it significantly harder to investigate certain files and programs. These techniques are as follows.

VM and Sandbox Detection

Virtual Machine (VM) and Sandbox detection are commonly used techniques to avoid analysis. To add some perspective, it is important to look back at a 2017 ransomware attack that affected 150 countries called WannaCry. To prevent analysis, WannaCry came with techniques to stop execution when it detected that it was in a sandbox or a virtual environment. By ceasing its functions, it was hard for analysts to find out the behavior of the ransomware. However, it was still analyzed using static analysis which involved the direct analysis of the code instead of the analysis of behavior. There are suspects that have tools that can do the same. When investigators get hold of these tools, they simply hibernate when they are run on virtual machines or sandbox environments. When this happens, the solution is to either analyze the raw code or run the tool on a sacrificial machine.

Search Engine Characteristics

To prevent the discovery of certain data by search engines, some suspects make data dynamic. Therefore, it is only generated when certain inputs are provided. An analyst who is not aware of this will visit a website and find nothing. At the same time, the suspect will visit the same website and provide some inputs and then data will be generated. It is an effective method of hiding sensitive data such as one that can be used as incriminating evidence.

Summary of the Chapter

This chapter has focused on the digital forensic exercises that are carried out for the purpose of obtaining evidence to prosecute suspects. The chapter has tied its discussions to real-world cases that have featured the same forensic exercises such as the arrest of the owner of Silk Road 2, a successful dark net marketplace. The chapter has explained the roles that cryptocurrencies have played, thus, making digital forensic investigations on the dark web more complex. They have eliminated the money trail that investigators used to rely on to track down suspects. The chapter has also discussed how cryptocurrencies have been used for money laundering thus making it easy for cybercriminals to cleanse dirty money. There has been a detailed explanation of the forensic investigation scope and models. The chapter has looked at the steps involved in a forensic investigation. It has then looked at the commonly used forensic investigation models. The chapter has also highlighted the Forensic Toolkit or known as FTK which is a tool commonly used for investigations. Lastly, the evasion techniques used to derail investigators have been discussed.

Questions

1. Explain why the dark web is not 100% anonymous.
2. What significant advantages have cryptocurrencies given cybercriminals on the dark web?
3. Explain how money laundering was done before the invention of cryptocurrencies.
4. Explain the steps followed in forensic investigations.
5. Why is it important to obtain warrants and authorizations during evidence acquisition?
6. State three forensic investigation models used today.
7. State and explain one FTK.
8. How is VM and Sandbox detection used as an anti-forensics technique?
9. How can data be hidden from search engines?

Further Reading

The following are resources that can be used to gain more knowledge on this chapter:

https://arxiv.org/ftp/arxiv/papers/1708/1708.01730.pdf.
https://arxiv.org/ftp/arxiv/papers/1710/1710.08705.pdf.
https://graduate.norwich.edu/resources-msisa/articles-msisa/5-steps-for-conducting-computer-forensics-investigations/.

Chapter 10

Open Source Intelligence

Introduction

With the rise of cybersecurity threats, organizations are not completely sure of their security status owing to the fact that even large organizations have found themselves victims of cyberattacks. The main target for hackers is data which has grown in value and demand in the dark web. There have been security companies set up with the goal of monitoring the dark web for listings of stolen organizational data. They use a myriad of ways to collect intelligence on the dark web in an effort to protect their clients. Simply by gathering intelligence available from open source platforms, they are able to uncover cybersecurity risks that might arise from underground markets. Open source intelligence can be hard to obtain from the dark web due to the obvious reason of anonymity. This chapter will discuss the methods of collecting intelligence using open source methods and platforms. It will do so on the following topics:

- Forensic introduction
- Crypto market and cryptocurrencies in the dark web
- Forensic investigation scope and models
- Forensic toolkits
- Anti-forensics techniques.

What Is Open Source Intelligence?

Open source intelligence is information that is publically available. It is not classi-fied or put under constraints. The manner in which such information is produced or presented does not matter. The information is perceived to be free and within reach to everyone. However, this particular definition does not exactly match what open source intelligence is on the dark web. In the dark web, open source intelligence is information that is available on the dark web platforms free of charge. However, there are some challenges in accessing the information on the dark web since some special software is required. To access some type of data, the creation of user accounts on the dark web is necessary.

Information available free of charge is not particularly readily usable. This is because of the content. There is too much of it such that it is almost impossible to find out the useful information without further analysis. This is why there are several tools that have been created to help users create meaning out of open source intelligence. These tools are mostly used by researchers, penetration testers, and legal agencies when collecting information about specific people, threats, and organizations, among other things. Data gathering is central to the process of gathering intelligence. A lot of useful information could be obtained from open source intelligence if carefully examined. There are many digital footprints that can be left on public domains, and these can be exploited for good reasons. For instance, in the quest to find the founder of Silk Road 2, security agencies used open source intelligence. They were able to track the username of the suspected founder to a Bitcoin chat forum where he was asking for coding assistance. In the process of asking for assistance, the founder, Ross Ulbricht, left his real email on the platform. From here, legal agencies were able to investigate him further having discovered his real identity. If it was not for open source intelligence gathering, probably Ross Ulbricht would never have been associated with the Silk Road 2. Agencies would still be getting zero results using sophisticated tools to breach the Tor network.

Security Intelligence and Its Challenges

There has been an increase in the number of threats that organizations are facing. This has prompted organizations to diversify their protection mechanisms. Previously, the focus was only put on cyber defense to deter attacks from occurring. However, this has proven to be inefficient as attackers have continually launched sophisticated attacks that have succeeded in breaching organizations. Additionally, the human element in the organization has caused a general weakness in all organizations. With perfected skills in social engineering, attackers can find ways to breach many organizations even without having to use a hacking tool. An attack might only consist of a simple email to an organizational worker. This is why organizations are diversifying their security portfolios and investing in two things. The first one is cyber resilience. This is aimed at making an organization capable of withstanding an attack without being overwhelmed. For instance, due to the rise in denial-of-service (DoS) attacks, organizations can invest in having additional processing capabilities in alternative sites such that if a DoS attack happens, normal users are still served as the DoS attack is handled. The second security mitigation that organizations are investing in is security intelligence. Instead of being sitting ducks, organizations want to be in the know of the threats facing them and how they can prevent them even before they happen. This is why some organizations have had clean records with regard to cyberattacks. They have put resources into getting threat intelligence of threats that have not yet been used.

One of the main focus points concerning obtaining threat intelligence is the dark web. This is where most of the threats arise from, and thus, it is prudent to gather intelligence from there. The dark web has formed a breeding ground for many malicious programs and codes that have been used in attacks. Even worse, one does not need to be an expert in coding to become a hacker, there are listings on the dark web for malicious code on sale. The following are the prevailing issues on the dark web.

Cybercrime-as-a-Service

On the dark web, for one to become a cybercriminal, only $10 is required to get one's hands on distributed denial-of-service (DDoS) botnets to perform an attack against an organization. There are ready hacking groups on the dark web charging different rates to hack organizations for other parties. Therefore, a disgruntled employee could just head to the dark web and give insider details about the organizations to be used for hacking and then pay the hackers. It therefore no longer requires technical training to hack, there are expert cybercriminals that can do just that at a price. This is a worrying fact for many organizations. It has been observed that cybercriminals for hire are ruthless and take their contracts seriously. This is because they want to earn reputation on the dark web so that they can get more valued hacking contracts. They will, therefore, unleash a wave of relentless attacks ranging from social engineering to DDoS. There are other cybercriminals for hire that just sell their malicious codes to script kiddies. Script kiddies are on the rise, and they are simply common people that do not have expertise in hacking and they only hack by buying already created exploits. Script kiddies can be a menace to organizations as they may obtain different types of exploit tools and continually use them against different organizations until they land on something valuable.

Based on the reported incidents so far, it seems that DDoS attacks are being preferred. An investigation into the dark web markets revealed that hiring a botnet to perform a DDoS attack starts at only $10 for an hour. A whole day might cost up to $200. There are merciless hackers that hire these botnets for several days. For instance, Kaspersky has reported that in the first quarter of 2018, there was a DDoS attack against an organization that lasted for 12 days and this was the longest attack reported in years. According to cybersecurity experts, DDoS attacks seem to be taking a while longer than in previous years.

Ultimately, cybercrime-as-a-service has now lowered the entry barrier for hacking. More hackers will be heading to the dark web to offer their services for hire for quick money. It can be likened to the taxi company called Uber where one can sign up their cars to be used as taxis just to make some cash. Since the demand for hackers is there, there is no doubt that the number of hacking incidents due to cybercrime-as-a-service will only go up. To survive this, organizations definitely need threat intelligence on the types of services for hire being sold and how to prepare themselves for such.

Rising Return on Investment for Cyber Weapons on the Dark Web

Another concern for organizations that amplifies the security threat is that the dark web is the rising Return on Investment (ROI) for cybercrime weapons. Unlike normal weapons, cybercrime weapons do not cost much. The section above has mentioned that a botnet for performing DDoS attacks costs only $10.

The consequences of the $10 attack may be devastating to a company that handles very many requests at any given time since all these will not be handled. A good example is the DDoS attack on DynDNS which is a leading DNS resolution company. The few hours attack caused global implications and some websites could not be accessed. There are several factors within the deep web that are making the ROI of cyber weapons to go up. The first one is the low barrier to entry. As discussed before, one does not need technical training to be a hacker today. One does not even need to have any sophisticated programs to attack. There are even free tools that are available that can be used for attacks. Another reason for the rising ROI is the low-risk high-returns nature of hacking today. Since the hacking tools are readily available, there are cloaking mechanisms by operating through the dark web and there are money-laundering services for the proceeds of hacking, cybercrime has become a profitable venture for some. The maturing cybercrime market is also a contributor to increased profitability from hacking. Everything is all set up in the dark web, ranging from hacking tools to the markets to sell things such as hacked personal data, bank records, and much more. Therefore, with the rising ROI of cybercrime, it is only prudent for organizations to prepare themselves for any event. This is why having security intelligence is paramount to ensure cybersecurity efforts are targeted at the current threats.

Dark Web Security Intelligence Companies

There are companies such as SurfWatch that charge clients to collect intelligence on the dark web and inform when they find something of concern. These companies help organizations in a number of ways. To begin with, they can protect a brand's reputation. For instance, the hacking of Yahoo followed by the sale of the hacked user data spoilt the name and reputation of Yahoo. There are very few people that still use Yahoo email in the face of more secure competitors such as Gmail. If Yahoo had a security intelligence collection strategy or had outsourced a company to do that, the stolen data that had been put for sale would have been detected early and the appropriate mitigations implemented. Alongside bad reputation is customer loyalty which these intelligence companies claim to protect. It is as simple as it sounds, if a company is not found out to be a victim of hacking, customers will not abandon it due to fears of losing personal data. Another focus of security intelligence gathering companies is to protect the intellectual property of a company. Even when a hack has taken place and data stolen, these companies will hunt it down in the depths of the deep web with hopes of finding someone that has listed it for sale. Once it is located, there are still hopes, though slim, of controlling the illegal redistribution of that data.

Intelligence Gathering Focus

There are many factors that are considered when dark web intelligence is being gathered. These factors are discussed below.

Hacking-as-a-Service

This is whereby the hackers that offer their services for hire on the dark web are focused on. The goal is to find out the techniques and tools that they may have or use in hacking. This intelligence will inform an organization of the types of defenses that they ought to put in place.

Exploits for Sale

The dark web is known for having markets that sell hacking exploits. These are bought by hackers that do not necessarily have technical know-how of creating their own exploits. Nevertheless, once they get their hands on these exploits, they pose a great threat to organizations. Therefore, part of the intelligence gathering process will include finding information about the specific exploits that are on sale on the dark web. The foreknowledge of the tools that hackers can get their hands on can help the information security team in an organization prepare for such attacks.

Vulnerabilities for Sale

In 2017, it is said that the NSA had found a vulnerability in Windows that could allow programs to issue commands with admin privileges. This vulnerability was exploitable, and even before Windows had patched it fully, a ransomware called WannaCry was released and it exploited the same vulnerability. Sold at varying prices, the dark web has different vulnerabilities on sale for different programs and operating systems. The charges go up with how recent a vulnerability has been discovered. The most expensive vulnerabilities are the ones sold for zero-day exploits. These are vulnerabilities that have not yet been discovered or patched. For instance, the Stuxnet attack on the Iranian nuclear facility featured several zero-day exploits. While dissecting the malware, experts said that this was a tell-tale sign that Stuxnet was sponsored since it was simply too expensive for a normal hacker to use up more than one zero-day exploit in a single attack while they can sell the vulnerability at a significantly high price on the dark web. The advantage of obtaining intelligence related to vulnerabilities that are on sale is that organizations can start preparing their systems to prevent such attacks.

Threat intelligence gatherers on the dark web have a task of finding out the new vulnerabilities that are in the hands of cybercriminals. In 2017, for instance, 12,517 vulnerabilities had been listed by the National Vulnerability Database. A comparative analysis by dark web intelligence researchers showed that 700 of these had already been listed for sale on the dark web even before they were published. It was also observed that there were 91 sellers that had the most number of vulnerability listings on the dark web. Clearly, these actors must have had multiple sources of vulnerabilities, and if well investigated, they could have possibly led law enforcement agencies to their sources.

Once a vulnerability is put on sale on the dark web, a race starts between the cybercriminals and cybersecurity personnel responsible for creating and deploying patches. The following is a diagrammatic depiction of the race.

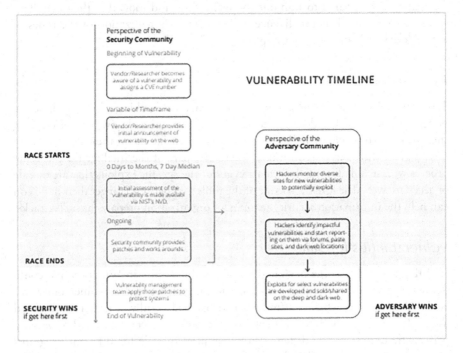

Stolen Intellectual Property

This has become an area of interest for many organizations that collect intelligence from the dark web. There are companies contracted to keep an eye on the dark web for listings of stolen data. When hackers have finally listed it for sale, the victim organization is notified. Sometimes, an organization is not sure that data has been stolen until they are notified that part of their sensitive data has been listed on the dark web. There are other hackers that seem to be focused on gathering business secrets. These are using them for economic gains. For instance, if company X steals business secrets from its close rival, it will be able to use these secrets to quash the success of the rivals. Also, if an overseas company steals the design prototypes of a US-based company, it can produce similar but counterfeit products based on the prototypes and sell at a very low price. The US-based company will only realize later on that there are counterfeits of its genuine products that are making it lose business as well as reputation. A good example is the shoe industry where leading market players such as Nike and Adidas have had their shoe designs copied by counterfeiters that sell similar designs that are counterfeit and cheaper than the originals.

Stolen Financial Data

It is a sensitive case when customers' financial data is stolen from an organization. The victim will be ready to use a lot of resources to protect this data, but when the worst happens and it is hacked, it becomes a big disaster. Quantifying the losses that will be accrued from fines, lawsuits, and lost customers, it is a painful ordeal that an organization will go through. This is the reason why there are many intelligence gathering companies on the dark web that are keeping eyes on financial data listed for sale.

Stolen Personally Identifiable Information

This information is so sensitive such that legislators have drafted tough laws for collecting and storing this type of information. Some types of data that are referred to as personally identifiable information (PII) include Social Security Numbers and medical records. The enforcement of tough legislations for organizations that collect and store PII data has not kept hackers from stealing it. This type of data is sold on the dark web at high prices. It can be used for many purposes such as tax fraud, identity theft, and extortion especially for notable people that would not want some of their information exposed.

Spam and Phishing Campaigns

Previously, phishing as an attack method was not much regarded as a big threat. This is because phishing emails could easily be detected from the spelling mistakes and lack of official formatting. The likes of the Nigerian Prince scam could only net a few people since they had been used over and over again. However, a new breed of phishers has come up and with a lot of force. In the United States, many people have been scammed by phishers when filing tax returns. Account holders of online banking platforms and systems such as PayPal have also become victims of these new phishers. The rising success rates of phishing today can be attributed to the dark web. There are dark web markets selling exact replicas of corporate emails formatted with corporate logos and similar content that can be used for phishing. For instance, the FBI and PayPal warned users of phishing emails claiming to be from PayPal bearing the same characteristics as official PayPal emails. These are the types of emails that are being sold on the dark web and with little expertise, a would-be hacker can send these emails to different recipients and successfully scam them. For instance, the American Internal Revenue Service scam known as IRS scam of 2017 was traced back to an Indian who was simply sending the well-formatted emails to US citizens. It is assumed that he had accessed their data from sources such as stolen medical or government records. The importance of getting intelligence on the scams and phishing emails for sale on the dark web is that an organization can warn its employees in time not to fall for these simple social engineering attacks.

The Value for Dark Web Threat Intelligence

The intelligence gathered from the dark web is directly applicable in cybersecurity efforts. It can be used for a broad scope of applications ranging from crime prevention to improving cybersecurity strategies in organizations. For instance, if a medical facility identifies that some of its patient data has been stolen, it can start the process of analyzing the deep web markets for listings of stolen medical records. It can then initiate mitigation measures when they find a seller with such data. There have been successful mitigation measures taken by organizations in recent past. For instance, a software company was recently able to prevent the sale of its Enterprise resource planning (ERP) software source code on the dark web. This source code could be analyzed by hackers for vulnerabilities that can be used to hack into organizations that use it. Thorough research into the incident showed that the software was being sold by an insider that wanted to make quick money. The source code had been listed for sale at $50,000 since it was from a renowned multinational software company.

There have been many other related cases where organizations have turned to intelligence gathering companies and law enforcement agencies to prevent stolen data from being sold on the dark web. It is a norm these days that any stolen data will eventually show up on the dark web since it is the ready market for that type of data. It is, therefore, an indispensable source for web threat intelligence.

Challenges of Security Intelligence

The cyberspace is currently filled with cyber threats. On the dark web, there are more threats that need to be monitored. However, one of the biggest challenges that organizations face is which threats to focus on. With their finite resources, they cannot possibly cover all the threats that are listed on the dark web. They can end up tying lots of resources to threats that will never be used against them. There are also false positives and fake threats. The dark web is not genuine of places to buy things because sellers have no obligation to be accountable. They may, therefore, advertise vulnerabilities and exploit toolkits that are false. Therefore, finding actual threat intelligence or references to them is quite challenging. Those that are found are normally in hundreds of thousands of messages shared on the dark web. Some of these chat rooms cannot even be accessed by researchers and law enforcement agencies. When the open chat forums are accessed, there is a lot of content to be scanned. It may also turn out to be irrelevant information and thus a wastage of resources.

Another challenge is that the process of getting threat intelligence from the dark web is itself complex and time-consuming. One needs to go to the depths of each hidden market. There are some markets that one cannot get into without invites or membership. Some organizations may give up at such stages; hence, the need for paid experts to handle the intelligence gathering work. Inexperienced people might also put the organizations that they are working for at risk. This is because some markets operate in a mechanism where the customer asks what they wish to have and is told whether it is or is not available. In an unfortunate incident, an inexperienced researcher enquired on penetration testing solutions for an infrastructure that was only known to be used on a few corporates. In a few hours, the organization he was researching for received a large number of malicious requests targeting the same thing he was asking about.

This shows that the dark web is potentially dangerous even to gather threat intelligence from. Therefore, researchers try as much as possible to avoid revealing certain information when gathering intelligence from the dark web. It is best to observe by reading and listening than to directly engage sellers and buyers on these platforms. There is sufficient intelligence that can be obtained from observation without having to engage actors on the dark web. However, experts who know how to approach the actors on the dark web without startling them or asking direct questions can be paid to do the threat intelligence collection work.

Lastly, there is a challenge of language barriers on the dark web since it is an expansive space on the internet. Those that end up selling stolen data on the dark web may not be from the same country as the victims. They may not even use the same language. For example, a US company could be hacked by Chinese hackers who list the stolen data on the dark web in Chinese. Investigators may search for keywords in English yet the hackers have listed the stolen data in another language. Therefore, searches may return no findings while the data being sought for is on the dark web but listed in a different language. The dark web is accessed in very many countries; therefore, covering all languages in searches is also a challenge.

Open Source Intelligence Monitoring Tools

The following are tools that can be used to analyze open source information.

Maltego

This is a tool that has been developed by Paterva that is commonly used in the cybersecurity industry. It runs on Linux and is an inbuilt program in Kali Linux OS variant. Maltego is known to carry out reconnaissance against a target. A user has to register with Paterva in order to be able to create machines to run transforms against a target. A machine should be configured and then started on the software so that it can start its operations. Maltego analyzes various footprints about a target. It can be anything ranging from a domain name to an IP address. The software can identify phrases as well contained in any amount of publically available data sources. Maltego is good at digging information about a target in depth. It can scour the internet searching for a certain phrase until it finds a match. For instance, if it was searching for stolen data listed on the internet, a user can just give a phrase such as "Stolen data XYZ bank." Any listing found with such a name on the internet will be flagged by the software.

Recon-Ng

This is another useful open source intelligence analysis tool. It also runs on Linux and comes with Kali Linux. Recon-Ng is made up of several modules, and it resembles the architecture of Metasploit.

```
[recon-ng][default] > show modules

  Discovery
  ---------
    discovery/info_disclosure/cache_snoop
    discovery/info_disclosure/interesting_files

  Exploitation
  ------------
    exploitation/injection/command_injector
    exploitation/injection/xpath_bruter

  Import
  ------
    import/csv_file
    import/list

  Recon
  -----
    recon/companies-contacts/bing_linkedin_cache
    recon/companies-contacts/jigsaw/point_usage
    recon/companies-contacts/jigsaw/purchase_contact
    recon/companies-contacts/jigsaw/search_contacts
    recon/companies-contacts/linkedin_auth
    recon/companies-multi/github_miner
    recon/companies-multi/whois_miner
    recon/contacts-contacts/mailtester
    recon/contacts-contacts/mangle
    recon/contacts-contacts/unmangle
```

The figure above shows a screenshot of Recon-Ng. There are different modules categorized. There are those that are categorized under discovery. These modules are for finding files or content of interest. There are modules under the exploitation heading. These are aimed at accessing content hidden by other tools. There is the import module for importing chunks of data into the tool for processing. Lastly, there is the most important category and that is Recon. This is where most of the action takes place when open source intelligence is being sought after. Probably if the law enforcement agencies that were looking for Ross Ulbricht used this tool, they would have used the Recon modules it provides. The Recon module covers many sources such as Who.is, Github, LinkedIn, and purchase contacts. In the case of Ross Ulbricht, it is said that the email the law enforcement agencies found was traced to a LinkedIn user called Ross Ulbricht. His profile had written content that was associated with what he was doing on the dark web with Silk Road 2. This tool can achieve the same result, it can resolve an email to a real user account on social media networks such as LinkedIn.

Recon-Ng works through workspaces whereby operations relating to a specific target will be done inside one workspace. Recon-Ng mostly works using URLs to where it should fetch the content to analyze. Therefore, when a user creates a workspace, they should provide a domain name with the suspected content. The different modules can extract more information about the domain and also from the domain. The tool can even use search engines such as Bing to find information related to the target domain. For instance, the Bing_LinkedIn_cache is a module used to mostly fetch emails related to a certain domain on the internet and the LinkedIn social network. Other modules can retrieve more types of information regarding a target from the open source.

theHarvester

It is a tool used to collect information about a target. It also runs on Linux and comes with Kali Linux OS. The tool is very good at gathering information related to an email address and domain names. The following is a screenshot that shows some of the options available in theHarvester.

```
Usage: theharvester options

       -d: Domain to search or company name
       -b: data source: google, googleCSE, bing, bingapi, pgp, linkedin,
                         google-profiles, jigsaw, twitter, googleplus, all

       -s: Start in result number X (default: 0)
       -v: Verify host name via dns resolution and search for virtual hosts
       -f: Save the results into an HTML and XML file (both)
       -n: Perform a DNS reverse query on all ranges discovered
       -c: Perform a DNS brute force for the domain name
       -t: Perform a DNS TLD expansion discovery
       -e: Use this DNS server
       -l: Limit the number of results to work with(bing goes from 50 to 50 results,
           google 100 to 100, and pgp doesn't use this option)
       -h: use SHODAN database to query discovered hosts
```

The tool can work with many data sources and is effective at collecting information about a target even on social media platforms. Sometimes, hackers decide to dump stolen data on social media platforms. This tool can find such data by searching through popular social media networks such as Twitter. The users of this tool appreciate its ability to extract information from open sources and the additional features it has to analyze such content.

Shodan

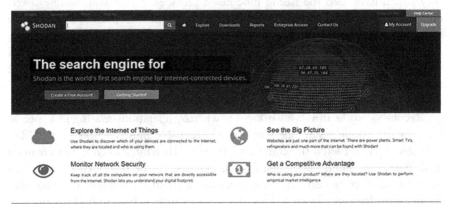

This has been named the search engine for hackers and there is a good reason why. Shodan is a goldmine for anyone wishing to trace digital footprints of a user, organization, or data. Shodan surpasses the capabilities of normal search engines such as Google in that it can search perform search queries on the dark web. The search engine has been put to use to search for servers, webcams, and other devices connected to the internet. It runs continuously and collects much information about the devices and services that are connected to the internet. This makes it a great open source threat intelligence collection tool. A quick search on Shodan can reveal traffic lights, CCTVs, and Internet of Things devices that are connected to the internet. It is, therefore, a potentially dangerous tool in the wrong hands. This is why it is touted as a hacker's search engine. There have been reports of users that have been able to find systems for water parks, gas stations, and a crematorium. The tool directed them directly to these systems on the internet. Expert users have been able to find control systems for nuclear power plants. Some of the discovered systems had no security access controls built into them, thus, any user could go on and directly manipulate them. The following article explains some of the things that have been discovered using Shodan.

A quick search for "default password" reveals countless printers, servers, and system control devices that use "admin" as their username and "1234" as their password. Many more connected systems require no credentials at all—all you need is a web browser to connect to them.

In a talk given at last year's Defcon cybersecurity conference, independent security penetration tester Dan Tentler demonstrated how he used Shodan to find control systems for evaporative coolers, pressurized water heaters, and garage doors.

He found a car wash that could be turned on and off and a hockey rink in Denmark that could be defrosted with a click of a button. A city's entire traffic control system was connected to the internet and could be put into "test mode" with a single command entry. And he also found a control system for a hydroelectric plant in France with two turbines generating 3 MW each.

Source: http://money.cnn.com/2013/04/08/technology/security/shodan/

In the search for open source intelligence, Shodan can be considered as a great tool. It can help find out a lot of information that is inaccessible using normal search engines. People make many mistakes when connecting devices to the internet including many IT departments. They are too lazy to change default passwords or put in place access controls for systems that they connect to the internet.

The founder of Shodan has had to make some modifications to prevent the overuse of his tool for malicious purposes. Without a Shodan account, search queries only return ten results. With an account, the search queries will return up to 50 results.

The tool has been used by cybersecurity researchers, law enforcement agencies, penetration testers, and inevitably cybercriminals to quickly access open source intelligence. The tool performs search queries on so many parts of the internet such that it is hard for one to miss a result for search queries. Security professionals are trying to alert those whose devices are accessible via Shodan to implement access control mechanisms to prevent hackers from taking control. The usefulness of the tool both for legal and illegal purposes cannot be discounted (Figures 10.1 and 10.2).

Google Dorks

This is not technically a different search engine than the normal Google. It refers to the use of advanced operators in search queries to make Google return specific or hidden results. These advanced operators can narrow a search query or specify the types of results to be returned by the search engine. It is also quite dangerous if in the wrong hands. It has been proven that advanced operators can be used for hacking purposes. The operators can be used to make Google show hidden systems and services running on a particular domain. These are things that are typically

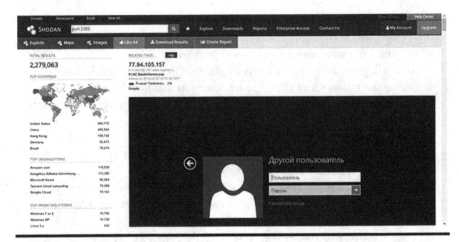

Figure 10.1 Shodan showing a login interface of a Windows-based server connected to the internet.

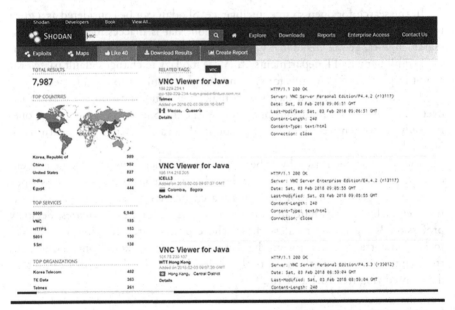

Figure 10.2 Shodan showing results for a search query for VNC (Virtual Network Computing) viewers on the internet. (More examples generated by the open source community can be accessed from: https://exploit-db.com/google-hacking-database/2/.)

hidden by the normal Google search. Table 10.1 lists some real-life examples of Google Hacking queries.

It might be useless to run these queries since they will only display the login pages. However, the fortunate thing is that many IT departments do not change

Table 10.1   Table Showing Examples of Google Hacking Commands

Date Tested	Command	Type of Results Expected
2018-06-04	inurl:/CMSPages/logon ext:aspx	Pages containing login portals
2018-06-04	inurl:/index.php/login intext:Concrete. CMS	Pages containing login portals
2018-06-04	"Powered by Open Source Chat Platform Rocket.Chat."	Pages containing login portals
2018-06-04	inurl:'listprojects.spr'	Sensitive directories
2018-06-04	inurl:'/blog/Account/login.aspx'	Pages containing login portals
2018-06-04	inurl:composer.json codeigniter -site:github.com	Web server detection
2018-06-04	allintext:'HttpFileServer 2.3k'	Sensitive directories
2018-05-31	intext:2001.-.2018.umbraco.org ext:aspx	Pages containing login portals
2018-05-29	AndroidManifest ext:xml -github -gitlab –googlesource	Files containing sensitive information
2018-05-25	allintitle:"Flexi Press System"	Pages containing login portals

their default passwords. Therefore, for each of these pages, one can just go trying common default username–password combinations such as "admin" for username and "123456" for password. According to password profilers "123456" is still the most commonly used password.

The following are even more malicious queries that can find more sensitive authentication details in domains:

"authentication failure; logname=" ext:log - Finds log files for failed logins, containing usernames and login paths.
inurl:/profile.php?lookup=1 - Will help find administrator name on most websites and forums. Very helpful in brute forcing.

Google Hacking or Dorking has been used for a long time to find open source intelligence. The fact that it utilizes an already powerful platform, Google search, this technique of gathering intelligence is reliable. It is very good at uncovering files hidden on the internet. For instance, if we are collecting intelligence on someone called Mark Weins, Google Hacking can help find his physical address, email address, phone number, organizations he is affiliated with, and even his CV. It is therefore very powerful. Hackers also use this technique mostly to find out misconfigured devices on the internet such as servers, printers, and CCTV cameras. In some cases, this mechanism can be used to unearth login credentials insecurely stored on web servers on notepads and SQL databases if they are not secured.

Data Gathering

Gathering data on the dark web is not a simple exercise. Many organizations fail to collect data on the dark web themselves and thus have to rely on third-party companies to do that. This section covers some of the ways that can be sued to gather data on the dark web and also on other open source platforms.

Chat Rooms

This is normally the main focus for researchers, law enforcement agencies, and companies. Information shared on chat rooms is very useful for intelligence gathering purposes. This data can be extracted for deeper analysis. Physical observation might be useful, but an automated analysis is much better. Most organizations pay companies to listen for the mention of their products, names of executives, or even the organizational names in these forums. When this happens, there are several possibilities. The first one is that the dark web users might be discussing on vulnerabilities discovered on a certain organization's system. For instance, if Amazon is mentioned, the topic of discussion may be a vulnerability that can enable hackers to get into Amazon and steal data. They may also be planning on effective strategies that can be used to attack the mentioned company. There have been some incidents where attackers have sought help in forums to attack a specific company. For instance, phishers normally post asking for expert HTML email creators and excellent in Photoshop to create clone emails that will be used for phishing. After the discussions are complete, the chatter left on the chat platform is sufficient evidence to warn a company that an attack is being plotted against it. Another possible case is that the dark web users may be discussing the sale of data owned by the mentioned company. They may be chatting on the sale of a data dump that was stolen from an organization's database. It is also probable that when an executive's name is mentioned, there may be plots to hack him or her. Business email compromise is a phishing scam where hackers first compromise an executive's email account and then use it to send emails to junior employees in accounts or finance departments to channel some money to overseas accounts. Therefore, if there are mentions of an executive of an organization, there are chances that an attack is being plotted against him or her.

Direct Conversations

Data can be gathered through direct conversations with actors on the dark web. This is however a risky venture since one may be coerced by the actors to give out some sensitive information. Law enforcement agencies have been known to use this tactic, especially when gathering data to be used as evidence in court against actors on the dark web. Therefore, this is a highly practical method of gathering data. All a researcher should know is the right people to talk to. There are famed usernames for releasing very powerful malware on the dark web for sale. These are contacts of interest. Therefore, one should start a chat with them as if interested in buying the newest and most powerful malware.

However, it is good for caution to be exercised when contacting these actors. This is because they can trace back the customer if they detect that they were simply using them. There is an instance that was mentioned before in this chapter where a non-experienced researcher asked a threat actors direct questions about a vulnerability that was only present on a system rolled out on very few firms. The threat actor was able to trace the organization and what followed was a wave of malicious activity targeted at the organization.

Threat actors on the dark web are experts in their fields, and it is therefore paramount that one is extremely cautious when engaging with them. They also hold very important pieces of information. They can be used to determine the new malware that is available or is being created. They can also be used to find out the targeted organizations since they have insider information. Getting into conversations with a few of these actors could yield a lot of information that can be used for security purposes such as informing organizations on what threats they should safeguard against. By appearing as a very serious client, the threat actors will not hesitate to let out some sensitive information such as exploits they are making or those that they have already made. It is therefore a great place to gather data to be used as intelligence. The good thing about direct conversations with the threat actors is that there is not much noise. Therefore, it is not going to be a big challenge to filter through the conversation to get the useful information. This is a challenge experienced in chat rooms where one has to filter through so much noise and useless messages to get to those messages that hold useful data.

Market Listings

Media houses discovered that Yahoo's user data had been stolen after it was found listed on dark web markets. Yahoo had not openly come out to declare that it had been breached and data was stolen. This is, therefore, a very important source of data in the markets. The challenge with markets is that some are restricted when it comes to entry. They operate using invites whereby a member or the admin of the market has to invite one to be able to view items that are put out for sale. However, there are still many dark web black markets that do not have these restrictions.

They have sellers that list out everything they are offering for sale to the public. The public in this context means all the users on the dark web. These black markets can help organizations track data that has already been stolen. In the case of Yahoo, it was too late to stop the data from being sold when it was discovered on the dark web. There had already been three buyers, and the listing was still active. The initial price of the data was $300,000, and this is what each of the three early buyers paid. Even after the hack was exposed, the stolen user data was still listed for sale, but its price had been reduced. Yahoo was at first denying that the data listed was from its data centers until later on, they accepted the claims.

There have been incidents where organizations have salvaged their data before it was bought by other parties. There is a common monitoring technique where organizations pay third parties to monitor the dark web for listings of their data on the dark web. When a listing happens, law enforcement agencies are informed to try and salvage the data before it is sold to a buyer on the dark web.

Apart from getting information about the stolen data that has been listed on the dark web, market listings can also be used to get information about the malware that are in circulation. The origin of most malware is the dark web where malware creators sell them to cybercriminals. As mentioned before, cybercriminals do not need to be experts in programming. Malware are available for sale at different prices on the dark web. Therefore, if a researcher could pretend to be a cybercriminal looking for malware, he or she can gather a lot of information on the dark web. The sellers will have given descriptions of the different malware and the systems that they can target.

Advanced Search Queries

A list of software that can be used to gather data was given earlier. It included two tools that were actually search engines, Google Dorking and Shodan. These are very useful tools for collecting data. Google Dorking or Google Hacking is effective when it comes to tracing the identities of individuals since it spans over all the data that the most powerful search engine has crawled. With the right operators, crucial data hidden on the internet will be churned out. Just that the normal Google search engine does not return results that are not on the surface web does not mean that its depth is so limited. It has crawled very many resources on the internet and will easily point out where a certain name or username was mentioned on the internet. The challenge is that Google Dorking is not very effective for information deep within dark webs. This is where Shodan comes in. Shodan is known to index data that is on the dark web. This is why the developers take the caution of limiting the number of results that can be returned to users.

Challenges in Gathering Data from the Dark Web

The process of gathering data from the dark web is not as simple as it may seem. It is a big challenge and that is why organizations opt to leave it to expert third-party companies. There are many hardships and complexities that are involved that require both human expertise and powerful tools. Organizations that opt to gather data using their own staff often fail due to the challenges listed below:

- Linguistic and cultural expertise—the dark web is not isolated to English speakers. There are Russian users, Chinese users, and many others from different countries. For most of these users, there are the ones that are most influential or dangerous and should be monitored. This, therefore, calls for the monitoring of a swath of languages such as Chinese, Russian, and Arabic, among others. On top of these, there are incidents where researchers will need to have the cultural expertise of the group that they are monitoring. They need to understand the slang used and the social norms. This is especially relevant when data is to be gathered by either monitoring chat rooms or directly engaging with the threat actors. If one is not knowledgeable of the slang used, they may fail to gather some important pieces of data. The lack of knowledge of cultural norms may upset the threat actors. This is a big challenge for organizations since they do not factor in this when doing their own research or data collection on the dark web.
- Determination of actionable intelligence—the dark web has highly relevant intelligence, but it is not going to be served on a silver platter to the researchers. It will often be covered upon layers of noise and irrelevant information. Without experience with data gathering on the dark web, one can end up wasting lots of resources on noise that will not benefit the organization. This may lead to the loss of trust by financiers thus the calling off of the data gathering efforts on the dark web.
- Penetrating trusted environments—all marketplaces are not the same. They will also not welcome every visitor with open arms since the FBI and other law enforcement agencies are known to masquerade as buyers and sellers. The marketplaces where most illegal of activities take place tend to be highly secured. Not everyone can get in. Those that have access are those that have established trust. There is a vetting process and it may include the number of years one has existed on the dark web space or the type of posts that one has made. Suspicious accounts and those that are deemed new to the dark web can hardly get access to these markets of interest. Therefore, there are limits to where some users can get and unfortunately for organizations trying to gather intelligence for the first time, their new usernames will not be welcome in the trusted environments.
- Resources required—it is not a small task to gather actionable intelligence from the dark net. There are many resources that have to be put into it. The process of mining this part of the internet for intelligence is often resource-intensive. Special software and skilled labor often have to be employed. Expert intelligence gatherers on the dark web work full time alongside actors. An organization can hardly put the same efforts into gathering intelligence.

They are going to be using employee that work 9 AM to 5 PM, and their output is nothing compared to what experts can do. There are some market-places or rooms that one has to monitor continuously so that no piece of communication passes without being analyzed. There are some markets that run based on trust, and users that are available on regular basis are the only ones allowed to continue to access the markets. There are all sorts of legitimacy checks from sellers and buyers on the dark web to filter out actual customers from law enforcement agencies and researchers.

It is therefore very difficult for organizations to put up their own dark web intelligence-gathering teams. The data-gathering exercise itself is very challenging and resource intensive. It might seem that the companies specializing in doing this for others are having it easy. This may not be the fact. They may have had to keep an account active on the dark web for years for them to get enough trust by the actors to be able to access the most secret marketplaces. They may also have formed alliances and relationships on the dark web to be able to be kept in the know of the latest happenings. Thus, it is most advisable for organizations to hire outside experts to monitor and collect threat intelligence from the dark web. By doing so, they also avoid putting their own employees at risk. Instead, they will be using experts that have years of expertise on the dark web and very useful connections with threat actors. These are the right people to gather data and actionable intelligence.

Summary of the Chapter

This chapter has focused on the issue of open source intelligence with attention to the dark web. It has defined what open source intelligence is and has given real-world examples of how such intelligence has been useful. The chapter has then delved into security intelligence where it has explained the significance of the dark web when it comes to gathering threat intelligence. There has been a highlight on the companies that have been established to gather security intelligence for others on the dark web and alert them when something of interest comes up. The chapter has explained the areas where security intelligence focuses on. These areas are hacking-as-a-service, exploits for sale, vulnerabilities for sale, stolen intellectual property, stolen financial data, stolen PII, and lastly the phishing campaigns on sale. The importance of these areas of interest has been stated. Mostly, this is where actionable intelligence on relevant threats can be found. For hacking-as-a-service, vulnerabilities for sale and exploits for sale, the intelligence that is mostly gathered is that of the available and the upcoming threats that organizations have to prepare for. As for the stolen intellectual property, financial data and PII, the intelligence gathered is that of stolen data to enable organizations to try and mitigate the situation before the data is sold to other parties on the dark web. In some cases, organizations are able to stop the sale of their stolen data. As for the phishing scam, the intelligence gathered is on the techniques being used by phishers such as cloned emails and websites. The chapter has looked at the main challenges of gathering security intelligence.

A focus has been made on the open source intelligence monitoring tool. The chapter has listed five tools which are Maltego, Recon-Ng, theHarvester, Shodan, and Google Dorking. Shodan and Google Dorking are search engines capable of gathering open source intelligence. All the five tools have been explained in fine detail. Advanced queries that can be used for Google Dorking to reveal sensitive information have been provided as a proof of concept. Lastly, the chapter has gone into data gathering for open source intelligence. The different areas where data can be gathered have been stated. These include chat rooms, direct conversations, market listings, and search queries. The process of gathering data from these has been discussed individually. Accompanying this has been the highlight of the challenges that occur when gathering open source data. These challenges include the lack of linguistic expertise, the inability to determine actionable intelligence, accessing trusted environment, and resource restrictions. The chapter has recommended that data gathering to be left out to the experts that are more familiar with the dark web and the actual threat actors.

Questions

1. Explain what open source intelligence is.
2. What is hacking-as-a-service?
3. What are zero-day exploits?
4. Why is it important for organizations to monitor the dark web for their stolen data?
5. What is Google Dorking or Google Hacking?
6. Give an example of a Google Hacking command and explain it.
7. What are the challenges of collecting data from the dark web?
8. In your own opinion, can open source intelligence be of any benefit to organizations factoring in that it is available to the public?

Further Reading

The following are resources that can be used to gain more knowledge on this chapter:

https://brookcourtsolutions.com/wp-content/uploads/2017/11/dark-web.pdf.
https://markmonitor.com/download/ds/ds-MarkMonitor_Dark_Web_Cyber_Intelligence.pdf.
https://surfwatchlabs.com/threat-intelligence-solutions/dark-web-threat-intel.
https://securityintelligence.com/the-high-roi-of-cyberweapons-five-factors-driving-the-rise-in-threats/.

Chapter 11

Emerging Trends in the Dark Web and Mitigating Techniques

Introduction

Despite the increasing security concerns on the existence of the dark web, it may seem quite perplexing why this part of the internet is still in existence. However, from the founders of the most famous dark net, Tor, there are many other applications that this part of the internet supports. Therefore, it has become a necessary evil that has to exist within the internet. Since it's unveiling, the dark web has undergone many changes. Most of the changes have been a reaction to changes in the cybersecurity industry. At the peak of interference from legal agencies that have been closing down black markets on the dark nets, there has been a reaction with new crime patterns evolving. With a closure of famous dark markets, some reaction has been always noted. Also, with the changes in the cybersecurity tools being used by many users, cybercriminals have devised new and more effective ways of attacking organizations. The dark web has become a well-established criminal economy through these changes that it has undergone and the trends that have been witnessed. The dark net has therefore grown in scope and resilience although law enforcement agencies have been and are still able to fish out notorious criminals from the dark net. This chapter will discuss the evolution and trends in the dark net and then give some mitigations. It will do so in the following topics:

- Recent evolution of dark web
- Crime patterns continuity, poaching

- Threats mapping
- State-of-the-art mitigating techniques.

Recent Evolution of the Dark Web

The main pillars that have built up the dark web are security and privacy. When normal internet users feel threatened of being spied on while on the normal internet, they turn to the dark web. It has enabled spies in restrictive areas and countries where democracy is not the rule of law to continue operating without being discovered. The dark web has also seen the creation of a suitable environment for whistle-blowers. High-profile cases have been exposed by WikiLeaks which gets some leaked information through the dark web. However, alongside all this is the main focus of the dark web which has come to be known from cybercrimes and the takedown of famous marketplaces. The following are some of the recent evolutions of the dark web.

Improved Security, Privacy, and Usability

One of the oldest dark nets is Freenet that was built in 2000 for the purpose of protecting opponents of restrictive regimes. The dark net was slow and had many usability issues. However, this was a price many were willing to pay for the type of anonymity that the dark net offered. Over the time, dark nets have improved both in privacy and security. They have made it easier for any user to access them. Taking Tor, for instance, it has upgraded from using modified old versions of Firefox to newer versions. The new version of Tor packs similar usability features as the latest versions of Firefox. Tor has also fixed a number of security gaps. There was a time the FBI was able to break into Tor and identify several users due to a security bug in the version of Firefox that the dark net used. Tor responded by keeping up with the newer releases of Firefox that did not have the bug. Also, Tor has been making security.

One of the most important and evolutionary improvements came about in 2017. In what was called the Alpha release, Tor was upgraded with many tweaks that fixed security weaknesses that had allowed rogue nodes to keep tabs on what was going on in a network. Rogue nodes are believed to have been used by security agencies to arrest users by identifying them in the network. In 2016, there was a zero-day vulnerability that was discovered inside Tor browsers that was identical to what the FBI was said to be using to expose Tor users. Malwarebytes reported it as a bug that was in Firefox that could allow attackers to run any code in a targeted system thus making the target visit a malicious website that had malicious JavaScript code. The malicious page was identified to be also sending hostnames, IP, and MAC addresses to 5.39.27.226. The biggest threat, however, was that the web page contained malicious JavaScript and SVG that were loaded to computers that visited it on Tor. Using this code, it was possible for an assailant (the FBI in this case) to leak details about a Tor user without leaving digital footprint of hacking them. The JavaScript code would not download, it would just be loaded directly on a computer's memory and execute. After Malwarebytes released this zero-day vulnerability, the 5.39.27.226 was shut down, and Tor released a patch for their browser. Malwarebytes also released an Anti-Exploit tool that could be used to protect Tor users from the vulnerability.

The following are some other vulnerabilities that are said to have allowed investigators to spy and get the identities of users:

■ Window and screen size—as minute as it might seem, this was a big security challenge for Tor. It led to a warning being brandished on all Tor browsers for users not to maximize their Tor window sizes. The software would open at a default width and height, and users were warned against changing from that default size. The issue was that with the version of Tor that was being used, it was possible for JavaScript to be used to detect a Tor browser from any other browser thus making users more vulnerable as their traffic could be monitored.

■ User profiling based on Mac Operating System (OS) window size—this was a unique flaw that faced Tor users that used Mac OS. When the Tor browser would launch, it would set its size as $1,000 \times 1,000$ px. For smaller screens, the window would be multiples of 200 and 100 px that would be ideal for the screen. There was a flaw where the Tor browser was miscalculating its window size on Mac OS leading to it occupying the height of the dock. This would make a user vulnerable since authorities could just hunt for browsers that were using window sizes of multiples of 200 px width but not 100 px height. The flaw uniquely would identify browsers accessing the Tor network and the users could then be profiled.

■ Scrollbar size—Tor browsers do not have a default size for viewports, which helped profitable scrollbars to be added to the browsers. The area occupied by the vertical and horizontal scrollbars could, therefore, be subtracted from the window size just to find out the individual thickness of the scrollbars. The scrollbar size could be used to identify the OS and type of computer that a user was on since different OS and computers have different scrollbar sizes. It was already known that Tor on Mac OS had 15 px-thick scrollbars, while on Windows it had 17 px-thick scrollbars.

Following these and other concerns, in April 2017, the Tor Project announced that it would run on Rust code developed by the makers of Firefox. This is where Tor began to take the face of new Firefox editions. Tor was essentially relying on the secretive features of the Firefox browser. Before then, Tor used to run on C and C++ software. Tor developers said that there was a risk in continuing with C since a small mistake could be used to undermine the security of its users.

Other than Tor, the other major dark net called Freenet has also seen improvements to improve its security and performance. Freenet has been upgraded to be able to support millions of users. To preserve their anonymity, the dark net has made it possible for its users to limit the peers that can engage them. This is quite different from other dark nets that allow peers to connect to each other without restrictions. Freenet has also made it harder for outsiders to discover Freenet users and also very hard for the activity of a user on the dark net to be known. Freenet is so much sealed such that it is hard for law enforcement agencies to interfere with it.

Improvements in User Interface Design

The dark web has seen increased efforts to make it more appealing to users. The improvements in user interface design have made it possible for novice users to access and use several dark nets without challenges. There are two levels of user interface designs that have been witnessed. The first level is on the individual dark nets. As was discussed before, Tor has been upgraded and now has the same look and feel as the new versions of Firefox browsers. The underlying code in Firefox has been reused in Tor. This has made it more appealing to users and quite user-friendly as most internet users are conversant with the Firefox browser. The second level of improvement in user interface design has been seen in services offered in the dark nets. For instance, the black markets in the Tor dark net have seen a wave of improved user designs. Markets feature interfaces similar to surface web e-commerce stores such as Amazon and eBay (Figures 11.1 and 11.2).

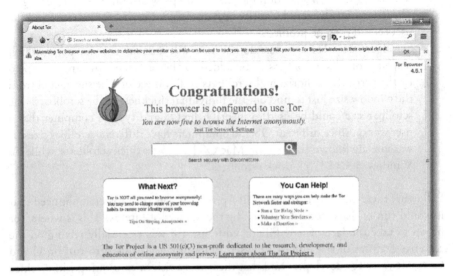

Figure 11.1   Old Tor browser interface.

Figure 11.2   New Tor browser interface.

Trust-Based Markets

Tor users have come to realize that law enforcement agencies have infiltrated the dark net. They pretend to be buyers or sellers with the aim of collecting evidence against a dark net user and arresting them. Therefore, there is a new trend that is being witnessed in markets where trust is being incorporated in transactions. There are markets where buyers cannot access or buy products without being invited in. This weeds out all the potentially law-agency-owned accounts seeking to incriminate sellers that deal in illegal items such as drugs. There are many other access controls being taken to ensure that a buyer is trustworthy. These include the ages of their dark net accounts, the users that know and can vouch for them and their style of communication. Normal law-agency accounts will either be new, not known by other users, or inquisitive in communication with the aim of gathering more information about how things go. Therefore, it is not as easy for law enforcement agencies to access trust-backed markets. On the side of sellers, there has been a noticeable pattern in markets aimed at reducing untrustworthy sellers (Figure 11.3).

Previously, it was easy for sellers to scam buyers. Since the payments were being done via cryptocurrencies, the transactions were not reversible; thus, it was too bad for customers that sent money to fake sellers. There was also a law enforcement presence in dark nets posing as sellers. When the law enforcement agents would take down marketplaces, they would infiltrate the accounts of sellers registered on the compromised sites and try to continue with normal operations. Buyers would think that they are dealing with the same sellers as before, only for them to realize later on that they were dealing with police officers. This strategy made it possible for law enforcement agents to nab several buyers. In reaction to this, it seems that a trust-based system borrowed from sites such as Amazon.com has been implemented

Figure 11.3 A marketplace that has implemented user reviews through a five-star score system.

in some marketplaces. This is where buyers leave a feedback after their purchase. In this part of the internet, a bad review could paralyze the operations of a seller by discouraging other buyers. If a buyer sends money and the items bought are not delivered, they can write that in the review of the shop thus cautioning other buyers. The trust-based buying and selling system seems to be the way forward for many buyers and sellers. It will therefore be hard for law enforcement agencies to purport to be buyers or sellers.

Continuity

The shutdown of a dark net marketplace can be likened to the cutting off of the mythological creature called Hydra. According to Greek mythology, if one tried to kill a Hydra by cutting off one of its heads, two more would grow to replace the head that had been cut. The Greek legend, Hercules, was only able to defeat the Hydra by having someone seal off the cut heads with a special substance so that new heads would not regenerate.

> In Greek mythology, the Hydra was a giant water snake with many heads that lived in a swamp near Lerna in the land of Argos. The number of heads is variously reported from as few as 5 to more than 100.
>
> *http://mythencyclopedia.com/Ho-Iv/Hydra.html*

The same behavior of regeneration of heads has been witnessed in the dark web. It is almost certain that when authorities shut off a dark net marketplace, a bigger marketplace is established. This has created a form of continuity that makes it hard for all illegal activities on the dark web to be stopped. The continuity wave started off in 2011 with the launch of Silk Road by Dread Pirate Roberts. In 2013, the FBI was able to completely shut down Silk Road. They even put a banner notifying visitors to the site that authorities had seized the website. It seemed that finally, the sale of drugs on the dark web had come to an end. However, it was not so.

There was so much coverage on media stations about the shutdown of a very sophisticated anonymous black market where people could buy drugs. Inadvertently, this brought more excitement to the purchase of drugs through the anonymous market. Demand therefore grew. At the same time, the buyers and sellers from the Silk Road market were also looking for another market to sell and buy drugs, fake currencies, driving licenses, and identification documents among others.

Therefore, two new black markets emerged. These were AlphaBay and Hansa. AlphaBay gained more prominence and attracted the most number of buyers and sellers. It gave room for the creation of the biggest dark net market ever. The marketplace operated successfully up to July 2017 where authorities composed of legal agencies from both the United States and European Union (EU) brought it down. They managed to arrest the founder who came to be identified as a 25-year-old called Alex Caves. He is said to have operated with ten other assistants that helped keep the site running. The United States claimed that AlphaBay had become a dangerous source of drugs and had led to many deaths due to overdosage. An 18-year-old girl was one of the victims that had died from overdosage of illegal substances bought on AlphaBay. Authorities uncovered that the market had 250,000 listed items for sale. There were 200,000 buyers and 40,000 sellers that had registered accounts with the website. Even more, since the start of monitoring of the internal activities in the marketplace, there had been 50,000 transactions done between sellers and buyers.

The FBI said that AlphaBay had grown to ten times the size of Silk Road that had been shut down 4 years earlier. The website servers were traced and seized, and they had been scattered over Lithuania, Canada, Britain, and France possibly for redundancy purposes. While this was happening, investigators are said to have already had taken over the Hansa marketplace. They were able to witness AlphaBay users migrate to Hansa. The traffic to Hansa grew by eight times the normal after the shutdown of AlphaBay. Thousands of buyers and sellers were creating accounts with the market without knowledge that authorities were already in control of the website (Figure 11.4).

The details about the money that had been transacted on the site were surprising to many. It was said that up to $4 million worth Bitcoin (at the exchange rate in July 2017) had been tracked back to AlphaBay. Another user claimed to have transferred $10 from AlphaBay to a different wallet. Due to the challenges of tracking Bitcoin, the details about the amount of money that was made in AlphaBay are not clear, but it is estimated that between May 2015 and February 2017, there was certainty that $450 million had been transacted on AlphaBay. Over its lifetime, it is estimated to have transacted up to 6 trillion.

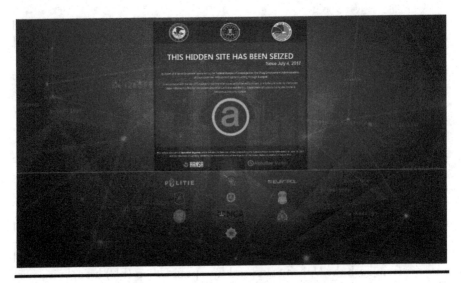

Figure 11.4   Notice left on the shutdown AlphaBay marketplace.

This amount, when compared to the $1.2 billion estimated to have been transacted on Silk Road, makes Silk Road appear as a very small marketplace. This affirms the continuity claims that whenever one marketplace is shut down, a bigger and more successful marketplace is established to replace it. The buyers and sellers that were using the shutdown marketplace will not simply vanish, they will wait for the creation of the new marketplace. Since the shutdown of other marketplaces, there is one that looks promising though it is hard to predict its future. This is the Dream market. Dream market seems to have survived the shutdown of many marketplaces in 2017. Its future is not, however, predictable since users have been raising an alarm that it seems that the market is being controlled by some law enforcement agencies of the sort. There are very many mirror links that users are being redirected to. Users that are logged in claim that when the mirror links redirect them, the mirror links do not recognize that they were logged in. It appears that there might be many versions of the market running and some are controlled by authorities. However, it has been quite some time, since 2013, and the marketplace has remained running while all other compromised markets have shut down. For now, it might seem that Dream market will be the continuum of the shutdown markets.

There is also the aspect of continued improvements. The errors in Tor that led to traffic analysis and then the arrest of Ross Ulbricht have most likely been fixed by Tor. The bugs that used to work at that time have also become ineffective against Tor. The loopholes that enabled law enforcement agents to register as vendors or clients and then collect information from other dark net users have also been fixed. There are markets with more restricted access which are hard to penetrate without special invites. The errors that previous site admins have made are also no longer being witnessed. Both the founders of Silk Road and AlphaBay met their downfall after their real emails were discovered in early communication. Alex Caves of AlphaBay gave out his real email address in initial messages on AlphaBay, while Ross Ulbricht of Silk Road gave out his real email when asking for coding assistance. Future site admins have most definitely taken note and will never post to the public their real email addresses. Therefore, the next big marketplace will be harder to take down than the previous ones.

Crime Patterns

The dark web has seen a new breed of crime. New patterns are coming up, and they have proven that the dark web is becoming an innovation hub for cybercriminals. The following are some of the patterns cropping up on the dark net.

Money Laundering Via Cryptocurrencies

Earlier chapters have talked about money laundering which can be simply said to be the process of making dirty money clean. Dirty money refers to the proceeds of illegal activities such as ransomware, sale of drugs, child porn sales, sale of ivory, and so on. The money that is collected from such activities has to go to someone. The money can and most likely will trigger searches from law enforcement agencies who will be looking at the perpetrators of crimes that led to the theft or extortion of the money. Till this decade, money laundering for illegal proceeds was only happening through fiat currencies. Banks such as those in Swiss that are very protective of their customers were being used. However, with the advent of cryptocurrencies, the dark web has become a center for money laundering. At first, cryptocurrencies were thought to be enough concealments of evidence due to their perceived anonymity. However, it came to be known that some cryptocurrencies were weak and could easily be traced back to their owners. Today, money laundering is done at a professional level on the dark web through mixers (Figure 11.5).

Mixers make so many transactions that effectively conceal the paths that law enforcement agencies could have used to trace the owners. Another tactic that is being used is through gambling sites. The holder of the cryptocurrencies just deposits them into a gambling site where he plays and wins. In most cases, it will be a sure win if the gambling company is on the money-laundering scheme. When the money is credited to the gambling company, it gets mixed with deposits from other players. When the game is over, the winner is given a lump sum that will include the mixed coins from many players. If authorities question the source of money, one will just say that it was from a lucky gamble.

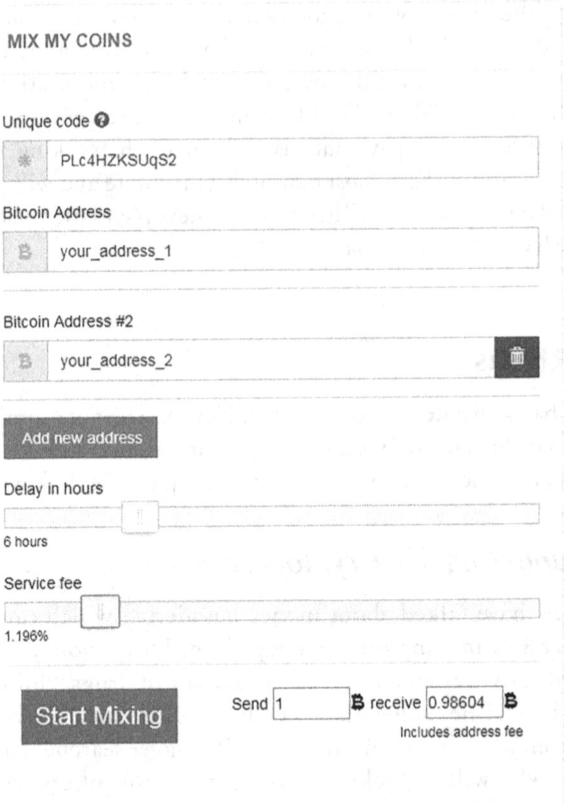

MIX MY COINS

Unique code ❓

※ PLc4HZKSUqS2

Bitcoin Address

₿ your_address_1

Bitcoin Address #2

₿ your_address_2   🗑

Add new address

Delay in hours

6 hours

Service fee

1.196%

Start Mixing   Send 1 ₿ receive 0.98604 ₿

Includes address fee

Figure 11.5   An example of a Bitcoin mixer on the dark net.

So how much are we talking here? So far, $4 million USD worth of Bitcoin has been tracked that could be related to AlphaBay—but that's likely just the tip of the iceberg. Another user claims to have tracked the money he or she was storing at AlphaBay to another wallet currently holding about $10 million in Bitcoin and which has seen over $6 trillion in Bitcoin transferred through it at one point or another. Dark net market Sheep Marketplace made off with nearly $40 million when it went offline in late 2013, and another market, Evolution, took $12 million with it when it abruptly shut down in 2015.

An article on estimated figures during AlphaBay exit.

http://nymag.com/selectall/2017/07/alphabay-exit-scam-may-be-the-biggest-one-yet.html.

Terrorism on the Dark Web

Terrorists have shown some appetite for technology in the last few years. Groups such as ISIS and Al Qaeda had opened social media accounts that they used to post propaganda videos. However, most companies clamped down on them and shut down these social media accounts. They therefore shifted attention to the dark web. The dark web provides an ideal environment for terrorists. It is anonymous and law enforcement agencies can hardly follow-up the activities that take place on the dark web. The dark web has also become an ideal place for terrorists to raise money. There are dark web websites that request for donations from the public to help the terrorists keep the fight going. There are crypto wallet addresses on these websites that can be used to deposit money directly to these terrorists. Singaporean authorities have been able to unearth one of such dark web pages that was requesting the public to give donations via Bitcoin (Figure 11.6).

The Rise of Botnets for Hire

There has been an upsurge of the number of denial-of-service (DoS) attacks that have been hitting organizations, and the dark web is partly responsible for this. There is a new crime pattern that is catching up of hiring or buying botnets. Botnets are the networks of zombie devices that have been infected with malware to make them participate in distributed denial-of-service (DDoS) and DoS attacks. The zombie

Figure 11.6 ISIS website on the dark web requesting for donations.

devices are the ones responsible for sending huge amounts of illegitimate traffic to organizational servers thus making them unable to attend to legitimate requests. It has also come to appear that DDoS attacks are being conducted to divert attention from another hack on an organization. When the organization will be struggling to respond to the DDoS attack, cybercriminals get enough room to carry out another attack against its systems. Since this type of an attack has been repeatedly successful, it appears that most cybercriminals are turning to the dark web to hire massive botnets to paralyze operations in organizations. The dark web has been reported to have very many botnets or hiring. The most current one is the Mirai botnet that has been associated with very many attacks. The Mirai botnet is based on Internet of Things (IoT) devices; hence, it has very many zombie devices in its army. IoT devices have been condemned for lacking security features that have made them too vulnerable to hackers. As a result, many botnets are being established based off of them. The Mirai botnet is estimated to include over 100,000 zombie devices that can be used to launch attacks against targets. They can hit a target with traffic exceeding 1 Tbps which is enough to make the targets go offline (Figure 11.7).

The prices for botnets on the dark web are particularly surprising. With only $10, there are botnets that can be hired for an hour. For a whole day, there are some vendors offering about $100–$200. These botnets can and possibly have disrupted the activities of very many businesses. There are other botnets that are on sale on the dark web. These are quite more expensive, but they give the buyer the privilege of using the zombie devices for an eternity.

Growth of Hacking-as-a-Service

The old hacking scenario was such that only the technically capable in coding used to hack. People that were not conversant in programming could not meet the cut

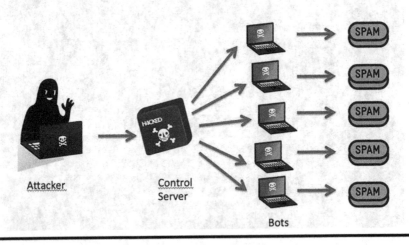

Figure 11.7 A diagrammatic depiction of a botnet.

as they lacked the skills that were needed to compromise networks and systems. However, there is a new pattern cropping up on the dark web whereby anyone can be a hacker. There are hackers that are offering their services for hiring. This therefore makes it very dangerous for organizations. For instance, disgruntled employees should now be considered as threats since that can easily hire third parties to hack for them. They can simply give out details about the organization they work for and hire the hacker to take out system after system. They need only to have money to cover the fees charged by the real hacker. This crime pattern is quite lucrative for the expert hackers. They no longer have to keep on searching for targets. They simply list their services on the dark web and wait for customers to hire them. The proceeds from providing hacking-as-a-service are not that bad either. It has made it less of a burden for them to monetize their skills. Instead of stealing money from organizations, going to money launderers, and then withdrawing just a percentage of their returns, expert hackers need just to charge by the hour. This brings in cleaner money that does not need to be laundered.

Increased Malware for Sale Listings

In the extension of the discussion that today's hackers do not need to be highly skilled programmers, there is a new observable pattern on the dark web of the sale of malicious codes, programs, and exploits. There is an uprising of a new type of hackers best known as script kiddies. These are hackers that do not necessarily have any hacking skills, but they buy malicious codes and programs and use them against targets. Script kiddies are known to be quite disastrous since they test out their acquired hacking tools and codes against many organizations. They can cause quite a menace as they attack organization after organization just for fun and also to steal money. Exploits are particularly of importance in this context. These are tools that can be used by other hackers to achieve something. For instance, if a hacker wants to encrypt a target's computer, he or she needs something to allow the encryption code to bypass the restrictions in place to prevent the unauthorized modification of files. The hacker can get such a tool or code from the dark web. Exploits are more costly and their cost varies with their applicability. Old exploits will retail for less since the target could have already received a patch to prevent the exploit from being used against his or her computer. New exploits tend to be costlier since they have a higher chance of succeeding. The sale of exploits on the dark web makes it more dangerous for organizations. It has lessened the workload for a hacker. A hacker can simply patch up codes bought from the dark web and then create a very effective hacking tool within a short period of time (Figure 11.8).

It has reached a point where organizations are in the dark against the exploits that are on sale on the dark web. They have therefore contracted third parties to keep an eye on all the malware markets on the dark web to document the type of malware on sale. This, in turn, enables organizations to know which

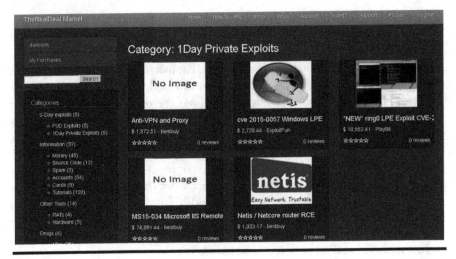

Figure 11.8 Exploits for sale on the dark web.

countermeasures they should put in place and which patches they need to install. For instance, the WannaCry ransomware was ineffective against organizations that had installed the latest patch from Windows. The patch was made and released to the users after a hacking group called Shadow Brokers released an exploit that could be used to bypass some security measures in Windows to prevent the modification of files. Therefore, if all the organizations had installed the patch, the exploit in WannaCry that was to bypass the security measures could not work, thus, making the attack fail. Malware for sale is definitely catching up, and with these tools of destruction at the disposal of small cybercriminals, many more attacks are going to be witnessed.

Sale of Stolen Data Listings

The dark web now acts as an economy of some sort. There are the hackers to steal data, money launderers to cleanse dirty money, and lastly the markets to sell or buy stolen data. Organizations have come to the realization that user data is very expensive, especially when it lands on the hands of today's cybercriminals. There are many vendors that are selling stolen data on the dark web, something that was previously unheard of. These vendors are selling the data to those that can make money out of it. For instance, the data could be bought by hackers that want to phish users. If a hacker buys a data dump that contains the actual names, addresses, and phone numbers of users, he or she could use the data to social engineer them. He could write emails claiming to be from a certain bank or government agency and demanding the payment of some amount of money. Since the email will appear to the recipients to have come from a legitimate source, they will not hesitate to pay (Figure 11.9).

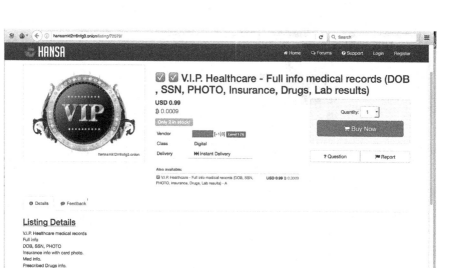

Figure 11.9   A listing of stolen data for sale on the dark web.

The sale of stolen data on the dark web has prompted organizations to have to incur the expense of paying third parties to monitor the dark web for listings of their data. Since not all hacks are discovered in time, an organization could end up finding its sensitive files being sold on the dark web even before they are aware that they have been hacked. Due to the prices that stolen data is attracting on the dark web, it has created a demand–supply force kind of reaction. Now, more hackers want to steal that data to meet the growing demand for user data that has led to high prices of this sensitive commodity.

Ivory/Rhino Horn Trade on the Dark Web

Interpol has confirmed that there is ivory trade taking place on the dark web. This is a new trend that had not been observed before. Smugglers have turned to the dark web to conduct their dirty business of selling ivory under the protection of the anonymity of communication and money transfer offered by the secure architectures of dark nets and cryptocurrencies. Ivory trade has become more difficult to be carried out on the open markets since there are very many agencies tasked with preventing such trade from taking place. However, most of these agencies operate on the surface web and physical markets. On the dark web, there are hardly any agents taking the same measures as those on the surface web. This vacuum has enabled ivory traders to resolve to communicate and also buy or sell these items through the dark web. There are very many anonymous shipping channels on the dark web. These have been used by drug traffickers with success. The payment part is protected through cryptocurrencies. The ease of money laundering has also made

Figure 11.10   Rhino horns posted for sale on the dark web.

it quite easy for proceeds of ivory trade to be untraceable by authorities. Therefore, ivory trade is catching up on the dark web (Figure 11.10).

Preferred Cryptocurrencies

For a long period, the preferred cryptocurrency to transact with on the dark web has been Bitcoin. However, the coin is fast losing preference due to the new concerns of its level of anonymity. Since it uses Blockchain and the distributed ledger, it is not as anonymous as other coins. The cryptocurrency that is seemingly replacing Bitcoin is Monero. Monero, which is abbreviated as XRM, is said to be by far more anonymous than Bitcoin. Monero is more difficult to trace back to its owners as it employs its own "mixing" techniques to prevent transactions from easily being followed up. For Bitcoin, mixing is only done by third parties, and it is quite expensive as these parties charge between 10% and 20% of the amount being mixed. Monero has also been more stable than Bitcoin. Bitcoin in 2017 and early 2018 kept on fluctuating from a low of $4,000 in August 2017 to a high of $19,000 in January 2018 and then falling back to an average of $8,000. This fluctuations definitely make it hard for business transactions to be carried out.

Threat Mapping

Cyber threat maps are maps showing active threats that are ongoing or that have been recorded all over the world. Cybersecurity companies are normally active in generating their own threat maps based on reports from their security devices or reports from credible sources. They map out the sources of threats and the destinations. This section will highlight some of the threat maps.

Kaspersky Threat Map

The Kaspersky threat map is renowned for its interactivity. It is produced based on the company's tools based on the threats collected on networks, websites, and even emails. Comparatively, the threat map has shown an increased the number of threats if the real-time threats of 2017 are compared with those of 2018. This is an indicator that the number of threats is on the increase. The threat map displays:

MAV—detections of threats made by the mail antivirus
OAS—on access scan or scans made by the tool automatically when accessing a device
ODS—On-Demand Scan or scans made by users themselves
WAV—web antivirus scans on pages visited by users
IDS—scans made by the company's intrusion detection systems
VUL—vulnerability scans of systems that Kaspersky products were running on
KAS—Kaspersky antispam scans for emails
BAD—botnet detection activity.

The following are the detections per second that were made at the time of writing this chapter (Figure 11.11):

- OAS-4944569
- ODS-6945897
- MAV-79578
- WAV-7571041

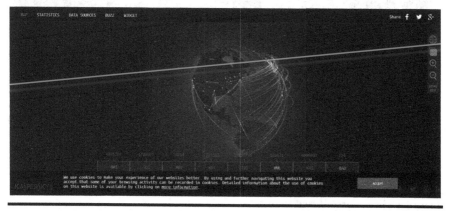

Figure 11.11   Kaspersky threat map.

- IDS-8067935
- VUL-199249
- KAS-3092227
- BAD-243.

Norse

Norse is another company that displays threat maps though they are not live but from recorded incidents. These threats are collected from its subset of honeypots that it uses to keep monitoring new attacks and preferred attack techniques. The following is a screenshot of a Norse threat map (Figure 11.12).

Fortinet

Fortinet, just like Norse, gives a threat map of recorded cybersecurity incidences. Therefore, its threat map is playback of the threats that have been recorded over a given duration. Fortinet gives the stats of the threats in the lower part of the screen to allow users to crunch down the numbers themselves. The following is a screenshot of the Fortinet threat map (Figure 11.13).

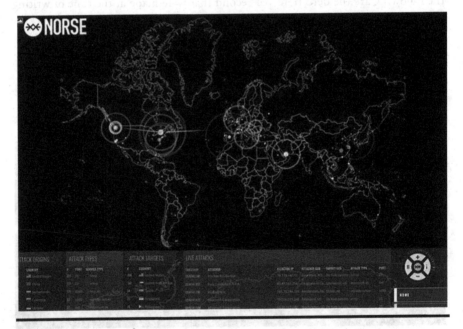

Figure 11.12   Norse threat map.

Figure 11.13   Fortinet threat map.

Checkpoint

Checkpoint also has a cyber threat map which shows threats recorded over a 24-h window. Each day at 12 AM, the website resets and starts creating a new threat map based on the detections that it has recorded. Checkpoint has a better visual appeal than other maps by companies such as Norse. The underlying structure is, however, similar to other threat maps. The main difference between Checkpoint and other companies' threat maps is that Checkpoint allows users to view historical data of interest such as the top attackers and top targets in a month, week, and so on. The following is a screenshot of the Checkpoint software threat map (Figure 11.14).

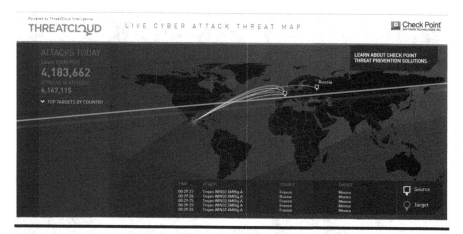

Figure 11.14   Checkpoint threat map.

FireEye

FireEye takes a simplistic approach when creating its cyber threat map. It removes most details that other companies attach to their threat maps. FireEye just keeps a map based on a subset of real-time data. The advantage is that the map data is separated into different industry segments and it shows the countries with the most number of attackers. The following is a threat map by FireEye (Figure 11.15).

Arbor Networks

Arbor generates a hybrid map that is created from the data collected from Arbor's threat intelligence system called ATLAS. Arbor is a big company, and its clients are mostly IP companies which make up 300 of its customer base. These companies in total contribute to 130 Tbps of all the global traffic. The threats that Arbor mostly shows on its threat map are DDoS attacks since they are the ones mostly used against ISP companies. Figure 11.16 is a screenshot of Arbor Networks threat map.

Trend Micro

Trend Micro has identified just a small niche that it creates a threat map for. This makes it a very accurate map, and richer details can be drawn from it. Trend Micro only generates a threat map for botnet connections. It maps the Command and Control servers that hackers use to control botnets around the world. The data on the maps is normally 14 days old as it takes time to map activities on these C&C servers.

Figure 11.15   FireEye threat map.

Figure 11.16   Arbor threat map.

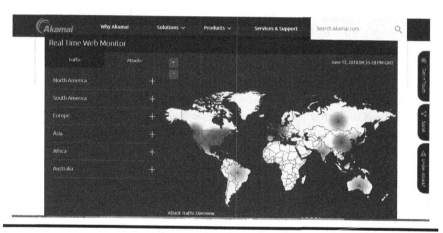

Figure 11.17   Akamai threat map.

Akamai

Akamai has a very good real-time threat monitor that tracks threats and attacks in addition to internet traffic. Once the map loads, a user is given two tabs. One tab shows the internet traffic from different parts of the world, and the second tab shows the regions that experience most attacks. Figure 11.17 is a screenshot of an Akamai threat map.

State-of-the-Art Mitigating Techniques

With current perception that the dark web is thriving in terms of cyber, it might appear that the law enforcement agencies are failing. Time and again the situation of law enforcement of the dark web has been likened to the game Whack-a-Mole. The thing is that the mole has kept on becoming more intelligent and thus more difficult to ack. However, the arrests and prosecutions of threat actors on the dark web as well as buyers of illegal items on the dark web mean that there is some progress when it comes to mitigating threats on the dark web. Alongside efforts from the law enforcement agencies, individual users and organizations have made some efforts to mitigate the threat that emanate from the dark web. However, through collaboration, much more can be achieved to put the dark web under control. The following are the current mitigating mechanisms.

Memex

The special browsers such as Tor that are used to access dark nets make it hard for users and their activities to be tracked by the law enforcement agencies. However, it seems that law enforcement agencies are coming up with their own solutions to overcome the anonymity challenge. Through DARPA, the United States has developed Memex which functions as a search engine but for the dark web. Memex has helped in the fight against human trafficking, an evil that shockingly still exists in the era, and has also helped combat some of the illegal activity that takes place on the dark web. Memex has a very powerful algorithm that is capable of scraping the contents of millions of dark web pages. After it scraps them, it indexes them such that search queries can be made against them. Memex supersedes the capabilities of the dark web search engines offered by browsers such as Tor (Figure 11.18).

Memex is, however, not able to beat the user anonymity of Tor and thus cannot unmask the actual IP addresses of the users on the Tor network. However, authorities are able to analyze contents all over the dark web that are used to uncover some striking relationships that can be used to track users instead. Users can only be so careful on the dark net, there are some careless mistakes that they do that expose their real identities or reveal information that can be used to track them. Memex is an attempt by authorities to make investigations of dark web-related crimes within the provisions of law. There have been some challenges in prosecutions involving the use of illegal means by law enforcement agencies to obtain evidence against suspects of dark web-related crimes. Courts can throw away evidence that is proven

In DARPA's MEMEX, DeepDive is used by law enforcement agencies to fight human trafficking.

Figure 11.18 Memex by DARPA.

to have been collected through illegal means. Memex makes it easy for evidence to now be collected using totally legal means.

Network Investigation Techniques

In a remarkable operation called "Operation Torpedo," law enforcement agencies were able to unmask the real IP addresses of 25 notorious dark web users that had been accessing child porn websites. The success behind the operation is tied to a method called "network investigative technique" (NIT) that the FBI used to unveil the addresses. The investigation kicked off in the Netherlands. Law enforcement agencies were able to create a web crawler that specifically searched for Tor websites on the dark web. They then isolated the websites that had content related to child porn. They monitored the users on these dark net websites and started unmasking their IP addresses. They were able to unveil the IP addresses of one of the websites that they were monitoring called Pedoboard. Once this information was available to them, doors opened that led to investigations that are part of the reason why there are hardly any child porn websites in operation today on the dark web. The FBI followed up on Aaron McGrath whose investigations showed that he was hosting these evil websites. In a yearlong operation, FBI was able to track down McGrath and seize his servers. With valid search warrants to help with the case, they were able to search all the recovered servers. The warrant allowed the FBI to modify the code on the servers such that their "NIT" could directly get traffic to and from the servers. This is what helped the individual users to be unmasked. Normally, users are protected by proxy IP addresses, but the NIT method had capabilities to unmask the actual IP addresses. The IP addresses of 25 users were unveiled, and then the FBI subpoenaed their ISPs to reveal the home addresses of these users.

Some Conventional Techniques

Law enforcement agencies do not always rely on high-tech tools to mitigate some threats on the dark web. There are incidents where traditional techniques that have been successful in other occasions are used. These traditional techniques go back to old cases such as the shutdown of Silk Road and the arrest of Ross Ulbricht. The techniques are as follows.

Informants

Since they are heavily used on the surface web and real world, informants are still used by law enforcement agencies to help uncover details about dark web-related crimes. There are prominent dark net users that are known and trusted by other users. These are commonly targeted by law enforcement agencies, and once they are identified, they can be made to help with investigations in the exchange of a favor or pardoning of their small crimes. These informants are able to access parts of the dark web where law enforcement agencies cannot reach and also communicate with people that cannot give a thought of talking to cops. Informants are great insider sources and can reveal the plans taking place in secretive dark net marketplaces. They can also help identify the main cybercriminals or hacking groups of interest that operate on the dark net to provide hacking tools and services.

Undercover Operations

This is where law enforcement agencies pretend to be part of the threat actors on the dark net so as to get closer to targets of interest. They can pose to be buyers or vendors on the dark net and then work their way up the dark web crime chain. They can even make regular purchases from a notorious vendor so as to appear as loyal customers. Definitely, the vendor will start having a soft spot for these loyal customers, and they can use that to find out more information such as the source of the illegal items or the distribution channel used. In the case of Ross Ulbricht, there were undercover government agents that were supposed to engage him on the dark web to keep him busy as his arrest plans were brewing. Ross Ulbricht was in a library trying to sort out an issue that had been raised by an undercover cop about his fake account on Silk Road. When Ross Ulbricht was trying to check up the issue, other undercover law enforcement agencies faked a fight in the library that Ross was in and this was enough distraction for them to arrest him before he could shut down or delete files from his computer. This shows that undercover operations are highly effective especially when it comes to the final part of arresting a target.

Tracking of Individuals

In 2017, there was an outcry by the general US populace that they were being spied on and tracked by the NSA. This was following an expose by Edward Snowden showing clearly that the NSA was spying on citizens. As it has become public knowledge, it has probably raised enough alarm on the dark web to make users more cautious of their activities in the outside world. Tracking of individuals is normally as a result of positive identification of a suspect of interest in dark web-related crimes. The tracking of every activity carried out by a suspect makes it easy for law enforcement agencies to mitigate threats on the dark web.

Postal Interception

There is a very weak and vulnerable point that authorities can use to beat illegal purchases of physical products on the dark web. For any order made on the dark web for a physical product, it has to be delivered to the physical location of choice given by the customer. When drug dealing was at the highest levels on the dark web, it came to be realized that the sellers were so successful because they were using clandestine ways to post the drugs to their users. While the destinations and sources of internet traffic can be made anonymous, postal packages cannot be anonymized at a similar level. Therefore, postal interception has been adopted as a means of curtailing illegal drug sales on the dark web. Vendors are becoming craftier though in response to the intensified monitoring of parcels. They are hiding drugs inside parcels containing other goods. When a random inspection is done on the parcel, it will be seen as a normal package carrying normal items while the drugs are hidden inside. Vendors are also using distractions to take away the attention of police officers from the actual shipments. After all, only a few samples of packages can be inspected; thus, it is easy for most drugs to go through. The success, however, is with the few packages that are intercepted. Officers can monitor their destinations and arrest the person that collects them. Officers can also trace back from where these drugs were shipped and lay traps there to catch the sender (Figure 11.19).

Cyber Patrols

Authorities have taken an active role in monitoring the activities that take place in the dark web. Areas of interest to them are popular drug markets, the listings made on dark net web stores, the renowned suppliers on dark net markets, and the cryptocurrencies in use. The regular monitoring has been yielding a lot of intelligence

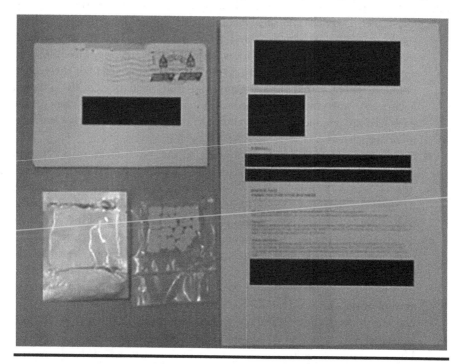

Figure 11.19   Intercepted parcel with MDMA (type of drug, ecstasy).

to the law enforcers that can be used to start off investigations. Cyber patrols have been a collaborative effort of experienced investigators in different fields. The identification of the current trends and patterns on the dark web has also been essential in helping law enforcers adapt to the changes. The following are six areas where law enforcement agencies have put most efforts in:

- Mapping of hidden services—earlier on in this section, we discussed a DARPA tool called Memex that is created with the purpose of mapping out or indexing the dark web. This is part of the efforts being taken to increase the visibility of the activities that take place on the dark web by the authorities. With regular runs to map out the hidden services or websites that are running on the dark web, it is easy for law enforcement agents to crush down any illegal marketplaces before they gain popularity.

- Customer data mining—the services on dark web exist because there are ready customers. Customers have been deluded that they are perfectly safe when they use the dark web due to the purportedly uncompromisable anonymity. However, there are many techniques that law enforcement agencies can use that have been successful in the past. For instance, law enforcement agencies were able to almost completely wipe out child porn sites from the dark web. They did not just go for the owners of the sites that had child porn, they went also after the visitors that used to frequent those sites. To quash illegal services and substances that are sold on the dark web, authorities have to discourage users from buying these items. The best way to teach internet users not to flock to dark web stores is by targeting, unveiling, and apprehending a number of them. Out of fear of being arrested, the general populace will be scared of buying anything from the dark web. The situation is currently worrying as false media reports have reported that users on the dark web are completely anonymous and cannot be traced by law enforcement agencies.

- Social sites monitoring—the chit chats on dark web forums and also on surface web forums that discuss dark net issues form a good source of intelligence. This is the intelligence that can be used by law enforcement agencies to know the latest news from the deep circles of the dark web. Social media posts have in the past been useful in tracking the progress of investigations or telling just how much the public knew about investigations. Reddit is a community that is known for having up-to-date posts about the dark web. When a deep web marketplace goes down, it is highly likely that Reddit users will be the first to know. Reddit users also keep giving an updated version of the dark web catalog known as the hidden wiki. The hidden wiki contains links to the new and old hidden services that can be accessed from the dark web.

- Hidden service monitoring—law enforcement agencies currently have a number of tools to keep an eye on new services and websites. As soon as they appear on the dark web, the authorities get notified. This helps them to plan on how to deal with the hidden service. If it is an illegal hidden service, authorities will start investigations and attempts to stamp it out before it gains popularity. This is also an effective technique that is being used to prevent the sale of stolen data on the dark web. As soon as a new listing is made on the dark web concerning the sale of stolen data, authorities can rush to the website and try and take the data offline as well as arrest the person selling it.

■ Marketplace profiling—this is a technique that has already yielded fruits. In 2017, authorities from all over the world were able to take down most marketplaces on the dark web that were selling illegal weapons and drugs. The takedown also involved the arrest of key actors such as site owners, staff, and customers. Marketplace profiling is where authorities keep tabs on the vendors, buyers, and any other agents that are involved in the illegalities committed on the dark web. When authorities were taking down markets on the dark web, they used to target site owners first. This was witnessed in both Silk Road and AlphaBay which were two of the most prolific takedowns. After the heads were taken out, the agents would start clamping down on the staff and the customers on the website. A number of vendors and buyers were arrested in different countries. For instance, there were quite a number of arrests of the customers that had bought illegal weapons from an illegal seller based in the United States called WeaponsGuy. WeaponsGuy had advertised his wares on different dark markets, and law enforcement agencies first arrested him then compromised his account to track down the people that he had sold weapons to. Profiling of different actors on dark net marketplaces was also used to wipe out child porn business on the dark web. The FBI used to seize servers and then run them with special codes to profile the visitors that accessed the child porn sites. With this, they would descend on the visitors and arrest them. Therefore, profiling of different actors in marketplaces and websites has been a largely successful technique in the past.

Dark Net Trade Disruptions

If the FBI would not have been able to take down Silk Road, the world would be in a worse state than it is right now. If Hansa and AlphaBay alongside many other marketplaces would not have been subsequently brought down, there would be a crisis of drug peddling and drug abuse all over the world. Therefore, disruptions in these markets have contributed to the world becoming safer and keeping at bay a societal problem that would be witnessed all over the world. Dark net market disruptions normally target the popular or upcoming marketplaces and also target specific individuals who are crucial to the running of certain marketplaces.

These disruptions also help authorities to know the scope of the problem of illicit drug and items trade on the dark web. There have been a number of operations whose aims were to disrupt dark net trade activities. The disruptions have been carried out at an international scale often involving authorities from different countries and continents. Some of these disruption operations include operation Onymous, Bayonet, and GraveSac. These were all successful at bringing down the largest market players on the dark web that were responsible for or were carrying out the sale of drugs. Let us take a look at one of the most interesting disruption activities that was carried out through the collaboration of several countries (Figure 11.20).

Operation Onymous was jointly undertaken in November 2014 by several agencies around the world and were targeted at the dark net markets that were running on Tor. Agencies from 16 EU nations with the support from US agencies successfully took down several marketplaces. It featured EU's European Cybercrime Center, the US FBI, US Immigration and Customs Enforcement, and Homeland Security. The objectives of the operation, which was to stop the illicit drug and weapons trade on the dark web, were achieved. In addition, 17 arrests were made of market admins and vendors. It was a big achievement since technical capabilities to beat anonymity that are available today were not yet so developed. Alongside the arrests, 600 onion addresses were also shut down as they were to be used by upcoming illicit drugs and weapon traders (Figure 11.21).

Funds were also recovered to the tune of $1 million worth Bitcoin and 180,000 euros. The impact of the success of this project was felt worldwide for a short time since illegal activities on the dark web fell. There had never been another similar partnership between authorities aimed at destabilizing the illegal items' trade on the dark web. This operation also led to the realization of the resilience of the dark web. After the shutdown of all these marketplaces, the dark web still responded with the creation of new marketplaces. Vendors and buyers moved to the new marketplaces and continued with their activities. That is why there have been continued

U.S. Immigration and
Customs Enforcement

THIS HIDDEN SITE HAS BEEN SEIZED

as part of a joint law enforcement operation by
the Federal Bureau of Investigation, ICE Homeland Security Investigations,
and European law enforcement agencies acting through Europol and Eurojust

In accordance with the law of European Union member states
and a protective order obtained by the United States Attorney's Office for the Southern District of New York
in coordination with the U.S. Department of Justice's Computer Crime & Intellectual Property Section
Issued pursuant to 18 U.S.C. § 983(j) by the
United States District Court for the Southern District of New York

EC3
EUROPOL

EUROJUST

Figure 11.20 Notice left by operation Onymous on shutdown websites.

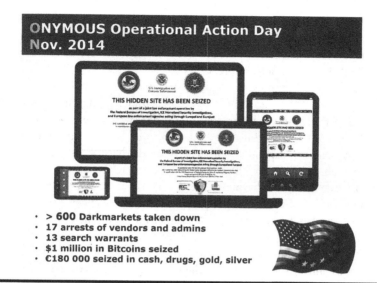

Figure 11.21   Accomplishments of operation Onymous.

operations undertaken by several agencies ever since then. These operations intensified most in 2017 leading to an almost complete wipeout of illegal marketplaces. Even though new marketplaces may still come up, these disruptions have been helpful in curtailing the speed at which the illegal trade of drugs and other items grows.

Summary of the Chapter

This chapter has looked at the emerging trends of the dark web and the mitigation measures that have been undertaken. It has first looked at the evolutions made in the dark web. The chapter highlighted that there is improved security, privacy, and usability of the dark web. These have made it quite friendly for novice users and more difficult for law enforcement agencies to compromise its security. Tor has been highlighted, and the upgrade of this dark net's browser from C and C++ to Rust has been explained. The factors that necessitated this upgrade such as the ease of profiling users through bugs have also been explained. Another evolution that has been discussed is the improvements in the user interface designs of both dark nets and their marketplaces. The chapter has also looked at a reactionary evolution to the infiltration of law enforcement agents in the dark net, the rise of trust-based markets. These are markets that run based on trust that vendors have for their sellers and buyers have for their sellers. The impact of this has been to eliminate the number of markets that law enforcement agencies can carry out undercover operations in. Lastly, the chapter has looked at the resilience of the dark web and its continuity even after it is shattered by law enforcement agencies. The impacts of several historic take-downs have been analyzed, and it has been noted that they have all mostly led to the establishment of new markets.

The chapter has also gone through the currently observable trendy crime patterns on the dark web. It has looked at money laundering that has quickly shifted from being done in banks to being done on the dark web through cryptocurrencies. The migration of terrorism into the dark web in a bid to request for anonymous funding has also been explained. Other new trends that the chapter has looked at include the rise of botnets for hire, the growth of hacking-as-a-service, increased malware for sale listings, a sharp increase of stolen data for sale listings, ivory trade on the dark web, and a shift in the preferred cryptocurrencies on the dark web. The chapter has then looked at cyber threat maps showing the different threats felt throughout the world as expressed by different security companies in maps.

The chapter has come to an end with a discussion of the mitigating techniques being used by authorities to combat illegal trade on the dark web. Memex has been highlighted as one of these techniques. It has been explained as a search engine created by DARPA that scraps and indexes data from the dark web to aid with the discovery of illegal trading activities that take place on this part of the internet. "NITs" have also been discussed as useful techniques that have been used during operations to unveil the actual identities of users on the dark web carrying out illegal activities. The chapter has also looked at the conventional but effective techniques that are still being used. These include informants, under-cover operations, tracking of individuals, and postal interceptions. Cyber patrols have also been discussed, and the areas that they are targeted have been given. These areas include the mapping out of hidden services, customer data mining, social sites mining, hidden service monitoring, and marketplace profiling. The last mitigation technique discussed is the dark net trade disruption. The chapter has explained how disruptions have helped in controlling the spiraling out of illegal trading activities on the dark net.

Questions

1. Explain how the Tor has improved its security.
2. How are dark net marketplaces incorporating trust in their dealings?
3. Explain the continuity of dark net marketplaces.
4. State and explain two trends of cybercrime on the dark web.
5. Why are cyber criminals preferring botnets?
6. What is Memex?
7. Give two conventional methods being used by law enforcement agencies to mitigate illegal activity on the dark web.
8. Explain the purpose of dark net trade disruptions.

Further Reading

The following are resources that can be used to gain more knowledge on this chapter:

https://ofdt.fr/BDD/publications/docs/Darknet171128JR.pdf -58.
https://osce.org/chairmanship/325666?download=true.
https://tandfonline.com/doi/full/10.1080/23738871.2017.1298643.

Index

Printed in the United States
by Baker & Taylor Publisher Services